T0202443

Communications
in Computer and Information Science

1609

More information about this series at https://link.springer.com/bookseries/7899

Andreas Holzinger · Hugo Plácido Silva ·
Markus Helfert · Larry Constantine (Eds.)

Computer-Human Interaction Research and Applications

4th International Conference, CHIRA 2020
Virtual Event, November 5–6, 2020
Revised Selected Papers

 Springer

Editors
Andreas Holzinger
Medical University of Graz
Graz, Austria

Markus Helfert
Dublin City University
Dublin, Ireland

Hugo Plácido Silva
IT - Institute of Telecommunications
Lisboa, Portugal

Instituto Superior Técnico
Lisboa, Portugal

Larry Constantine
Madeira Interactive Technologies Institute
Funchal-Madeira, Portugal

ISSN 1865-0929   ISSN 1865-0937 (electronic)
Communications in Computer and Information Science
ISBN 978-3-031-22014-2   ISBN 978-3-031-22015-9 (eBook)
https://doi.org/10.1007/978-3-031-22015-9

This Springer imprint is published by the registered company Springer Nature Switzerland AG
The registered company address is: Gewerbestrasse 11, 6330 Cham, Switzerland

Preface

The present book includes extended and revised versions of a set of selected papers from the 4th International Conference on Computer-Human Interaction Research and Applications (CHIRA 2020), held during November 5–6, 2020, as a web-based event due to the COVID-19 pandemic. CHIRA 2020 received 44 paper submissions from 22 countries, of which 18% were included in this book.

The papers were selected by the event chairs and their selection is based on a number of criteria that include the classifications and comments provided by the Program Committee members, the session chairs' assessment, and also the program chairs' global view of all papers included in the technical program. The authors of selected papers were then invited to submit a revised and extended version of their papers having at least 30% innovative material.

The purpose of the conference is to bring together professionals, academics, and students who are interested in the advancement of research and practical applications of interaction design and human-computer interaction (HCI). Five parallel tracks were held, covering different aspects of HCI, including interaction design, human factors, entertainment, cognition, perception, user-friendly software and systems, pervasive technologies, and interactive devices.

The papers selected to be included in this book contribute to the understanding of relevant trends of current HCI research and applications, including cognitive interfaces, both from the perspective of supporting future users of autonomous vehicles and of controlling user interfaces based on workload level; designing of shape-shifting technologies capable of promoting user engagement; augmented reality applied to music embodiment and digital experiences; and using eye tracking to understand nutritional behavior and choices.

We would like to thank all the authors for their contributions and also the reviewers who have helped ensure the quality of this publication.

November 2020

Andreas Holzinger
Hugo Plácido Silva
Markus Helfert
Larry Constantine

Organization

Conference Co-chairs

Markus Helfert	Maynooth University, Ireland
Larry Constantine	Madeira Interactive Technologies Institute, Portugal

Program Co-chairs

Andreas Holzinger	Medical University Graz, Austria
Hugo Plácido Silva	Instituto de Telecomunicações, Portugal

Program Committee

Iyad Abu Doush	American University of Kuwait, Kuwait
Alessandra Agostini	University of Milano-Bicocca, Italy
Nizar Banu P. K.	Christ University, India
Juan-Manuel Belda-Lois	Instituto de Biomecánica de València, Spain
Jens Binder	Nottingham Trent University, UK
John Brooke	Independent Researcher, UK
Juan Calleros	Universidad Autónoma de Puebla, Mexico
Eric Castelli	Laboratoire d'Informatique de Grenoble, France
Luis Castro	Instituto Tecnológico de Sonora, Mexico
Bongsug Chae	Kansas State University, USA
Christine Chauvin	Université de Bretagne Sud, France
Ahyoung Choi	Gachon University, South Korea
Yang-Wai Chow	University of Wollongong, Australia
Cesar Collazos	Universidad del Cauca, Colombia
Lizette de Wet	University of the Free State, South Africa
Achim Ebert	University of Kaiserslautern, Germany
Vania Estrela	Universidade Federal Fluminense, Brazil
Peter Forbrig	University of Rostock, Germany
Silas Formunyuy Verkijika	University of the Free State, South Africa
Peter Fröhlich	AIT Austrian Institute Technology, Austria
Diego Gachet	European University of Madrid, Spain
Valentina Gatteschi	Politecnico di Torino, Italy
Toni Granollers	University of Lleida, Spain
Martin Hitz	Alpen-Adria-Universität Klagenfurt, Austria

Sadanori Ito	National Institute of Information and Communications Technology, Japan
Victor Kaptelinin	Umeå University, Sweden
David Kaufman	SUNY Downstate Medical Center, USA
Gerard Kim	Korea University, South Korea
Josef F. Krems	Chemnitz University of Technology, Germany
Gerhard Leitner	Alpen-Adria-Universität Klagenfurt, Austria
Wen-Chieh Lin	National Chiao Tung University, Taiwan, Republic of China
Youquan Liu	Chang'an University, China
Arminda Lopes	Interactive Technologies Institute (LARSyS/ITI)/Instituto Politecnico de Castelo Branco, Portugal
Eurico Lopes	Instituto Politécnico de Castelo Branco, Portugal
Lorenzo Magnani	University of Pavia, Italy
Federico Manuri	Politecnico di Torino, Italy
Frédéric Mérienne	Arts et Metiers, France
Daniel Mestre	Aix-Marseille University/CNRS, France
Giulio Mori	ISTI-CNR, Italy
Lia Morra	Politecnico di Torino, Italy
Max Mulder	TU Delft, Netherlands
Jaime Muñoz-Arteaga	Universidad Autónoma de Aguascalientes, Mexico
S. Musse	Pontifícia Universidade Católica do Rio Grande do Sul, Brazil
Helen Petrie	University of York, UK
Prashan Premaratne	University of Wollongong, Australia
Laura Ripamonti	Università degli Studi di Milano, Italy
Andrea Sanna	Politecnico di Torino, Italy
Shamus Smith	University of Newcastle, Australia
Frédéric Vanderhaegen	University of Valenciennes, France
Gualtiero Volpe	Università degli Studi di Genova, Italy
Marcus Winter	University of Brighton, UK
Diego Zapata-Rivera	Educational Testing Service, USA
Gottfried Zimmermann	Stuttgart Media University, Germany
Floriano Zini	Free University of Bozen-Bolzano, Italy

Additional Reviewers

Fu-Yin Cherng
Navid Razmjooy

Invited Speakers

Giancarlo Fortino	University of Calabria, Italy
Ann Blandford	University College London, UK
Yvonne Rogers	University College London, UK
Anind K. Dey	University of Washington, USA

Contents

Cognitive Control: Transitions in Control Modes Under Different Level of Workload and fNIRS Sensitivity

Philippe Rauffet[1]([✉]) [ID], Farida Said[2] [ID], Amine Laouar[1,3], Christine Chauvin[1] [ID], and Marie-Christine Bressolle[3]

[1] Lab-STICC, Université Bretagne Sud, 17 bd Flandres-Dunkerque, Lorient, France
{philippe.rauffet,amine.laouar,christine.chauvin}@univ-ubs.fr
[2] LMBA, Université Bretagne Sud, 17 bd Flandres-Dunkerque, Lorient, France
farida.said@univ-ubs.fr
[3] IYDN Department, Airbus, Toulouse, France
mariechristine.bressolle@airbus.com

Abstract. This paper aims to deeper study the relations between cognitive control and mental workload. Indeed, cognitive control is a contemporary concept in neuroscience and cognitive ergonomics, that can explain the metacognition carried out by operators in their multitasking activity, as well as the regulations that operators implement to manage their level of mental workload. In this paper, an experiment was conducted, where a main task was presented to participants in different conditions of multitasking and difficulty. The scenario was designed with the aid of the Multi-Attribute Task Battery (MATB-II) microworld, which reproduces basic multitasking that a pilot can carry out in an aircraft. The performance and the neurophysiological responses of twenty participants were recorded, especially by analyzing cardiac activity and oxygenation and deoxygenation of the prefrontal cortex. The findings particularly emphasized a link between the level of task difficulty and the control modes, which is highly significant for the tactical mode. Furthermore, fNIRS signals were significantly related to cognitive control modes. Indeed, the tactical mode was found to be the most efficient one, since it is associated with a satisfying performance and with low mental strain, contrary to the other modes with a worse performance and a higher mental strain. These results about the dynamic of cognitive control and the specific sensitivity of fNIRS to tactical control mode open new perspectives for proposing new ways to support this mode in naturalistic situations, particularly in the domain of aviation.

Keywords: Cognitive control modes · Mental workload · fNIRS

1 Introduction

Supervising and controlling complex systems in dynamic and uncertain situations are characterized by risk mitigation and multitasking [1]. This activity relies on cognitive processes associated to situation assessment and decision-making that use both internal

A. Holzinger et al. (Eds.): CHIRA 2020, CCIS 1609, pp. 1–16, 2022.
https://doi.org/10.1007/978-3-031-22015-9_1

(i.e. mental models related to the knowledge on supervised systems) and external data processing (i.e. information that is available in the current situation). Thus, in dynamic contexts, the drivers or the pilots of a transportation system can be proactive (when they base their decisions on mental models) or reactive (when their actions are mainly driven by external data).

This paper aims at deeper exploring the adaption mechanisms implemented by human operators, who transit between different cognitive control modes. It presents an experimental study that was already partially presented at CHIRA 2020 [2].

The following paragraphs first present a literature review on the main research works achieved on cognitive control in the domain of cognitive ergonomics and cognitive neuroscience. Then the next section develops an experiment conducted on the MATB-II microworld to study how participants adopted cognitive control modes when undertaking a multitasking activity with different level of difficulty. The results from this experiment are finally given and discussed, in terms of theoretical and methodological contributions.

2 Literature Review on Cognitive Control

Behavioral flexibility is closely related to the concept of cognitive control, which is at the center of two important models in the field of cognitive ergonomics: Rasmussen's Skills-Rules-Knowledge (SRK) model [3] and Hollnagel's Contextual Control Model (COCOM) [4]. If these models are well-known, the different modes of control they identify have rarely been "quantified" or evaluated from a neurophysiological point of view [5]. Several questions arise regarding the relationships between the control mode that operators may adopt and their performance, but also concerning the control mode adopted and the operators' workload.

2.1 Ergonomic Models of Cognitive Control

Cognitive control is one of the key concepts in modern cognitive science. It is defined as a set of processes that support information processing and behaviour to vary adaptively from time to time, depending on current objectives, rather than staying rigid and inflexible on the strategies used to implement actions.

In cognitive ergonomics, two models of cognitive control have been proposed to account for the behaviour of operators in dynamic situations: the SRK taxonomy of Rasmussen [3] and the COCOM model proposed by Hollnagel [4]. As Hoc and Amalberti [6] underlines, these two models focus on two different aspects of cognitive control. The SRK taxonomy considers the level of abstraction of the data processed during supervision activities (sub-symbolic vs. symbolic data), whereas the COCOM model stresses the reactive or proactive nature of the observed behaviours.

The taxonomy defined by Rasmussen distinguishes three different levels of control. The skill-based level results in the implementation, without conscious attention, of cognitive automatisms and automated patterns of actions. At the rule-based level, behaviour is guided by known rules or procedures. The knowledge-based level finally support the activity undertaken to solve new problems requiring the definition of new rules and creativity.

The COCOM model puts the emphasis on temporality. It distinguishes among four main control modes [4, 7]: strategic, tactical, opportunistic, and scrambled. The strategic mode is used when time is abundant, and when one must generate or optimize new plans for solving a novel or complex situation. It requires considerable attentional resources. The tactical mode uses known rules to process a limited number of goals. It can be considered as the most efficient one. The opportunistic mode occurs when time is just enough; actions are therefore driven by the most salient information. Finally, the scrambled mode is used when time is extremely limited. And actions are random. In that case, planning is impossible, and the choice of action is random, that might generate errors and performance decrement.

2.2 Dynamics of Cognitive Control and Relationship with Mental Workload

Many studies have already used the concept of control modes to explain operators' performance variations in dynamic situations [8–11]. Stanton et al. [8] have especially shown people move between cognitive control modes (coded with COCOM models) in a linear manner when the situation does not change too abruptly. They did not observe any disruptive transitions (for instance between scrambled and strategic modes), but instead slight variations towards neighbour modes (like from tactical mode to opportunistic mode).

Research conducted in the domain of cognitive neuroscience has also identified some links between control modes and neurophysiological responses [12]. Proactive control is characterized by the maintenance of goal-relevant information in working memory, which optimizes attention, perception, and response preparation. It relies on a sustained activity of the dorsolateral prefrontal Cortex (dlPFC). In the reactive control mode, attention is mobilized as part of a late correction mechanism, and decision-making is guided by stimuli [13]. This mode of control is related to a more transient activation of the dlPFC [14]. As summarized by Braver [12], "proactive control relies upon the anticipation and prevention of interference before it occurs, whereas reactive control relies upon the detection and resolution of interference after its onset". In cognitive neuroscience, various experimental studies have shown a relationship between cognitive workload and cognitive control, as a heavy workload leads to the adoption of a reactive control mode [15].

Moreover, Cegarra, Baracat, Calmettes, Matton & Capa [16] examined the relations between cognitive control modes and mental workload. In this study, the notion of cognitive control was viewed from the perspective of Rasmussen's Skills, Rules, Knowledge (SRK) taxonomy [3]. Cegarra et al. [16] have especially shown that the skill-based level is associated with a lower mental load than the rule-based level.

2.3 Research Question

However, to our knowledge, the relationship existing between the four modes of the COCOM model and the mental workload of operators has not been investigated yet.

In this paper, mental workload is considered with two dimensions, mental stress (i.e., the constraints imposed upon operators) and mental strain (i.e., the cognitive cost of the task for the operators), following the standard DIN ISO 10075-1:2017 [17].

This study aimed at: (a) investigating how cognitive control transits from one mode to another one (as defined by the COCOM model) when the mental stress varies between low and high constraints, and (b) exploring if some physiological measures of mental effort could be sensitive and related to different control modes.

3 A MATB-II Experimental Approach for Studying Cognitive Control

The experiment was conducted by using the MATB-II microworld [18], which has already been used to examine the relations between cognitive control modes and mental workload [16]. The experiment entailed asking participants to execute a main task for which optimum performance would require adopting a strategic mode. The task involved managing fuel tanks, by keeping them at a given level. The task was repeated three times, and its complexity (i.e. mental stress) increased each time.

3.1 Participants

Twenty male participants were recruited among the student population of Université Bretagne Sud in the 18–21 age group (M = 18.55; SD = 0.83). All had normal vision (or corrected to normal vision). The participants were informed of their rights and provided written consent for their participation, in line with the Helsinki Declaration.

3.2 Experimental Set-Up

Participants were asked to carry out tasks in the MATB-II environment, as shown in Fig. 1. MATB-II is a microworld that enables people to execute four tasks that are characteristic of multitasking activity in an aircraft. The communication task was excluded from the protocol because this involves the listening to an audio message in English, which could cause a bias effect due to the heterogeneity of the linguistic level of our participants.

In this experiment, one of these tasks was used as a "main task". This main task, called "Resource management", simulated a continuous process controlling. This task takes the form of a diagrammatic representation of an aircraft fuel system. The task consists of a set of six rectangular tanks, two of which are depleting at a constant speed. There are pumps between the tanks to make it possible to transfer fuel from one tank to one another at a fixed and specific rate. Participants are required to maintain the two depleting tanks at a given fuel level (here at 2, 500 units, symbolized by blue marks on the tanks), by turning the available pumps on and off by means of numpad keys. Sometimes, the pumps failed for a certain amount of time, forcing participants to find a new path to fill in the two depleting tanks.

The secondary tasks were defined as follows. On the one side, there was a tracking task that involved keeping a target inside a rectangular target area (cf. the upper middle of Fig. 1). This task is designed to replicate continuous compensatory actions inherent in piloting an aircraft. The cursor movements follow a forcing function corresponding to a sum of sinusoidal waves for the X and Y axes. This task is manually controlled by participants with the aid of a joystick. On the other side, participants must manage a system monitoring task, consisting in watching six visual indicators, and in correcting any abnormal behavior. The abnormal behavior corresponded to discrete alarms, that the human operator must acknowledge in a given time budget with predefined numpad keys (see the dial in the upper left corner of Fig. 1). For this monitoring task, six parameters needed to be monitored; they related to the colors of the boxes and the position of the marks on the scale. The top two boxes should normally be green for the left one, and white for the right one. The bottom four marks should be approximately in the middle of each scale. Deviations could be observed: the top two boxes could change color (red for the left one, green for the right one), and the bottom marks could move and touch the extremities of each scale. These deviations represent abnormal situations that must be remedied by pressing the key corresponding to the incriminated element: F5 and F6 for the top boxes. Participants needed to press these keys within a time budget of 30 s.

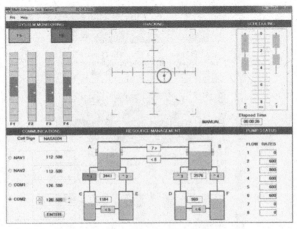

Fig. 1. Screen capture of the MATB-II window (source: https://matb.larc.nasa.gov). (Color figure online)

3.3 Experimental Protocol

A preliminary phase was used to explain the tasks to be executed during a 15-min training session followed by a test session aimed at ensuring that participants had fully understood the instructions. The experimental phase was broken down into three 7-min sequences (see Fig. 2). The first sequence involved the main task only (referred to as "resman"), the second one involved the main task and the secondary system monitoring task (named "with track"), and the third one required participants to execute both the main task and the secondary tracking task (named "with sysmon"). It should be noted that the main task ("resman") was a continuous task, since the participants had to manage the levels of the two reservoirs that changed every second, and whose dynamics (filling or emptying) could change when failures occurred. Furthermore, as explained by Philips et al. [19] and Gutzwiler and Wickens [20], we can also distinguish the two different secondary tasks of our scenario: tracking is a continuous task, which requires permanent control of the trajectory, whereas the monitoring system is a discrete task, consisting of acknowledging alarms when they appear on the screen. Thus, the succession of sequences in our scenario resulted in an increase in difficulty: first there was a continuous task alone, then a continuous task with a discrete task (generating "discrete" stimuli occasionally disturbing the participants in the main task), and finally two continuous tasks (which required the control of two processes whose dynamic evolution must be managed).

Furthermore, Fig. 2 shows that each sequence itself was broken down into two periods: one 3-min period during which executing the main task was less complex and a second 4-min period during which the long breakdown of one pump made the task more complex. At the end of each 7-min sequence, a NASA-TLX questionnaire [21] was given to the participants through the MATB interface.

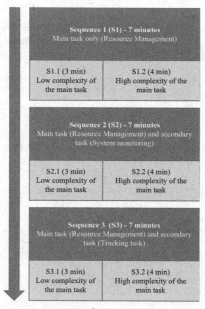

Fig. 2. Three experimental sequences, each with two levels of complexity of the main task (from [2]).

3.4 Measures and Coding

The performance of the main task was coded to identify the modes of cognitive control likely to be adopted by the operator. To do this, we examined whether the participants complied with the instructions for the task (i.e. keeping the level of each of the two reservoirs between 2000L and 3000L), and how they managed their safety margin in relation to the low threshold of 2000L (the low threshold was more difficult to comply with than the high threshold, since pump failures accelerated the emptying of the reservoirs). Table 1 shows the characteristics of the operations used to operationalize each control mode likely to be used for the main task of fuel tank management. In accordance with Hollnagel's model [4], the strategic and the tactical modes are associated with a satisfying performance, whereas the opportunistic mode is associated with some errors and the scrambled mode with a poor performance.

Table 1. Characteristics of the cognitive control modes (from [2]).

Control mode	Performance
Strategic	Complying with instructions and high margins for at least one of the two tanks (maximum upper value between 2,750 and 3,000)
Tactical	Complying with instructions and lower margins for both tanks (values oscillate between 2,000 and 2,750 around the target value of 2,500)
Opportunistic	Errors for at least one tank; the participant takes action when the minimal value (between 2,000 and 1,950) is exceeded
Scrambled	Serious errors for at least one tank; the minimum value (inferior to 1,950) or the maximum value (superior to 3,050) is exceeded by a large margin when the participant intervenes

Two types of physiological data were collected and analyzed as indicative of mental strain: cardiac activity with Bioharness 3 belt (Zephyr, Medtronic, Ireland), and oxygenation and deoxygenation of the prefrontal cortex with the 8-channel functional near-infrared spectroscopy (fNIRS) system (Octamon, Artinis Medical, Netherlands).

These sensors were especially chosen for their known and robust relationships with mental strain (see Table 2), as well as their ease of implementation in real world application, with a few interferences with ambient factors, such as light variations.

Concerning the activity in the prefrontal cortex, the electrical activity of neurons is dependent on their metabolic activity, and more precisely on their need for oxygenated blood. The more the activity of the neurons increases due to a higher mental strain, the more the blood flow in the surrounding arterioles and capillaries increases. This phenomenon is known as neurovascular coupling, and it is possible to assess it to deduce brain activity. Indeed, hemodynamic variations can be measured from the transmission of light in the brain area of interest, with functional Near InfraRed Spectroscopy sensors (fNIRS). This non-invasive imaging technique can distinguish between the concentrations of oxygenated hemoglobin ($[HbO2]$) and deoxygenated hemoglobin ($[HHb]$) since, depending on their state (oxygenated or not), hemoglobin molecules have a different absorption spectrum for the near infrared light range. The processing of fNIRS data was performed using a bandpass filter (0.01 Hz–0.09Hz). To select the cutoff frequencies, we followed the approach of Pinti et al. [27], which advocates a low frequency of 0.01 Hz and a high frequency lower than the Mayer wave frequency (0.01 Hz).

Table 2. Relationships between neurophysiological indicators and mental strain (from [2]).

	Indicators
Cardiac activity	Heart rate variability (HRV), computed within time-domain parameters with the standard deviations over 100 successive RR intervals *Relationship with mental strain:* decreases with an increased mental workload [22, 23]
Prefrontal cortex activity	Concentrations of oxygenated hemoglobin (HBO2) and deoxygenated hemoglobin (HBB) on the 8 optodes of the Fnirs. T1 to T4 capture relative changes in cerebral activation of the right hemisphere of the prefrontal cortex (PFC), and T5 to T8 capture changes in the left hemisphere. Specifically, T1-T7 capture changes in the dorsolateral PFC, T2-T8 capture changes in the ventrolateral PFC, T3-T5 capture changes in the ventromedial PFC, and T4-T6 capture changes in the orbitofrontal PFC *Relationship with mental strain:* neuronal activity is associated with an increase in concentration of oxygenated hemoglobin and a decrease in deoxygenated hemoglobin [24–26]

3.5 Data Analysis Method

The analyses conducted are part of an exploratory study. We used a two-step methodology to analyze the data. Bhapkar and McNemar analyses were conducted to investigate possible links between mental stress (viewed as an independent variable) and control mode (viewed as a dependent variable). Additionally, we used R [28], and especially the lme4 package [29], to perform linear mixed effects analyses of the relationship between sequence and complexity (viewed as independent variables) and the neurophysiological indicators presented in Table 2 (viewed as dependent variables). Visual inspection of residual plots did not reveal any obvious deviations from homoscedasticity or normality. As fixed effects, we entered sequence (single or double task), complexity (low or high, corresponding to whether the main task had few or many incidents on the pumps) and cognitive control mode (with interaction terms) into the full model. As random effect, we had intercept for participants. Regarding fixed effects, a stepwise model selection by AIC (stepAIC) was conducted. During each step, a new model was fitted, in which one of the model terms was eliminated and tested against the former model.

4   Results

4.1   Effect of Mental Stress upon Cognitive Control Modes

First, we conducted a multinomial logistic regression between control modes and the two factors related to mental stress (sequence and complexity). No effects of interaction were found between these two factors. Next, we examined the effect of the complexity of the main task by comparing the control modes adopted when complexity is low (first period) and when it is more important (second period) as shown in Table 3.

Table 3. Contingency table crossing complexity levels and control modes (from [2]).

	Scrambled mode	Opportunistic mode	Tactical mode	Strategic mode
Low complexity	4	3	26	23
High complexity	15	10	3	28

We observed that tactical and strategic modes are largely adopted when the task complexity is low. The strategic mode is still used when the complexity increases but the tactical mode disappears.

A Bhapkar test revealed that the level of complexity has a significant effect on the control mode regardless of the secondary task: resman ($\chi 2(3, 19) = 30.38$, $p < 0.001$), resman with sysmon ($\chi 2(3, 19) = 11.08$, $p = 0.01$), and resman with track ($\chi 2(3, 18) = 20.79$, $p < 0.001$). McNemar post-hoc tests with Bonferroni adjustment revealed that, for the main task alone (resman), the scrambled mode is significantly more frequent when the level of complexity is high ($p = .03$). Besides, the tactical mode is significantly more frequent in tasks with low complexity level than in tasks with high complexity level: resman ($p < .001$), resman with sysmon ($p = .043$) and resman with track ($p = .019$).

The probability of moving from an X mode when the complexity is low to a Y mode when the complexity is higher was calculated from a transition matrix (see Table 4).

Table 4. Matrix of transition between the mode adopted when complexity is low and the mode adopted when complexity is high (from [2]).

	Scrambled mode	Opportunistic mode	Tactical mode	Strategic mode	Total
Scrambled mode	4				4
Opportunistic mode	3				3
Tactical mode	5	9	3	9	26
Strategic mode	3	1		19	23

Examining the transitions between the two periods (hence between the two complexity levels) shows (see Fig. 3) the stability of the strategic mode (among the 23 participants who adopted the strategic mode in the first period, 19 maintained it in the second one) and the instability of the tactical mode (among the 26 participants who adopted the tactical mode in the first period, only 3 maintained it in the second one).

In contrast, the comparisons conducted for each complexity level between sequence 1 (main task alone) and sequences 2 and 3 (main task and secondary tasks of system monitoring and tracking) do not show any negative effect of the secondary task upon the control modes. As a matter of fact, the majority of participants kept the control mode they had adopted for sequence 1 (main task alone), or else they adopted a more effective control mode, which shows the effect of learning.

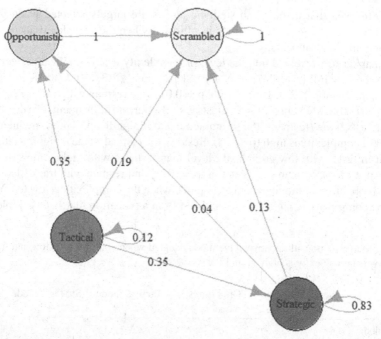

Fig. 3. Transitions between modes between low complexity - S1.1, S2.1, S3.1- and high complexity periods - S1.2, S2.2, S3.2 (from [2]).

4.2 Relations Between Mental Stress and Mental Strain

We conducted different linear mixed-effect analyses to test the effects of task, complexity and cognitive control modes (CCM) on physiological responses. The significant effects (figures in bold in Table 5) are given relative to the reference condition. For example, we can observe the effect of the sequence on HRV, which decreases by 13.72 ms between the single task condition "resman" only" and dual task condition "resman with sysmon", and by 12.46 ms between the single task condition and "resman with tracking" (see Table 5 and the left part of Fig. 4).

These analyses show that HRV can be explained by mental stress, i.e. by sequence, complexity and their interactions (see Table 5 and Fig. 4).

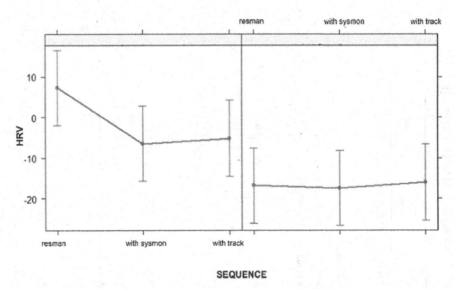

Fig. 4. Interactions of sequence and complexity on HRV (from [2]).

We found a significant main effect of complexity, with HRV more likely to decrease in the high complexity than in the low complexity condition ($\beta = -24.03$, SE = 3.60, $t(63) = -6.67$, $p < 0.001$). Moreover, there is also a significant effect of sequence. We found lower HRV when the main task was carried out with the secondary tracking task ($\beta = -12.46$, SE = 3.69, $t(63) = -3.38$, $p < 0.01$) or with system monitoring task ($\beta = -13.72$, SE = 3.60, $t(63) = -3.81$, $p < 0.001$), than when it was conducted as a single task.

This effect of sequence upon operator strain is also observed, on the mental demand dimension of the NASA-TLX. A one-way between subjects ANOVA shows that the single task condition involved a significantly lower mental demand than the double task conditions ($F(2, 48) = 4.32$, $p < 0.05$). The interaction between complexity and sequence is also found to be significant, with a higher contrast between single task and double task conditions when the complexity is low. Moreover, there is no significant correlation between neurophysiological indicators and NASA-TLX scores.

Table 5. Estimates of fixed effects from linear mixed-effect model for HBO2 on the 8 fNIRS optodes and for HRV (from [2]).

	HBO2 T1 ~ CCM + Sequence	HBO2 T2 ~ CCM	HBO2 T3 ~ CCM	HBO2 T4 ~ CCM + Sequence	HBO2 T5 ~ CCM	HBO2 T6 ~ CCM	HBO2 T7 ~ CCM	HRV ~ Complexity * Sequence
(Intercept)	0.13 (1.66)	3.08 (0.95)**	0.26 (2.56)	1.39 (1.16)	0.36 (2.53)	2.66 (0.95)**	1.3= (0.94)	7.25 (4.66)
CCM (reference = Tactical)								
Opportunistic	0.94 (0.21)***	1.11 (0.32)***	0.69 (0.30)*	0.99 (0.34)**	0.48 (0.29)	0.97 (0.32)**	0.5= (0.28)*	
Scrambled	1.08 (0.24)***	0.71 (0.36)*	1.26 (0.33)***	0.84 (0.39)*	0.62 (0.33)	0.85 (0.35)*	0.71 (0.32)*	
Strategic	0.63 (0.18)***	0.78 (0.27)**	0.76 (0.25)**	0.53 (0.29)	0.71 (0.25)**	0.74 (0.27)**	0.7= (0.24)**	
Sequence (reference = single task resman)								
with sysmon	0.23 (0.15)			0.30 (0.24)				-13.72 (3.60)***
with track	0.48 (0.15)**			0.69 (0.24)**				-12.46 (3.69)***
Complexity (reference = low complexity)								
high complexity								-24.03 (3.60)***
Sequence:Complexity								
with sysmon : high complexity								13.07 (5.09)*
with track: high complexity								13.24 (5.19)*
Num. obs.	100	100	100	100	100	100	100	82
Num. groups: Participant_	17	17	17	17	17	17	17	14
Var: Participant_ (Intercept)	46.61	14.82	110.76	21.72	108.17	14.62	14.=2	212.55
Var: Residual	0.36	0.82	0.70	0.93	0.69	0.80	0.6=	90.84

4.3 Relations Between Cognitive Control Mode and Mental Strain

The linear mixed-effect analyses also showed a significant effect of the control modes (CCM) upon the concentration in oxy-hemoglobin (HBO2). According to the stepwise model selection by AIC, HBO2 can be explained by control modes only, for optodes T2, T3, T5, T6 and T7, whereas HBO2 for optodes T1 and T4 can be explained by two main fixed effects, CCM and sequence. We followed the same procedure for concentration in deoxy-hemoglobin (HBB), but no significant results were found.

It should be noted that, for all the optodes from T1 to T7, the tactical control mode (set as reference condition in the linear mixed model) always produces a significant lower HBO2 concentration, in comparison with the less effective modes (scrambled and opportunistic control) or the more anticipatory one (strategic control).

5   Discussion

The study findings are both theoretical and methodological in nature. First, regarding the stress-strain relationship, we observed a significant effect of mental stress on HRV, which was expected. There is especially a main effect of the complexity of the reservoir management task on cardiac activity. In addition, we investigated, in a more original way, the relation between the cognitive control modes and mental workload, from the perspective of both mental stress and mental strain. Our analyses reveal two main theoretical contributions.

On the one hand, there is a significant effect of task complexity on the adoption and the variation of control modes. In particular, we found an instability of the tactical mode, showing attraction between this mode and low complexity, and repulsion between this mode and higher complexity. We observed that an increase in complexity mainly leads to transitions from the tactical mode to a less effective mode (54% of the transitions). In contrast, the strategic and scrambled modes were mostly stable when complexity increased (respectively 83% and 100% of participants in one of this mode remained in the same mode). Furthermore, and congruent with the study of Stanton et al. [7], we observed that a major part of the transition is between two "close" modes (70% of transitions from tactical to opportunistic or strategic modes, and 100% of transitions from opportunistic to scrambled modes). This result suggests that people move between control modes in a linear manner. On the other hand, we found links between the modes of control and operator strain, as it was shown by Cegarra et al. [16]. The present study indicates that the tactical mode is associated with lower mental strain, when considering the HBO2 concentration indicator of mental workload. As stated by Leon-Carrion et al. [30], "the hemodynamics of inter-individual differences in this region may reflect different cognitive strategies used in task resolution". Our study shows that the tactical mode is the most efficient one, since it is associated with a satisfying performance and with the lowest mental strain off all control modes.

This result underlined the advantage of studying brain activity to detect changes in control mode. If, in our study, the cerebral activity seems little correlated with mental stress variations, we nevertheless observe, on almost all the areas of the prefrontal cortex, a significant difference in HBO2 concentration between the tactical mode and other modes. Thus, an increase in cortical activation helped reveal the shift away from the tactical mode towards less effective and more reactive control (the opportunistic or scrambled mode, where control of the situation is no longer guaranteed) or on the contrary towards more proactive control (the strategic mode, requiring more anticipation).

This potential detection ability opens new perspectives to design and trigger assistance aimed at keeping operators in the tactical mode, since it appears to be the most efficient one. Such perspectives are worth considering in all areas where operators have to control dynamic situations and where they have therefore to make, in real time, compromises between speed and efficiency, between performance and risk, or between understanding and action [31]. Such circumstances cover the field of transport but also the supervision of industrial processes, or the field of crisis management.

Finally, it should be noted that this research work has some limitations. The experiment was run with novice participants only, who may be more heterogeneous in terms of cognitive control than an expert population. One may thus wonder whether some individual factors might not explain the propensity of some participants to adopt a particular control mode. Therefore, it would be necessary to verify whether the same findings would apply to experts (e.g. a population of aircraft pilots).

6 Conclusion

This study aimed to better understand the decision-making mechanisms that occur in dynamic situations. More specifically, it aimed to explore the relationships between mental stress, cognitive control, and mental strain. The work carried out allows us to better understand these links, to explore the influences exerted by these three factors as well as their interactions.

It was observed in this study that the control modes, defined according to the COCOM model, support the regulations of operators' mental workload, and cab be considered as a moderator of the stress-strain relationship, as previous authors assume [16, 32–34].

Particularly, the classical relationship between mental stress and mental strain was retrieved, with a significant effect on task difficulty on physiological activation, especially on HRV. Moreover, an effect of mental stress on cognitive control was also found, with notably an instability of the tactical mode, instantiated preferentially when the task difficulty was low, and abandoned in favor of more reactive modes when the task difficulty increased. The scrambled and strategic modes showed some stability regardless of the task difficulty. Finally, the results underlined links between cognitive control and mental strain, notably through lower brain activity measured with fNIRS when participants adopter the tactical mode instead of more reactive (scrambled or opportunistic) or proactive (strategic) modes. As suggested by Hollnagel et al. [4] and Stanton et al. [8], these findings showed that the tactical mode can be considered as the most efficient one, with a satisfying performance and a lower mental workload.

This study also stressed the interest for the neuroergonomic measurements performed with the fNIRS. The results obtained with this sensor allowed to discriminate different levels of brain activity related to different levels of mental workload, that can be related to different modes of cognitive control, as assumed by Braver et al. [12] and Ryman et al. [14].

Finally, the potential ability of fNIRS system to detect the tactical mode with HBO2 concentration could, in the future, help trigger adaptive assistance so as to keep operators in this efficient mode, especially in the domain of aviation where pilots can face dynamic situations and need to adapt very promptly their cognitive activities.

References

1. Hoc, J.M.: Supervision et contrôle de processus: la cognition en situation dynamique. Presses universitaires de Grenoble, Grenoble (1996)
2. Rauffet, P., Saïd, F., Laouar, A., Chauvin, C., Bressolle, M.C.: Cognitive control modes and mental workload: an experimental approach. In 4th International Conference on Computer-Human Interaction Research and Applications (CHIRA), pp. 17–26 (2020)
3. Rasmussen, J.: Skills, rules, and knowledge - signals, signs, and symbols, and other distinctions in human performance models. IEEE Trans. Syst. Man Cybern. **13**, 257–266 (1983)
4. Hollnagel, E.: Human Reliability Analysis – Context and Control. Academic Press, London (1993)
5. Borghini, G., et al.: EEG-based cognitive control behaviour assessment: an ecological study with professional air traffic controllers. Sci. Rep. **7**(1), 1–16 (2017)
6. Hoc, J.M., Amalberti, R.: Cognitive control dynamics for reaching a satisfying performance in complex dynamic situations. J. Cogn. Eng. Decis. Making **1**, 22–55 (2007)
7. Hollnagel, E.: Time and time again. Theor. Issues Ergon. Sci. **3**, 143–158 (2002)
8. Stanton, N.A., Ashleigh, M.J., Roberts, A.D., Xu, F.: Testing Hollnagel's contextual control model: assessing team behaviour in a human supervisory control task. J. Cogn. Ergon. **5**, 21–33 (2001)
9. Eriksson, A., Stanton, N.A.: Driving performance after self-regulated control transitions in highly automated vehicles. Hum. Factors **59**, 1233–1248 (2017)
10. Chauvin, C., Said, F., Langlois, S.: Does the type of visualization influence the mode of cognitive control in a dynamic system? In: Karwowski, W., Ahram, T. (eds.) IHSI 2019. Advances in Intelligent Systems and Computing, vol. 903, pp. 751–757. Springer, Cham (2019). https://doi.org/10.1007/978-3-030-11051-2_114
11. Chauvin, C., Said, F., Rauffet, P., Langlois, S.: Analyzing the take-over performance in an automated vehicle in terms of cognitive control modes. Le travail humain **83**(4), 379–405 (2020)
12. Braver, T.S.: The variable nature of cognitive control: a dual mechanisms framework. Trends Cogn. Sci. **16**(2), 106–113 (2012)
13. Mäki-Marttunen, V., Hagen, T., Espeseth, T.: Proactive and reactive modes of cognitive control can operate independently and simultaneously. Acta Physiol. **199**, 102891 (2019)
14. Ryman, S.G., et al.: Proactive and reactive cognitive control rely on flexible use of the ventrolateral prefrontal cortex. Hum. Brain Mapp. **40**(3), 955–966 (2019)
15. Mäki-Marttunen, V., Hagen, T., Espeseth, T.: Task context load induces reactive cognitive control: an fMRI study on cortical and brain stem activity. Cogn. Affect. Behav. Neurosci. **19**(4), 945–965 (2019)
16. Cegarra, J., Baracat, B., Calmettes, C., Matton, N., Capa, R.L.: A neuroergonomics perspective on mental workload predictions in Jens Rasmussen's SRK framework. Le travail humain **80**, 7–22 (2017)
17. DIN EN ISO 10075-1. Ergonomic principles related to mental workload—Part 1: general issues and concepts, terms and definitions (ISO 10075-1:2017) (2018)
18. Santiago-Espada, Y., Myer, R.R., Latorella, K.A., Comstock Jr., J.R.: The multi-attribute task battery II (MATB-II) software for human performance and workload research: a user's guide (2011)

19. Phillips, C.A., Repperger, D.W., Kinsler, R., Bharwani, G., Kender, D.: A quantitative model of the human–machine interaction and multi-task performance: a strategy function and the unity model paradigm. Comput. Biol. Med. **37**(9), 1259–1271 (2007)
20. Gutzwiller, R.S., Wickens, C.D., Clegg, B.A.: Workload overload modeling: an experiment with MATB II to inform a computational model of task management. In: Proceedings of the Human Factors and Ergonomics Society Annual Meeting, vol. 58, no. 1, pp. 849–853. Sage CA, Los Angeles (2014)
21. Hart, S.G., Staveland, L.E.: Development of NASA-TLX (task load index): results of empirical and theoretical research. In Advances in Psychology, vol. 52, pp. 139–183. North-Holland (1988)
22. Malik, M.: Heart rate variability: standards of measurement, physiological interpretation, and clinical use: task force of the European society of cardiology and the North American society for pacing and electrophysiology. Ann. Noninvasive Electrocardiol. **1**(2), 151–181 (1996)
23. Durantin, G., Gagnon, J.F., Tremblay, S., Dehais, F.: Using near infrared spectroscopy and heart rate variability to detect mental overload. Behav. Brain Res. **259**, 16–23 (2014)
24. Fairclough, S.H., Burns, C., Kreplin, U.: FNIRS activity in the prefrontal cortex and motivational intensity: impact of working memory load, financial reward, and correlation-based signal improvement. Neurophotonics **5**(3), 035001 (2018)
25. Causse, M., Chua, Z.K., Rémy, F.: Influences of age, mental workload, and flight experience on cognitive performance and prefrontal activity in private pilots: a fNIRS study. Sci. Rep. **9**(1), 1–12 (2019)
26. Causse, M., Chua, Z., Peysakhovich, V., Del Campo, N., Matton, N.: Mental workload and neural efficiency quantified in the prefrontal cortex using fNIRS. Sci. Rep. **7**(1), 1–15 (2017)
27. Pinti, P., Scholkmann, F., Hamilton, A., Burgess, P., Tachtsidis, I.: Current status and issues regarding pre-processing of fNIRS neuroimaging data: an investigation of diverse signal filtering methods within a general linear model framework. Front. Hum. Neurosci. **12**, 505 (2019)
28. R Core Team. R: A language and environment for statistical computing. Foundation for statistical Computing. Vienna, Austria (2012)
29. Bates, D.M., Maechler, M., Bolker, B.: lme4: linear mixed-effects using S4 classes. R package version 0.999999-0 (2012)
30. León-Carrion, J., et al.: The hemodynamics of cognitive control: the level of concentration of oxygenated hemoglobin in the superior prefrontal cortex varies as a function of performance in a modified Stroop task. Behav. Brain Res. **193**(2), 248–256 (2008)
31. Hoc, J.M.: La relation homme-machine en situation dynamique. Rev. d'intell. Artif. **14**(1), 55–71 (2000)
32. Hockey, G.R.J.: Compensatory control in the regulation of human performance under stress and high workload: a cognitive-energetical framework. Biol. Psychol. **45**(1–3), 73–93 (1997)
33. Kostenko, A., Rauffet, P., Chauvin, C., Coppin, G.: A dynamic closed-looped and multidimensional model for Mental Workload evaluation. IFAC-PapersOnLine **49**(19), 549–554 (2016)
34. Kostenko, A., Rauffet, P., Moga, S., Coppin, G.: Operator functional state: measure it with attention intensity and selectivity, explain it with cognitive control. In: Longo, L., Leva, M.C. (eds.) H-WORKLOAD 2019. CCIS, vol. 1107, pp. 156–169. Springer, Cham (2019). https://doi.org/10.1007/978-3-030-32423-0_10

Eyetracking Nutritional Behaviour and Choices

Julius Schöning$^{(\boxtimes)}$ ⓘ and Shoma Berkemeyer ⓘ

Osnabrück University of Applied Sciences, Osnabrück, Germany
{j.schoening, s.berkemeyer}@hs-osnabrueck.de

Abstract. Visual attention on nutritional outcomes are currently under investigation. Across a variety of disciplines, visual analytics currently offers many new applications with easy-to-use tools. In this interdisciplinary pilot study, we are refining a novel visual analytics software for assessing dietary and food choices. The goal is to improve our understanding of nutritional behavior when individuals are hungry or satiated. In addition to developing a software toolchain, two null hypotheses were investigated: *1*) there is no difference between visual search patterns on food when subjects were hungry and satiated and *2*) there is no difference in visual search patterns between subjects when vegetarian and non-vegetarian. The experimental data suggest that food choices may differ from dietary patterns and are slightly correlated with dish gazing. Using visual analytics of food scene perception our study suggests there is likely variation in food gazing pattern when hungry and when satiated. Our study further suggests that participants' dish-gazing probably could be generalizable; the participants' gazes on dishes were predicted by shallow artificial neuronal networks (ANN). The mean squared error of the predicted to the real gaze points were 11.1%, probably indicating that study participants' scene perception of food could be dirigible. In conclusion, to understand the complicated relationship between scene perception and nutritional behavioral patterns, this pilot study needs to be scaled up to a full study.

Keywords: Scene perception · Dietary patterns · Food choices · Nutritional behavior · Gaze analytics · Artificial Neuronal Networks (ANN) · Visualization · Nutritional patterns

1 Introduction

Visual attention on nutritional outcomes are receiving greater research focus [3,20]. Studies in this interdisciplinary research area have though classically concentrated largely on consumer purchase behavior for food products alone [7,20]. Nutritional outcomes though encompass far broader and far-reaching outcomes, such as, dietary patterns, food perception, health status and as well nutritional status. In our previous pilot study, we investigated gazing patterns on dishes in the state of being hungry and in a state of satiation, and our initial results indicated that there could be variations, which itself is a complex outcome of physiological and behavioral processes in food choices and dietary patterns [3]. The attitude towards food, including food culture, and individual emotional state relate to perception of and preference of food as well and can, thus, co-determine food choice. Short-term food choices and long-term dietary patterns affect

A. Holzinger et al. (Eds.): CHIRA 2020, CCIS 1609, pp. 17–31, 2022.
https://doi.org/10.1007/978-3-031-22015-9_2

nutritional status, all of which have a bearing on etiology and therapy of nutrition-based diseases [4, 12, 14].

The field of visual analytics offers applications for the acquisition of gaze data and the visualization of gaze as the perception of the scene. In the research field of nutrition, the use of visual analytics is still in its early stages. In our previous work [3], we have combined therefore these disciplines. Observing visual search patterns on food opens up attractive nutrition research opportunities and provides insight for, e.g., new treatment options.

In addition to developing an easy-to-use toolchain to conduct and analyze food scene perception studies for nutrition research, a first pilot study was was conducted. The aim of our pilot study was to examine scene perception concerning gazes on food when hungry, i.e., before lunch, and the gazes on food when satiated, i.e., after lunch. Prior knowledge of dietary patterns was also included. The underlying assumption of the pilot study was that *involuntary* gaze movements on dishes would be an index of spontaneous nutritional decisions. Taken into account the prior knowledge of dietary patterns, gaze movements to preferred dishes should be more focused, i.e., not *involuntary*.

In the context of this paper, the aims of our pilot study are presented, the developed tooling is introduced, and the hypotheses are stated. Section 3, Methodology, describes the setting, the participants, the development of the visual analysis tool used to analyze gaze data to index scene perception, and the data analysis conducted. Based on the results in Sect. 4, Sect. 5 describes the prototype prediction of participants' gaze using slightly modified versions of the LeNet [11] and AlexNet [10] ANN architecture. The interplay of recorded scene perceptions, predicted viewpoints, and food selection is discussed in Sect. 6. Note that all survey data were collected just before the COVID-19 pandemic. Thus, due to the ongoing pandemic situation, it was not possible to collect new data, and thus this work mainly extends our work [3] with a detailed bootstrap analysis and individual gaze pattern prediction by ANN.

2   Structure of the Pilot Study

Gaining interdisciplinary knowledge from nutritional, computer, and behavioral sciences, three goals were determined:

I creating software for conducting surveys with low-cost eye-tracking devices at the site of food consumption,
II testing the analysis toolchain for first insights on the null-hypothesis introduced in Sect. 2.2, and
III prototyping an AI-based prediction of participants' gaze position and scene perception on dishes.

2.1   Study Design

Nutrition studies considering scene perception required data collection directly in the places such as canteens or food courts where food is consumed. For our study, the university cafeteria setting was chosen because of its proximity and ease of pilot testing. It

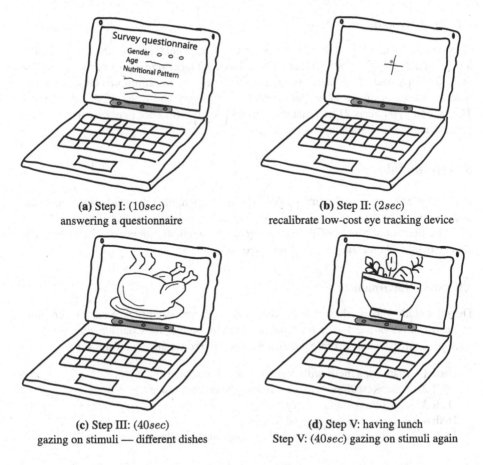

(a) Step I: (10sec)
answering a questionnaire

(b) Step II: (2sec)
recalibrate low-cost eye tracking device

(c) Step III: (40sec)
gazing on stimuli — different dishes

(d) Step V: having lunch
Step V: (40sec) gazing on stimuli again

Fig. 1. Steps of the study designed [3]; not illustrated: Step IV have lunch.

can be assumed that individuals have limited time for their lunch break, including food intake, classically half to three-quarters of an hour is granted by organizations for lunch breaks. Therefore, with a mobile hardware-software solution, the study had to be feasible without requiring special equipment such as chin rests, and the execution of each experiment was made possible with minimal participant's time investment in their lunch break. In addition to collecting questionnaire-based information from participants, the implemented survey tool allowed to record gaze points on stimuli types such as photos, video footage, and animations.

Besides data collection, data storage for an interdisciplinary team was the second challenge. Using multimedia container formats for storing data series [17, 18] facilitated this study an initial exploratory visual data analysis without the requirement of using a dedicated tool. By improving this existing concept, a more meaningful visualization was implemented, as illustrated in Fig. 7. The storing data series in multimedia container formats allowed nutritionists to explore the collected data without the need for self-compiled or costly proprietary software. This approach enables new dimensions in nutritional analytics.

2.2 Null-Hypotheses

Prior to the data collection, two hypotheses were generated to test the complete toolchain and gain the first insights without having a large number of participants. The first null hypothesis *1)* defined was that there would be no difference between visual search patterns of dishes when participants were hungry and when they were satiated. The second hypothesis *2)* was that there would be no difference between visual search patterns and a priori stated dietary patterns.

3   Methodology

In January 2020, prior to the first COVID-19 lock-down, the pilot study was conducted to the terms of the Declaration of Helsinki [21]. Informed consents were obtained before study participation. Since there was no unique personal and identifiable data that was collected, ethical clearance was not required for this pilot study.

3.1   Study Environment

The pilot study was conducted in the university canteen Osnabrück. Students, employees, and visitors of the university canteen were among the study participants. Four different main dishes and several side dishes were offered on the day of the survey:

Dish 1. organic spaghetti with organic soy bolognese
Dish 2. chicken escalope with peach and hollandaise sauce
Dish 3. gemstone pumpkin curry
Dish 4. beef Esterhazy in vegetable sauce
Dish 5. side dishes i.e., potatoes, salad, soup, and noodles.

3.2   Variables and Software Tooling

A cross-sectional study design was used for this early-stage feasibility study. Therefore, the exploratory study was conducted with a total of ten participants, which generate a visualizable set of gaze pattern data on food. On the survey day, visitors to the cafeteria were randomly selected as study participants. Given willingness to participate in the study and informed consent, participants underwent a computerized gaze tracking experiment once before and once after eating lunch. Inclusion of ten participants for pilot feasibility was determined by the duration of the lunch break period, of approximately half to three-quarters of an hour per person, over a total lunch period between 12:00 and 14:00 on the survey day, and the use of a single computer-based terminal with eye-tracking device for data collection. Study participation, although stochastically randomized, cannot rule out bias in study participation by those who were naturally more interested in nutrition compared with those who were less interested in nutrition. A study staff member conducted the study on the day of the interview. The software developed for this pilot study integrated a self-reidentification sequence for study participants, allowing for ease of use and applicability for matching data collection before and after having lunch.

Dietary patterns were divided into the two classes of non-vegetarian and vegetarian. The class non-vegetarian includes omnivorous, healthy omnivore nutrition [6], and paleo-diet. The vegetarian class included ovo-lacto-vegetarian, ovo-vegetarian, lacto-vegetarian, vegan diets; raw food, whole food, flexitarian diets; and pesco-vegetarian diets. It was assumed that the dietary pattern chosen indicated long-term dietary behavior. Furthermore, we also assumed that food choices indicated ad hoc decision-making by participants. The dishes of the cafeteria menu determined the food choices that could be selected by the study participants on the survey day. Therefore, for this exploratory study, food choices were assumed to indicate short-term dietary behavior. On the study day, the five menus, dish 1 to dish 5, were available for selection. In addition to dietary patterns, background data on age, gender, and country of birth were collected. All data were collected anonymously, so ethical clearance was redundant.

A standard mid-class laptop with a built-in or detachable low-cost eye-tracking device was used as the mobile hardware platform. After estimating the required computing power, it was determined by the research-group, that a low-cost laptop was not capable to synchronously display the stimuli and perform the data storage of the gaze data. Thus multi-threading was required for the mobile software solution. For the pilot study, a standard mid-class laptop with an *Intel i5* CPU and a *Tobii EyeX* eye tracker was used.

The self-developed software covered, as shown in Fig. 1, the entire process of data collection. This process also included the human-machine interaction, e.g., the questionnaire and the calibration of the eye-tracking device. Our software was designed as free, open-source software and can be downloaded from our project website[1]. The software written in the programming language C++ can provide timed graphical user interfaces for, e.g., the presentation of the stimuli at a defined time and thereafter to synchronize with different low-cost eye-tracking devices. Based on the free widget toolkit QT, our software is available as open-source for public research.

For improving the accuracy of low-cost eye-tracking devices, a simple calibration routine was implemented that allowed recalibration of the gaze points in a few seconds. In this calibration routine, the participant was therefore asked to fixate on a cross in the center of the screen, refer to Fig. 1(b). Based on the detected fixations over a period of one second, the software recalibrated the gaze points. Fixations with an offset greater than 50 pixels were neglected during the calibration routine.

In each of the university canteen dishes change daily. These daily changes, were taken into account in the study and software design. Thus, a flexible switch between the stimuli without programming was made possible. As shown in Fig. 1(c), the stimulus showed photos or videos of university canteen dishes. These stimuli could be easily placed in a specific file folder next to our study software. Through the naming convention, the software recognized and knew the order and the duration of the stimulus. For example, if a video of a dish was to be shown for 5000 msec, the video sequence was named "Dish1_5000.mp4". In case, if a 4500 msec photo was shown as the next stimuli, this was named "Dish2_4500.jpg". There was no limit to the number of stimuli, and one could continue the list of stimuli following this pattern. In this way, a lightweight,

---

[1] Software source code can be downloaded at https://www.hs-osnabrueck.de/prof-dr-julius-schoening/nba.

(a) dish 4: before having lunch   (b) dish 4: after having lunch

(c) dish 5: before having lunch   (d) dish 5: after having lunch

Fig. 2. Cumulated gaze patters off all participants on stimulus dish 4 and dish 5, after having lunch the participants explore the outer areas of the stimulus [3]. (Color figure online)

simple, and flexible solution for interchangeable stimuli was developed in this pilot study.

To avoid repeated restarting of the software for each participant, a guided dialogue was provided to the survey instructor, which allowed back and forth movements with command repetitions. This user interface design reduced the training time for survey instructors, as the guided dialogue makes the software applicability—almost intuitive.

A reward for study participants was incorporated into the study design and to facilitate re-recruiting participants after lunch. As a reward, the participants received her/his gazes on the stimuli visualized in a multimedia format compatible with standard multimedia players [16]. The visualization in multimedia format is described in the following section in detail.

3.3   Analysis

For the analysis of scene perception, the gaze trajectories on each plate were visualized for our study. For this purpose, a simple Python script was used to generate static heat maps for each shown dish per participant, as shown in Fig. 2. In addition to the five different dishes, see Subsect. 3.1, a white screen was also shown for zero-error correction calibration. For further analyses, differences in gaze patterns were visualized for hunger and for satiety.

For visual inspection focusing on the hypotheses *1)*, the resulting heat maps were plotted side by side. In addition to the heat maps per participant, cumulative heat maps per dish were created for all participants, cf. Fig. 2. With the focus on hypotheses *2)*, cumulative heat maps were also generated across vegetarians and non-vegetarians.

The visual search pattern at hunger and satiety as an assessment of nutritional behavior was compared with the participants' food choices at the midday meal. In doing so, we visually examined and thus tested the possibility of using visual search pattern heat maps to assess nutritional behavior.

We additionally analyzed the difference in stated meal preference when hungry with actual meal chosen when hungry in a bootstrap analysis using data of the ten participants and generating bootstrap replicates of $10,000$. Likewise we ran bootstrap replicates of $10,000$ for correlation between stated meal choice when hungry with age, sex, ethnicity and dietary patterns: As a corollary we also ran bootstrap replicates of $10,000$ for correlation between actual meal chosen on the day with age, sex, ethnicity and dietary patterns. An alpha of 0.05 was considered significant for all bootstrap runs. For age, sex and ethnicity the runs served the purpose of study intern validity check. The run for dietary patterns was targeted to estimate how much short-term food choice and long-term dietary patterns correlate.

4   Results

A detailed tabular overview of all study participants is presented in the appendix of our previous paper [3]. Briefly, we provide the characteristics of the ten study participants. Of the ten, seven had a non-vegetarian dietary pattern and three had a vegetarian dietary pattern. Of the three vegetarians, one had a vegan dietary pattern, one had a vegetarian dietary pattern, and the third had a pescovegetarian dietary pattern. Of the total participants, three were female and seven were male in an age range of 23–40 years. Of the seven non-vegetarians, two were female and five were male, and of the three vegetarians, one was male and two were female.

Based on the individual gaze data the hypothesis *1)* was tested. As Fig. 3 suggests that there was no significant difference between visual search patterns when hungry and at satiety. Visual inspection indicated that there could be gaze discrepancies in cumulative gaze patterns, i.e., during hunger and during satiety. However, this observation could also be due to the fact that the same photographs were presented before and after lunch, which remains a confounding factor in the study. In a corollary analysis, cf. Fig. 3, the cumulative similarity in visual search pattern over the five dishes yielded concordance in the range of 0.53% and 9.72%, indicating that there is likely variation in food gazing pattern when hungry and when satiated, which our study currently is not powered enough to detect it.

Gaze pattern of the seven non-vegetarians showed that three gazed at dish 2, and two chose dish 2 (chicken schnitzel with peach and hollandaise sauce), one chose an undisclosed dish 5; two gazed at dish 4, and one chose it and the other chose dish 2. The seventh non-vegetarian was undecided and chose dish 1 (organic spaghetti with organic soy bolognase). Of the seven non-vegetarians, six were decided and one undecided as to meal choice when hungry, and of the six only three chose what they gazed at.

Gaze pattern Of the three vegetarians showed that the vegan participant gazed and chose dish 3 (gemstone curry). One was undecided and chose an undisclosed dish 5. The

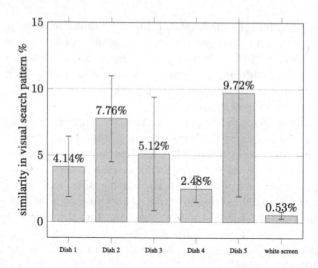

Fig. 3. Similarity of visual search pattern when hungry and when satiated, accumulated over all participants [3].

third vegetarian (pescovegetarian) gazed, and chose dish 2. Of the three vegetarians, two chose different dishes than at onset; one food-choice was different from the dietary pattern, one remained undisclosed.

In this exploratory analysis only four (one vegetarian and three non-vegetarian) out of the ten ten participants, i.e. 40%, made food choices that coincided with what they gazed at when hungry. Two were undecided in food-choice from onset on (one vegetarian and one non-vegetarian). Of the remaining four participants (one vegetarian and three non-vegetarian), three food choices were different from what was gazed at, yet within the dietary pattern (non-vegetarian) and in one case food choice was different from the stated dietary pattern (vegetarian).

The bootstrap results on difference in stated meal preference when hungry with actual meal chosen when hungry yielded a t-value of 3.3 $[CI\ 2.2, 4.0]$ at a bias of 0.0045 and standard error of 0.4518 for when hungry and a t-value of 3.0 $[CI\ 2.0, 3.7]$ at a bias of 0.0007 and standard error of 0.4210 when satiated. In that, the confidence interval (CI) of both the t-statistic overlap there was no significant difference in meal preference when hungry and actual meal chosen when hungry.

The bootstrapping results on age, sex and ethnicity confirmed that the study retained internal validity.

Results on short-term food choice and long-term dietary patterns indicated a t-value of 0.05 $[CI\ -0.7, 0.6]$ at a bias of 0.0056 and standard error of 0.3105 for meal preference when hungry and a t-value of 0.29 at a bias of -0.0013 and standard error of 0.3057 for meal actually chosen, indicating that there can be significant differences in long-term dietary pattern, which is a long-term preference, and short term food choice, which is largely short-term decision-making.

5   Predicting Users Gazes on Dishes

As stated by Hornik et al. [8] "standard multilayer feedforward networks are capable of approximating any measurable function to any desired degree of accuracy, in a very specific and satisfying sense". Therefore, in theory, if an ANN can predict the gaze points on a dish, the scene perception on food might be generalizable and could not be a pure coincidence.

5.1   Prototypical ANN

For the prediction of the gaze points, the general architecture of LeNet [11], and AlexNet [10] was chosen. Since both network architectures were originally designed for image classification, the output layers had to be altered. As in Fig. 4 bluely high-lighted, the output layer in both architectures were replaced by an output vector for 20 gaze points. Each gaze point comprised out of one x and one y coordinate representing the gaze position on the stimuli. For ensuring that the ReLU activation function of the output layer was cable to return valid gaze coordinates, both the x and y coordinates had to be converted from $[1, 1920]$ for x and from $[1, 1080]$ for y to $[0, 1]$. For reducing the number of trainable parameters within the modified version of the LeNet and AlexNet, the stimuli images were rescaled from 1920×1080 to 960×540 pixel. For both ANN architectures, gray-scale input images were used. Thus, the modified LeNet had $9, 401, 216$ and the modified AlexNet had $303, 829, 776$ trainable parameters.

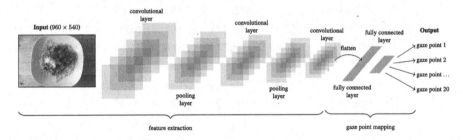

Fig. 4. Sketch of ANN architects used for gaze point prediction; for both the LeNet [11] and AlexNet [10] the stimuli image is rescaled to 960×540 pixel, and the output layer–marked blue– is altered to a vector of 20 gaze points; for all layers, the ReLU is used as activation function. (Color figure online)

For the training data set, 20 gaze points on the dishes 1, 2, 3, and 5 per participant are randomly selected. Figure 5 exemplary shows the 20 randomly sampled gaze points of participant P280413. Note the training data set generation for participant P284111 and P285611 failed due the high number of invalid measurement point on dish 5 therefore no ANN could be trained for these to participants. As unseen validation data set the gaze point on dish 4 were chosen.

Based on the training data, for each participant both the modified LeNet and AlexNet were trained over 100 epochs of training. Avoiding overfitting the training data set was augmented by mirroring the data, input images as well as corresponding gaze points, horizontal and vertical.

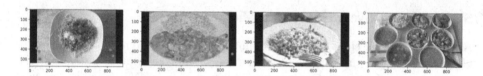

Fig. 5. Training data set, dish 1, dish 2, dish 3, and dish 5 of participant P280413; red dots 20 randomly sampled gaze points. Dish 4 is excluded from training, it serves as unseen validation data. (Color figure online)

5.2   Evaluation

Table 1. Predicted gaze patters by the modified LeNet and AlexNet ANN; Minimum and maximum values of the mean absolute error (MAE) and mean squared error (MSE) highlighted.

	LeNet		AlexNet	
Participant	MAE	MSE	MAE	MSE
P280413	**21.42 %**	8.59 %	**11.55 %**	**5.00 %**
P281612	27.55 %	14.44 %	30.61 %	16.04 %
P283111	23.46 %	9.75 %	23.04 %	7.21 %
P283312	24.17 %	9.29 %	**37.45 %**	**17.97 %**
P283811	28.69 %	12.83 %	29.87 %	15.83 %
P284811	22.41 %	**8.49 %**	19.05 %	6.21 %
P285111	**30.96 %**	**15.72 %**	25.68 %	11.65 %
P285710	23.79 %	9.55 %	21.51 %	8.77 %
Average:	25.31 %	11.08 %	24.84 %	11.09 %
Top-3 average:	22.43 %	8.79 %	17.37 %	6.14 %

Based on the unseen validation data set, dish 4, the participant-specific trained ANNs were evaluated. As evaluations metrics mean absolute error (MAE) and mean squared error (MSE) between the 20 predicted gaze points and 20 randomly chosen real gaze points were calculated, cf. Table 1. The minimum MAE is 21.42% for the modified LeNet and 11.55% for the modified AlexNet, where the minimum MSE are 8.49% and 5,00%. This difference between MAE and MSE might have been caused by our data augmentation technique of mirroring the training data. Independent of the ANN architecture, the average MSE overall participants was 11.1%. Nevertheless, the AlexNet, as more complex architecture, outperformed the LeNet in the top-3 average of MAE and MSE by more than 2%.

The visualization of predicted gaze points showed, that in cases where the ANN predicted less gaze points on the edges of the stimuli image, the MSE value is below 10%, cf. Fig. 6 (a) and (b). In cases where a hight MSE value occured, Fig. 6 (c) and (d), more than 9 predicted gaze points were on the edges of the stimuli image. The height number of predicted gaze points on the image edges might have been caused due to insufficient training data for a participant, where insufficient was defined in terms of the number of gaze points considered during training as well as of the corner case covered by the randomly picked points.

To avoid predicted gaze points on the image edges, the ANN training process requires to be altered so that at training time, 20 gaze points could be randomly selected from certain stimuli. The gaze point selection at training time ensured that the ANN would consider the significant corner case of participants' gazes during training, and in consequence, the exploitative pattern of a participant would be mapped into the ANN. As the second option, with all participant gaze-data, a participant independent ANN was trained. This ANN was then used as a pre-trained ANN for training participant dependent, i.e., participant-specific, ANN for predicted the participants' gazes on dishes.

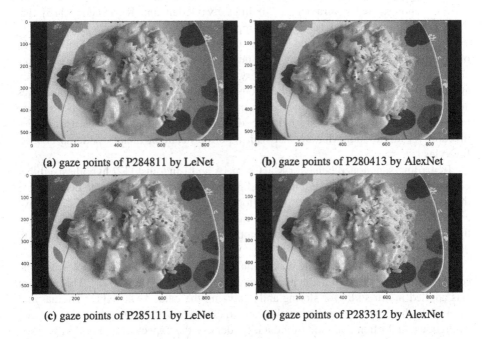

(a) gaze points of P284811 by LeNet   (b) gaze points of P280413 by AlexNet

(c) gaze points of P285111 by LeNet   (d) gaze points of P283312 by AlexNet

Fig. 6. Visualization of predicted gaze points; predicted gaze points are marked with a blue start; real gaze points are marked with a red dot; (a) and (b) have the minimum mean squared error values between predicted and real gaze points; (c) and (d) have the maximum mean squared error values between predicted and real gaze points. (Color figure online)

6   Discussion

Our exploratory study indicates that the stated dietary pattern, i.e. being vegetarian or non-vegetarian, does not alone suffice to explain ad hoc food choices and decision-making. Our exploratory study indicates thus that food choices can be different from participant stated dietary pattern. This key new input in our bootstrap run of the original results [3] indicate that to some extent why studies to date, which gather largely data on dietary patterns, have not been efficient enough in determining health status and nutrition status, since as our exploratory study indicates, that person-related short-term food choices can well be different from overtly stated dietary patterns.

On this sparse data, two shallow ANN architectures were capable of predicting participant gazes on dish 3 with an average MSE of below 11.1%. Since ANN are function approximators, this result might indicate that individuals' scene perception of food is generalizable and therefore dirigible. If individuals' dish gazing can be generalized and trained by an ANN, the dish gazing of certain groups like obese people might also be generalizable. In this case, food arrangements on dishes can be evaluated by an ANN for regulating food choices regarding participants' dietary patterns and health status.

Guiding and directing individuals in food decision making might increase healthier food choices and contradict the findings by Ogden and Roy-Stanley [13] that greater autonomy in food decision making or food-choices does not automatically imply healthy food choices. Food choices and nutritional behavior relate to the burden of diseases of civilization [4], as while statistics indicate larger population segments are increasingly following healthier dietary patterns [5]. Thus, our exploratory study attempts to explain this observed dichotomy in health and nutrition status outcomes and observed dietary patterns, indicating that our current body of research literature reporting on obesity, metabolic syndrome, diabetes, cancers and other diseases of civilization [1] might somewhat coexist with reported healthier dietary patterns or food lifestyles [5].

Regarding sanctioned behavior MacCormack and Lindquist [12] hypothesized that people experience hunger as emotions and misattribution process [14], to demonstrate that hunger [2,15] shifts affective perceptions in negative but not in neutral or positive contexts. A role for intuitive eating to promote health has also emerged requiring further investigation [9,15] which remains another viable option in nutritional advice with diseases [1].

To explore and analyze scene perception spatially and temporally, we improved the concept of using any multimedia player for exploratory analysis [16–18]. This concept was applied in our study for storing and analyzing the data. As stated by Thomas and Cook [19], the purpose of visual analytics is to derive insights from massive, dynamic, ambiguous, and often contradictory data, to identify the expected, and to discover the unexpected. In consequence, the prediction of the ANN, cf. Sect. 5, must also be integrated within the concept of using any multimedia player for exploratory analysis.

Instead of using the purely text-based universal subtitle format (USF), we added transparent heatmap images as subtitle tracks. Through these heatmap images, we increased the meaning of the gaze points per frame without losing the ability to playback through the use of standard multimedia players such as the *VLC Player*. Visualization with colored heatmap layers increased the information content since multiple gaze sample points can be color-coded on a single pixel. The increase in the information content became obvious when comparing the Figs. 7(b) with the USF and Fig. 7(a). Even so we implemented these extensions ino ur study, our implementation remained still compliant with the multimedia container format and allowed both instantaneous visualization

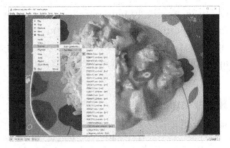

(a) universal subtitle format (USF) for visualization

(b) transparent image as sub station alpha overlays as subtitles for visualization

Fig. 7. Gaze visualization with standard multimedia player; (a) former approach [16] and (b) our new approach providing a heatmap in each frame [3].

with multimedia players and storage of all data in raw formats within a single file.

As implied, an applied application of our study results is how restaurants prepare food and arrange dishes. Many of the processes within professional kitchens are pre-defined, starting from the food preparation, such as chopping, slicing to preparing basic sauces and slides. Making it easier for the kitchen staff to access the same objects, everything has its place and order in a professional cooking process. The use of visual data analytics in scene perception and the AI-based prediction of scene perception in this field of professional cooking could aid in training staff in simulations or real practice evaluations in food presentation. An adequate food presentation influences the food selection of individuals [13].

Due to the ongoing COVID-19 pandemic, the main limitation of this pilot study is the number of participants that could be addressed in a full-scale study. The dichotomous classification of vegetarians and non-vegetarians might be insufficient, requiring a third intermediate class of semi-non-vegetarians, including pescovegetarians, flexitarians and other classes of mild animal protein sources. In addition, our being hungry-satiated, before-after study can be improved by considering additional factors determining diet and nutrition, such as, cultural and emotional factors that would also contribute to food choices. The acquisition of healthy eating habits can be improved by reeducation incorporating emotional association with food, which is also an additional application dimension of the current pilot study that requires future focus. Finally, despite random recruitment of participants on the day of the survey, we cannot rule out participation bias among individuals interested in food, which is a limitation of the study. The use of cumulative heat maps would require more significant optimization. Future studies will need to use different sampling methods to recruit participants to generate valid and reliable results in the long term.

Our pilot study indicates that by understanding scene perception and gaze data on dishes and food, the understanding of dietary patterns increases as well. Combined with the AI-based predicting of participants' dish-gazing, a novel basis for developing innovative nutritional therapies and innovative ways of preparing and serving food are established. For example, a small inconspicuous bay leaf in the right place could likely instinctively help people make better food choices— a food-nudging cue or perhaps a learning cue. As in this study, interdisciplinary research is the mainstay for new, open, easy-to-use tools for data collection and analysis and uniting different scientific approaches to create new perspectives.

References

1. Berkemeyer, S.: Acid–base balance and weight gain: are there crucial links via protein and organic acids in understanding obesity? Med. Hypotheses **73**(3), 347–356 (2009). https://doi.org/10.1016/j.mehy.2008.09.059
2. Berkemeyer, S.: Starvation versus calorie restriction: our road to food insecurity or health. J. Nutr. Food Sci. **01**(S1) (2012). https://doi.org/10.4172/2155-9600.s1.004
3. Berkemeyer, S., Schöning, J.: Feeling hungry–association of dietary patterns with food choices using scene perception. In: Proceedings of the 4th International Conference on Computer-Human Interaction Research and Applications (CHIRA). Scitepress (2020). https://doi.org/10.5220/0010146101880195
4. Breer, N., Gendig, C., Berkemeyer, S.: The relationship of migration, age, income and dietary patterns with body mass index in a cross-sectional analysis of ebagil-study. In: Eighth EUSPR Conference and Members Meeting (2017)
5. Deutsche Gesellschaft für Ernährung e. V.: Jahresbericht der deutschen gesellschaft für ernährung e. v. 2020 (2020). https://www.dge.de/fileadmin/public/doc/wueu/DGE-Jahresbericht-2020.pdf. Accessed 23 Aug 2021
6. Deutsche Gesellschaft für Ernährung e. V.: Vollwertige ernährung (2020). https://www.dge.de/ernaehrungspraxis/vollwertige-ernaehrung/. Accessed 23 Aug 2021
7. Graham, D.J., Roberto, C.A.: Evaluating the impact of US food and drug administration–proposed nutrition facts label changes on young adults' visual attention and purchase intentions. Health Edu. Behav. **43**(4), 389–398 (2016). https://doi.org/10.1177/1090198116651082
8. Hornik, K., Stinchcombe, M., White, H.: Multilayer feedforward networks are universal approximators. Neural Netw. **2**(5), 359–366 (1989). https://doi.org/10.1016/0893-6080(89)90020-8
9. Keirns, N.G., Hawkins, M.A.W.: Intuitive eating, objective weight status and physical indicators of health. Obes. Sci. Pract. **5**(5), 408–415 (2019). https://doi.org/10.1002/osp4.359
10. Krizhevsky, A., Sutskever, I., Hinton, G.E.: ImageNet classification with deep convolutional neural networks. In: 25th International Conference on Neural Information Processing Systems (NIPS). NIPS 2012, Curran Associates Inc. (2012). https://doi.org/10.1145/3065386
11. Lecun, Y., Bottou, L., Bengio, Y., Haffner, P.: Gradient-based learning applied to document recognition. Proc. IEEE **86**(11), 2278–2324 (1998). https://doi.org/10.1109/5.726791
12. MacCormack, J.K., Lindquist, K.A.: Feeling hangry? when hunger is conceptualized as emotion. Emotion **19**(2), 301–319 (2019). https://doi.org/10.1037/emo0000422
13. Ogden, J., Roy-Stanley, C.: How do children make food choices? using a think-aloud method to explore the role of internal and external factors on eating behaviour. Appetite **147**, 104551 (2020). https://doi.org/10.1016/j.appet.2019.104551
14. Payne, B.K., Hall, D.L., Cameron, C.D., Bishara, A.J.: A process model of affect misattribution. Pers. Soc. Psychol. Bull. **36**(10), 1397–1408 (2010). https://doi.org/10.1177/0146167210383440
15. Rubin, O.: The precarious state of famine research. J. Dev. Stud. **55**(8), 1633–1653 (2018). https://doi.org/10.1080/00220388.2018.1493196

16. Schöning, J., Faion, P., Heidemann, G., Krumnack, U.: Providing video annotations in multimedia containers for visualization and research. In: IEEE Winter Conference on Applications of Computer Vision (WACV). Institute of Electrical and Electronics Engineers (IEEE) (2017). https://doi.org/10.1109/wacv.2017.78

17. Schöning, J., Gert, A., Açik, A., Kietzmann, T., Heidemann, G., König, P.: Exploratory multimodal data analysis with standard multimedia player – multimedia containers: a feasible solution to make multimodal research data accessible to the broad audience. In: Proceedings of the 12th Joint Conference on Computer Vision, Imagingand Computer Graphics Theory and Applications (VISAPP), pp. 272–279. Scitepress (2017). https://doi.org/10.5220/0006260202720279

18. Schöning, J., Gundler, C., Heidemann, G., König, P., Krumnack, U.: Visual analytics of gaze data with standard multimedia player. J. Eye Mov. Res. **10**(5), 1–14 (2017). https://doi.org/10.16910/jemr.10.5.4

19. Thomas, J.J., Cook, K.A. (eds.): Illuminating the Path: The Research and Development Agenda for Visual Analytics. IEEE, Los Alamitos (2005)

20. Turner, M.M., Skubisz, C., Pandya, S.P., Silverman, M., Austin, L.L.: Predicting visual attention to nutrition information on food products: the influence of motivation and ability. J. Health Commun. **19**(9), 1017–1029 (2014). https://doi.org/10.1080/10810730.2013.864726

21. World Medical Association: World medical association declaration of Helsinki. JAMA **310**(20), 2191 (2013). https://doi.org/10.1001/jama.2013.281053

Reshaping Thinking for Shape-Shifting Technology: Adapting a MAS Agent Design to Encourage User Engagement

Helen Hasenfuss(✉) [iD]

Abbeyfeale, Co., Limerick, Ireland
helenh2009@gmail.com

Abstract. The aim of this paper is to present an adaptation of an agent design to facilitate the dissemination of shape-shifting technology research. This research is based on the development of a multiagent system (MAS), with a particular focus on designing an individual agent (the Dod). The gap between the creative and actual representation of such technology is still large. Because of this gap, design challenges exist for which solutions will emerge as the technology and knowledge of its end application become more apparent. Detailing communication protocols of existing MAS and defining a design guideline to assist in accommodating unknown variables in the design process are explored in the first half of this paper. After establishing the context for this research to date, the second half of this paper illustrates how 3D thinking and manipulation can be made more accessible through the development of a game, by adapting the Dod design as a game piece, a Dodlen. Thereby aiming to introduce concepts of shape-shifting technology to a larger audience in a gradual, and multi-modular fashion.

Keywords: MAS agent design · Communication · Shape-shifting technology · Game development

1 Introduction

This paper is an extension of the conference paper, Emerging Complexity: Communication between Agents in a MAS for shape-shifting TUIs , presented at CHIRA conference in 2020 [1]. The paper explored communication methods between agents, which are part of a multiagent system (MAS). The overall context of the research on which it is based, relates to the development of MAS in their use for shape-shifting technology and further implementation for tangible user interfaces (TUIs). To date a large portion of research relating to this field has been divided between agent-to-agent communication methods [2, 3] and the process of self-assembly [4–7]. The study on which the research described in this paper is based, focused on designing a physical agent: the Dod [8]. The Dod is a blueprint for an agent design, to be used as part of an artificial MAS. The design itself is highly adaptable and versatile as it reflects the changing developments in technology and material sciences. In refraining from creating a high-fidelity prototype during the original study, it was possible to explore a larger breadth of possibilities with respect to

A. Holzinger et al. (Eds.): CHIRA 2020, CCIS 1609, pp. 32–53, 2022.
https://doi.org/10.1007/978-3-031-22015-9_3

the overall function of the Dod itself and an entire MAS based on the Dod agent. The physical design of the Dod and how it can potentially communicate have been presented in the following papers [1, 9, 10]. This paper will explore a design guideline that can be used in a situation whereby significant design criteria were still unknown, as well as exploring an avenue of future work that had been detailed in the original PhD study: developing the Dod as a game-piece.

As it emerged, there is a large gap between, how shape-shifting technology should ideally work, what it should look like, and what is currently possible. Aside from the technical and design challenges of realising such technology, another obstacle is the uptake into the public realm. If there is no engagement or understanding for this kind of technology, it is questionable how successful it can be. Therefore, the Dod design as a game-piece can begin to introduce essential qualities of shape-shifting technology into social consciousness as well as foster the art of 3D thinking. As technology develops, and if the Dod design is still viable, it will be possible to integrate for use as a MAS agent design more easily. An analogy can be draw with the initial development of computer technology - since its introduction into mainstream society, even though the shape, size and construct of the computer has altered, the fundamental principle of how users interact with them are still the same: visual screen for representation of digital data and some sort of interface to enable interaction with this data (e.g. keyboard, mouse, trackpad, etc.). From an interaction perspective, shape-shifting technology represents a slightly stronger focus on the haptic modality. This modality is present in the majority of humans from a very early stage in their conceptualisation process of their environment. A function of touch is to create a sense of grounding in one's reality and is a key element in being able to act on or in one's environment. Unique to a person's haptic sense is the quality of bi-directionality [11]; the ability to receive sensory input but also being able to exert a change in the environment. For example, it is possible to see a leaf on a table; its texture, colour, shape, and size, but it is not possible to affect the leaf only by looking at it (sensing). Without vision it is possible to lift the leaf, feel it to discover its size, shape, weight, temperature, and texture - it is also possible to change its size or shape by folding or tearing edges (sensing and acting). In conjunction with this sense, the act of play is not only an integral part to socialisation but also the creation of holistic experiences that aids in the process of contextualisation and the sharing of ideas and knowledge.

In turn, an important aspect of play is communication. Communication is integrated in several different levels in a project of this nature. Because the final application of shape-shifting technology is not yet clearly defined, it is necessary for MAS agent to have a degree of autonomy that enables them to interact, interpret and adapt to their environment. For example,

- User to technology interaction,
- Agent to environment interaction,
- Agent to agent interaction,
- Agent to itself interaction

Despite the physical appearance and design of the agent (the Dod) taking precedence throughout the original study, a portion of research was given to defining the type of communication method that was possible as a result of the design itself. To highlight the variety of communication techniques available to implement in MAS, section two will detail the journey of communication techniques in relation to how the original ideas for shape-shifting technology have evolved.

Section three will continue to expand on a specific design guideline that was very influential in development of the Dod: emulation rather than replication. Due to certain design parameters being unknown, it is important to explore design guidelines that do not limit the scope of creative potential and can still maintain a structured framework in order to produce viable results. Applying this kind of guideline to various stages of research ensures that there is a consistency of approach throughout the project's development.

The existing and fictional games that influenced the development of the final game design will be presented in section four. These not only help to contextualise the Dod game-piece, but also to highlight how specific game strategies can influence players' interactions and engagement with a game, e.g. being able to see patterns. Being able to identify patterns is fundamental to Gestalt psychology as it provides a person with grounding and the ability to organize their reality.

Lastly a description of the proposed Dod game-piece, the Dodlen, and several suggestions for game play rules will be detailed in section five. The primary concept for this avenue of research is that in order to facilitate user interaction with the concept of MAS, and in the future with shape-shifting technology, people must become familiar with it, play with it and explore it long before they actually need it. Therefore, even if the Dod design could potentially no longer be relevant, the behaviour of interacting with 3D structures may have become more familiar in general society.

2   Related Work

The Tangible Interface classification scheme provided the parameters within which the Dod was developed [12]. The categories of constructed assemblies and continuous plastic TUIs being of particular relevance. However, the initial ideas and research that inspired the Dod, were strongly influence by William Butera's work in 2002: a *paintable computer* [13], Ishi's conceptual exploration of Radical Atoms [12] and Horev's work into the affordances presented by shape-shifting technology [14]. Going back further to research that inspired these studies, is Sutherlands vision of the *Ultimate Display* [15]: *'a room within which the computer can control the existence of matter'*[16]. In the domain of science fiction, the Ultimate Display concept can be said to be represented by the Holodeck in the Star Trek franchise [17]: a room that uses holographic projections and that gives a person the ability to interact with digital representations in the same manner as physical ones, i.e. a digital table would be as real and solid as its physical counterpart. The gap between reality and fiction is continuously reducing as is evidenced by the advances in Virtual Reality (VR) technology. Being able to introduce haptics into VR, via shape-shifting technology would represent a significant development in a number of different STEM disciplines.

Changing reality in real-time, and exerting control over that new reality, are interesting perspectives to consider and reference, in the development of shape-shifting technology. The question as to which forms or shapes, digital representations would take once they are made tangible, is the open-ended question with respect to this kind of technology's design. In Butera's work, he suggests the concept of a paintable computer; enhancing surfaces, making them interactive and intelligent. The concept is a blend of the internet of things (IoT) approach, whereby objects are connected to one another and communicate over a shared network, and multiagent computing [13]. He suggests that future computer technology could become so resilient, small and cheap, that it would be possible to deal with it in bulk and that it will be small enough to potentially blend into the background and be applicable to everything in the environment. Butera describes agents that function on a basic level, ideally suspended in a liquid, so that they can be dispersed evenly but also be used to enhance the surface onto which they are painted. An agent consists of a 'brain', in terms of memory, communication and energy manipulating ability [13]. The predominant method of functioning of such agents is through self-organisation. It is possible to see the correlation between digital pixels and their possible physical representation through the agents suggested by Butera. At this point it becomes clear that whilst a paintable computer cannot form 3D structures, it is beginning to address the concept of a reactive reality that a user can influence in real-time.

Expanding this concept, it is possible to envision a computer liquid that could change its physical shape, i.e. it would be able to create 3D relief structures or even be used as an independent 3D object. Such an interface would be in a quasi-liquid state when inactive and could become solid when in use, comparable to an augmented Non-Newtonian fluid (specifically rheopectic fluids [18]). These types of interfaces are described in Horev's work, primarily highlighting the value of haptic affordances of shape-shifting structures [14]. In his work the method of communication shifts from the traditional visual interpretation of digital information to haptic representation. Communication is facilitated through textural or shape change, temperature and movement. As a result, Horev also highlights behaviours to which a shape-shifting interface may be ideally suited that are currently difficult to convey: "Hidden statuses...Process Guidance...Adaptation to Context" [14]. This kind of research is the valuable counterpart to the digital exploration of agent-to-agent communication because it considers novel ways of user interaction with shape-shifting technology but also focuses on the haptic modality. In order to accomplish 3D structures, the necessity to focus research on self-assembly techniques became evident. It could be argued that self-organisation is a product or physical manifestation of a communication protocol, whereas self-assembly used in the context of construction, indicates that an agent can use knowledge that is communicated amongst agents and apply it to form more complex structures.

As is evidenced by Butera's work, the MAS approach appears to be the most efficient system to achieve independent, artificial, 3D structures and communication between these agents is essential. The work done by Lifton illustrates how communications between a large quantity of agents can function in a network configuration [2, 19]. He poses the questions of how to process, communicate and apply the voluminous influx of data gained through large sensor matrices contained in current machinery, particularly with respect to the robotics domain. This aspect becomes relevant when considering that the scale of these agents is envisioned to be 2–6 mm [6, 7]. Lifton presents a distributed sensory network in the form of hardware and software embodied through pushpin computing. His research supports a system whereby it is possible to incorporate the following functions:

- add more agents to an existing system and have them integrate faster because they can benefit from the agents that came before them,
- the ability of a system to self-repair,
- compensate for possible failures in specific areas,
- localise and isolate problems rather than affecting the whole system.

In research projects whereby MAS communication protocols were implemented via physical prototypes, the outcome resulted in successful agent-to-agent interaction [3, 20, 21]. However, these systems often exhibited self-organising behaviour as opposed to the required self-assembling ability. Despite this behaviour, the value of these projects resides in the behaviours that were coded into the agents. For example,

- A MAS must be capable of dealing with agents that malfunction or, if for example a shortage of energy is detected, function with a reduced capacity of agents [21]. This requires adaptive communication protocols.
- The ability of agents to decide which 'role' or function they must provide in any given situation. This is reflective of behaviours evidenced in natural systems [22] but also becomes more relevant for an agent's spatial orientation and position in creating 3D structures.
- Similar to natural systems being based on specific blueprints, each artificial agent can also have a range of variations based on the quality of its components (motion, learning, communicating, material makeup, etc.) [3].
- Rare or unforeseen events that cause errors ranging in severity, either from within or due to external environmental influence (e.g. internal influence: short circuit, external influence: poke) [3].
- Communicative errors such as multiple messages per channel, chatter between agents, random noise. This can have a domino effect on other dependant factor, e.g. failing to sense boundaries [3].

These behaviours (deciding, coping, acting, learning, sharing, etc.) should ideally be transferable to any kind of agent, requiring adaptation only to accommodate changes in physical design of the agent, i.e. analogous to the act of walking, irrespective of whether it is on two or four legs. Whilst the listed examples demonstrate the complexity and variation of scenarios, outside of the original purpose for such a system (self-assembly into user-defined 3D structures), it also indicates the layers of awareness that are funda-mental to an agent's ability to act autonomously. Self-assembly adds the conditions of structural cohesion and the physics involved in 3D construction. Similar to the necessity for agents to be able to self-assemble into 3D structures, communication protocols also have to become 3D. This not only refers to the traditional spacial axes and the natural flow of communication, but includes the levels of awareness that translate between the internal and external world of agent perception [1, 23], see Fig. 1. The model of aware-ness proposed by Thórisson indicates the bi-directionality of awareness but also the balance between 'hardcoded' behaviours found in the innermost layer and the flexible, adaptability of the remaining layers in their participation of information exchange.

Each layer is interlinked with the other, and once the process of awareness begins to include environmental influences, a range of behaviours emerges. Even though each layer or level may be clear in its function, in isolation; similar to the nature of complexity, it is the combinations of these layers that can help define the degree of intelligence for artificial agents. It is becoming clear that, in conjunction with intelligence, communication plays an integral part in defining agent autonomy. Exploring the development of agent communications can also provide valuable insight into the degree of autonomy required for shape-shifting technology. Evolving from a) functional communication: agents moving in their environment, completing a task; to b) basic autonomy: coping with an unexpected event, getting pushed and eventually c) intelligent autonomy or AI: learning from experiences, forgetting irrelevant data, making decisions, interpreting situations.

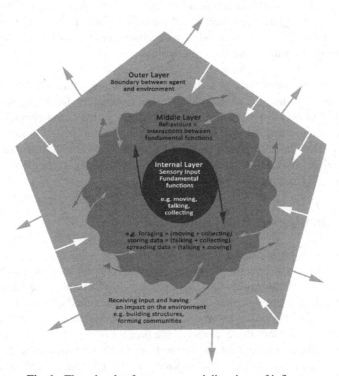

Fig. 1. Three levels of awareness and directions of influence.

At this point it is important to consider again that an appealing aspect of digital, is the ability to control it; its predictability, and its order. Does intelligence enhance these qualities or does it detract from them? Is it possible to find the balance between control and artificial autonomy? What would happen if artificial agents are given a degree of autonomy and allowed to develop their own form of communication? These questions again can only truly be answered closer to a time in which MAS based shape-shifting technology becomes more clearly defined. However, as the design process develops, and in researchers' engagement with the subject of agent autonomy, it is important to consider that certain peripheral questions as those suggested above, may become more relevant earlier than expected.

Having highlighted pivotal research that informed the technical communication methods relevant to MAS, another key influence is the discipline of biomimcry. It is important to recognise the vast diversity in how biological entities can communicate with each other and within a social setting but also the diversity that individuals themselves can present, using different combinations of their senses. For example, consider the range of influences, with respect to communication alone, in the design of the Dod:

- with its moving arms, the Dod shares a physical likeness to an octopus or sea anemones,
- The Dods implementation requires it to be part of a MAS, like ants or bees,
- Being made by humans, includes the elements of creativity; drawing from a rich diversity of communicative adaptation: spoken, pictographic, sign, numeric, written languages, to name but a few variants. It not only ensures a rich variety of learning and perspectives but can accommodate adaptability and the means to convey shared experiences over multiple channels of cognition.

Considering the complexity of shape-shifting technology that is to be based on a MAS, there are still a number of undefined design parameters. Deciding which avenue of research would be most worthwhile to pursue and which could provide the greatest probability of success, it is necessary to develop versatile design guidelines. In the instance of the Dod the design guideline *replication versus emulation* emerged. Applying this guideline assisted in achieving rigorous, theoretical suggestions whilst still accommodating the required scope for creativity.

3   Replication Versus Emulation

An advantage of exploring the discipline of biomimicry, is the diversity of biological systems and in particular how they have developed to function successfully, being optimized for their specific purposes and environments. For example, communicating via the olfactory modality through pheromone trails [24], aural modality via echo location, or kinesthetic modality represented in dance (e.g. bees communicating through dance). To understand and research these methods, the process of replication provides a good starting point for the initial exploration. Replication entails recreating what already exists and fulfils an essential quality of deductive reasoning. Conclusions reached as a result of this approach are formed as a logical progression from an original premise(s). This also means that even if the original premises were to be incorrect, the conclusion would still be logical.

Deductive reasoning finds resonance within the STEM disciplines and in conjunction with the process of replication, allows system variables and behaviours to be determined. It is a process that can help unravel complex systems. Physicist Richard Feynman described complex systems as being constructed-of or based-on very simple rules / algorithms and that it is the interaction of these simple rules, with each other and the environment, that underlie complexity [25]. In isolating and defining the number of system variables in order to discover these 'simple rules', the potential to create constrained or singular conclusions is increased and each new variable may require the repetition of the entire deductive process. Following this process, if a system can be replicated near to exactness and it functions as the original, then it can be understood. It also creates a strong and secure knowledge foundation. From this point it is conceivable to gain further insight into the relationships these variables have on each other, not just as the whole system, but it is also possible to postulate further questions: 'What if…', 'Consider this…', which indicate the stage of research where the system variables are altered. Studying the effect or consequences of these alterations indicate that a system is understood to such a degree that there is potential to predict the resulting behaviour to a high probability of accuracy.

Whilst deduction is favourable to the exploration of systems that are known to exist, what aspects of reasoning change when the questions originate from a purely conceptual or idea-based perspective, where there is no previously proven data, clear evidence or a possible correlation? In this instance, the previous process of exploration, through replication, does not occur on an external system but rather on an internal one: intuition. The internal system of intuition, experience and perception often produces connections between elements that cannot occur from a grounded perspective. Lifton, Feynman and mathematician Dirac use terms such as *elegance* and *beauty* in the description of scientific processes because the emotional connection and interpretation of knowledge, has as strong an influence in the manner in which researchers interact with knowledge as would a process that is documented and which produces tangible results [19, 25, 26]. The process of analysing, connecting and living experiences in order to create a different kind of knowledge base, is a valuable asset in research that deals with significant unknown variables, e.g. how will tangible shape-shifting technology be used? what can it actually do? how sentient does it need to be? how will users react?, etc.; it incorporates a researchers phenomenology. This essentially means, that even if a core piece of research is being explored by several different researchers, each individual will be able to contribute a unique insight and perspective. As shape-shifting technology in its current vision is still hypothetical, it is a subject that benefits greatly from an inductive reasoning approach. It broadens the scope of research and allows for the variable of uncertainty. As different, individual elements of this kind of technology are being explored (e.g. communication, self-assembly, agent shape, metamaterials, etc.), it will eventually be possible to combine this research.

In contrast to deductive reasoning, the conclusions drawn from the inductive process of reasoning are based on the surrounding evidence, or comparable theories, more so than an actual, specific premise itself. They promote a probability of truth or fact (as opposed to a clear certainty), but do not need to be correct. The greater the volume of relevant data that is available in the construction of the premise(s), ensures a higher probability that the conclusions will be true. For example, consider the following conclusions from the question: 'can a human fly as a bird does?'.

- Deduction: A bird flies as a result of its overall design (premise). This ranges from body shape, skeletal density and muscle distribution, etc. to the shape of its wings, the function of the feathers and the mechanics and physics of air flow. Humans cannot fly exactly as birds do (conclusions).
- Inductive: 'if a bird can fly, and the mechanism is mimicked (premises), then can humans fly too (conclusion)?'. The variety of shapes and sizes of birds, as well as

other flying creatures such as bats or insects indicates that if the proportions are correct and relative to human dimensions, it should be possible.

In the latter example the premises were true (if a bird was to be replicated as is in every detail, [27, 28]), but the conclusion that this mechanism could work for humans was false - humans cannot fly *as* birds do. However, it establishes the scope to consider that humans could fly *like* birds. In the original PhD study surrounding the Dod, it was found that inductive reasoning was a useful tool for generating questions, whereas deductive reasoning helped answer these questions. Applying this cyclical process in the same manner as the user centred design (UCD) method is applied, ensured that the Dod design could undergo testing as well as maintain an adaptive design process in order to help accommodate the unknown design variables. Furthermore, for the purposes of the study, these two types of reasoning approaches were represented in the processes of replication and emulation. As has been established deduction and replication are mutually beneficial. Inductive reasoning focuses on the essence of a system or idea, and emulation can aid in establishing this concept. Emulation entails qualities also conveyed through imitation and replication; however, an important difference is that the system that is emulating another, is not designed to be applied in the same manner as the original - it aims to surpass the original. It entails the utilisation of knowledge and adaptation to a different or new application. Using the example of flight, a key element or essence of flight is the physics of airflow over the wing structure. This knowledge, among other contributions, produced a wing shape that could enable humans to fly - not replicating the exact mechanism.

Another example of using emulation as a guideline in the design process can be seen in the development of the foot prosthetic. Whilst exact replicas of the foot / leg were initially the point of relevance for research, it is also worthwhile considering the prosthetic seen in Fig. 2.

Fig. 2. Purpose-orientated leg/ foot prosthetic.

The prosthetic in Fig. 2 is dissimilar to the biological counterpart that it aims to replace, but it represents the essence of how the leg / foot structure functions and simulates that action. In the research of the Dod, the essence of what is represent by a fire ant colony and rheopectic Non-Newtonian fluids, was researched.

- Most ant colonies represent successful and efficient, biological MAS and not only use material from their environment to build structures larger than themselves but in times of need can also use themselves as building blocks [29–31].

- Non-Newtonian fluids provided valuable insight into particle characteristics that enables a fluid to be both liquid and semi-solid given specific forces it is exposed to.

These explorations lead to the following design criteria from which the Dod emerged:

1. A semi-spherical shape with an irregular, cratered surface.
2. Non-hierarchical chain of command: autonomy to function as individuals
3. The ability to morph: surface topology and fundamental form
4. One material make-up and scalability – structural affordances and inherent material qualities
5. Bi-directionality – the ability to assemble and dis-assemble
6. Behavioural simplicity

The design guideline, emulation versus replication, has been useful in this instance to facilitate a degree of adaptability in the design itself. As research continues it is important to return to the original concepts overarching the individual areas of research entailed in shape-shifting technology: Sutherland's Ultimate Display and Ishii's Radical Bits. What is the essence of shape-shifting technology? One interpretation could be that it is giving an ethereal substance (digital data) a physical manifestation. Consider extrapolating this concept further to encompass quantum computing; what connotations are entailed in this avenue of research?

4 Game Context

Having considered the potential of the Dod design, the next stage in the research of such a project is the application of knowledge gained throughout the research and making it accessible. A strong motivation to design the Dod primarily as an adaptable and versatile blueprint for an agent design, was to accommodate the fast-paced or short-lived lifespan of such research. A large portion of proposed shape shifting devices rarely leave a lab environment because of the possible expertise, specialist equipment or material cost involved in the project [32–41]. With the developments in material science, 3D printing, biological engineering [42–44] it is necessary to continuously develop research in order for it to stay relevant. In the original study regarding the Dod, four main sections of future work that explore the potential of the Dod with respect to considering further adaptations to its physical form as well as possible variations to its overall behaviour, were detailed. These are as follows:

- developments of the Dod design (facet and arm function, methods of motion),
- energy manipulation,
- boundary conditions and
- 3D thinking

The subject of 3D thinking will be addressed in this section. The importance of 3D thinking in shape-shifting technology relates to user interaction, and creative application but also eventually commercial uptake and social engagement. Thinking 3 dimensionally should be innate to people (e.g. strictly speaking even a piece of paper is 3D). However, there is a discrepancy between how people represent and convey designs, and how people actually interact with 3D space. In general, the first point of reference for the expression of ideas or designs, whether 2D or 3D, occurs predominantly through sketching. Whilst sketching is a powerful tool, it is primarily focused on visual representations on a 2D plane. The illusion of 3D can be created; however, it can be argued that an important 1st step in the act of interacting and communicating with digital data that has a tangible form (i.e. shape-shifting technology), is that of 3D visualization. An analogy can be drawn from sewing, whereby drafting a paper pattern occurs on the 2D plane, whereas draping a pattern occurs on the model; on the 3D plane. Each process, designing in 2D or 3D, provides unique insights with respect to interaction techniques and produces very different results.

The nature of digital structures has enabled technology to develop based primarily on the visual sense which is unidirectional. Large volumes of data can be processed and it is accessible by a large majority of any society. In contrast 3D exploration (e.g. sculpting, multimedia prototyping, construction) is primarily based on the haptic sense which is bidirectional. A reason as to why it is important to upgrade or adapt the manner in which people can represent 3D thinking and manipulation is because if they cannot express their ideas, and are limited by the medium they use to convey ideas, it may result in a lack of creativity and hinder the potential of 3D exploration. This has since been recognized in both academia and industry. For example, in the digital domain, 3D modelling software is available and more readily accessible via high quality open source software that can be introduced into schools more easily (e.g. Solidworks, zBrush, Maya, Blender, SketchUp, etc.). 3D printing technology has changed the prototyping and fabrication process, and is also becoming more accessible through 3D printers aimed at Hobbyists and the development of Fab Labs (e.g. Ultimaker, Form1, Makerbot, etc.). Even the process of sketching itself which was traditionally done through pen and paper has been augmented through the development of 3D pens. These tools are taking the next step into realizing 3D concepts and encouraging 3D manipulation, without first translating it into a 2D representation (e.g. 3D Magic Imagi Pen, IDO3D Vertical, AtmosFlare, 3Doodler, CreoPop, etc.). In other domains such as human computer interaction (HCI), the importance of multi-material prototyping and the process of involving users in the design process itself, including hands-on modelling, has been recognized and is being encouraged. The various forms of user research already illustrate the multimodal nature of the design discipline and how different insights are possible through the variety of engagement / exploration (e.g. multimedia brainstorming, shadowing, game-play, diary studies, simulations, verbal interviews, quantitative or qualitative questionnaires).

To date the research surrounding designing MAS for their use in shape-shifting technology for TUIs has been purely academic. To reduce the gap between theory and practice it is necessary to consider how the Dod, in its concept of being an agent, can A) become more publicly disseminated, B) how it can encourage haptic exploration through play and C) how it can potentially help train 3D thinking. A viable avenue of development that encompasses these three requirements is adapting the Dod into a game-piece or a toy, both as analog and eventually as digital format (e.g. the cuboid shape: as an analog toy is represented by Lego®, and as a digital game-piece is represented by Minecraft). This development would have an immediate benefit of public dissemination. As the technology becomes more refined, it would have the later benefits of the general public being more familiar with MAS, or programmable matter concepts. This process is comparable to how the cuboid shape has become integrated into public consciousness, in Western society.

A strong element that supports the approach of game-play, is that of learning and establishing conceptual frameworks through the act of playing. As children learn, they explore their environment through multimodal sensing thereby generating experiences that are not purely theory based. For example, Gupta and Khanna are educators that have made physics principles accessible and applicable for young children through the development of toys, e.g. a race car built on a twisted rubber band [45–49]. The children can create these toys themselves using readily available materials. The understanding gained through this process is invaluable because they not only learn how the toy works but also how to construct it. This type of learning encompasses a wider range of modalities than the traditional classroom setting, i.e. haptic learning as opposed to a purely cognitive uptake of knowledge. Using this core approach, other toys such as Topobo [50], Meccano, K'Nex, Baufix (Fig. 3a–3c) and Lego® all aim to foster an understanding of physics, engineering, electronics and construction concepts, among others, but also inherently encourage 3D manipulation and an understanding of a 3D environment through playing. The act of playing also supports contextualizing experiences in relation to others, encompassing a variety of behaviours and emerging social strategies[1].

Fig. 3. 3D thinking – (a) Meccano, (b) K'Nex, (c) Baufix.

Some of the mainstream toys (e.g. Lego®, Meccano) are a simplified representation of the world, i.e. straight lines and 90° angles. There is however a much larger scope of shapes for achieving the same and sometimes even better results. For example, in Buckminister Fuller's childhood he was very short-sighted which lead him to perceive only elements in his immediate presence. In one classroom exercise the children were asked to create a structure using peas and toothpicks. By comparison to the children who perceived their environment and mimicked the structures they saw, e.g. square, blocked houses, Fuller created what he later patented as the geodesic dome. He could only draw

---

[1] A greater trend exists nowadays for children to play on flat computer screens more often; therefore, 3D manipulation may be done artificially through digital representation. In the long term, this may have an effect on the ability for 3D conceptualization and may be the reason why thinking & designing in 3D is still viewed as more challenging.

on his own haptic experiences, thereby creating and using an alternative building block (a triangle) and producing a unique structure [51, 52].

Ideally a multimodal learning style of learning should also be continued into adulthood as it continuously assists in developing motor skills and neuro-connectivity. Therefore, considering the benefits of haptic exploration through play and considering the construction-based toys that already exist, to base a building block on a semi-spherical shape, like the Dod, can open opportunities for a new range of creative solutions.

The following games, projects and hypothetical concepts provided inspiration regarding the potential of the Dod to be developed as a game-piece, with the primary aims of becoming more publicly accessible as well as encouraging 3D thinking and manipulation: Cellulo, Tantrix, Domino, Jenga and Kal-toh.

4.1 Cellulo

Cellulo is a project that uses swarm computing to link macro-sized robots to affect motion, haptic sensation and visual perception. The aim of the project is to make *"tangible what is intangible in learning"* (Özgür *et al.* 2017). Three primary requirements have guided the development of this project to make the interaction with data more accessible: ubiquity, practicality and flexibility. The inspiration from this project relates to the classroom environment in which it is used. Whilst the system provides valuable insights to communication techniques for MAS, the qualities necessary for encouraging interactivity are also valuable. For instance, by designing the robots to be *ubiquitous* follows in the recommendations of Mark Weiser's description of an *'excellent tool'*. The tool itself should be intuitive and easy to learn and so natural to use that the focus and attention of the user is directed towards the task itself rather than be distracted by the implement used to carry out the task [53]. *Practicality* is an essential component of these types of robots and in this instance more accurately refers to the necessity for robustness of the materials - not only the physical outer appearance but also the interior circuit components. Cellulo is intended to be used regularly in a classroom setting, for a variety of subjects and by children of varying ages. Being able to cope with the unexpected is an advantageous design consideration.

Since Cellulo is designed for the scenario of robots in education, *flexibility* and *versatility* are key factors. Being applicable to a multitude of subjects encourages the integration of this type of technology but also ensures that the robot design is focused towards ease of use, i.e. it should not take up any of the teacher's time to set up thereby potentially detracting from teaching the subject material itself.

4.2 Dominoes and Tantrix

Both games are based on the placement of tiles with specific values on them and can be played solo or as part of a group. A Dominoe[2] tile is a cuboid with a number of dots

---

[2] Dominoes are also famous for their alternative application in their use as a tool to initiate and facilitate chains of reaction (e.g. Dominoe Day). Variants of 3D Dominoe also exist, the 2012 version uses cuboid prisms (divided into 2 cubes through colour) that have one of two colours printed on every side [60] and a version where triangular prism tiles were used that could connect to create larger 3D structures s.

printed on either side ranging from 1–6, like a die. A Tantrix tile is a hexagonal prism and has three lines of different colours and orientation printed on one surface going from one edge to another. In each game, a variety of other puzzles developed from the basic game play: each player chooses a number of tiles whilst the rest remain unallocated and can be used throughout the game when the player's own tiles cannot be played.

In Dominoe tiles must be placed adjacent to each other whereby a following tile can only be placed at one of the two ends of the previously played tile, doubles act as branching points whereby tiles may be placed at one of the four sides of the tile. In Tantrix each player choses a colour and must attempt to lengthen their coloured line by the placement of other tiles. As each tile contains three colours in total it is necessary for the player to ensure that the other colours on the tile also match the previously played tiles. Whilst this can mean one player enhances another player's position (by lengthening their line), the line orientations on the tiles (i.e. straight, curved, etc.) ensure that it is not a reliable method of gaining an advantage because the line may also be curtailed, e.g. if it does a U-turn.

In both of these games the simple aim of adjoining matching numbers or colours is enhanced and elaborated on by the physical shape of the tile. They are good examples of the principle that complexity can emerge through the interaction of a simple set of rules. These games start from a single origin point and build-up to generate a larger playing field - similar to the concept of having a seed agent that communicates throughout the entire network. Dodlen would act as a tile that allows players to build into the 3D space as opposed to remaining on a '2D' surface.

4.3 Jenga

Jenga is a game based on cuboid building blocks. 54 blocks are stacked in alternating orientation of 90°, in rows of three until a tower of 18 rows is standing. Players alternate in turn each taking one block from any layer (apart from the top two layers) and placing it on the topmost layer in alternate orientation to the existing layer, i.e. the layers of blocks must lie perpendicular to each other. A player may only use one hand but can bump or nudge a block to check its willingness to depart from its current location. A steady hand, as well as good spatial awareness and dexterity are skills practised in this game. The game ends when the tower can no longer retain a stable equilibrium and topples.

This game highlights how the visual and haptic sense combine in order to assess and anticipate the reaction of the structure via interaction with it. It is also a good example of how 3D thinking is inherently fostered.

4.4 Kal-Toh

Many sources of inspiration in the sciences could not exist without the element of creativity. The last game suggestion (Kal-toh) is first mentioned in the science fiction series Star Trek. It is a geometric, shape-shifting based game, whose aim is to train patience as well as logical and rational thought of the user in their attempt to create the final shape of two nested icosidodecahedra. The inner shape is connected to the outer shape by the centre points of the edges [54]. Similar concepts such as the 3D interlocking wooden puzzles already exist today, however the interesting difference is that the player's moves in Kal-toh have the potential to initiate a chain reaction of shape-shifting that can work towards achieving the final structure or, contrary to the players advantage, can work towards creating greater chaos (similar to the game snakes and ladders), i.e. the game is reactive to the user's actions. This latter quality is another important challenge for any kind of technology, current and future: coping with the unpredictability of human behaviour. Figure 4 illustrates the starting and end position of Kal-toh.

Fig. 4. The beginning and end stages of the fictitious game of Kal-toh [54].

A key feature of the game is finding the "*seeds of order even in the midst of profound chaos*" [54]. The player adds or moves the thin rods to specific locations to set in motion a change of shape that eventually leads to the final structured geometric shape (like the reapplication of Dominoes, regarding chain-reactions). The icosidodecahedron is an Archimedean solid based on two primary polygons: pentagon and triangle, which meet in identical vertexes. Each side of a pentagon is connected to a triangle which has pentagons attached at the remaining two sides until they meet each other, i.e. similar to the Hoberman sphere. The rods used in the game enable the player to create the icosidodecahedron by outlining the edges of the required polygons.

The following points highlight the crossover between existing games and the academic findings relating to MAS agent design. They demonstrate the relevance and ability to link current and future research into agent design.

- be robust,
- facilitate quick learning (i.e. clear affordances),
- be versatile, possibly have multiple puzzles in one (i.e. shape and size change),
- pattern matching,
- playing with others or individually,
- haptic engagement through 3D exploration (i.e. bi-directionality)

The scope for creativity in this domain is substantial because the objectives and boundary conditions have altered. It brings a new set of challenges, but also considers the importance for momentum in research to continue developing the Dod, as well as developing the overarching concept of MAS agent design.

5   The Dodlen

The nature of the games or interactive pieces (i.e. shape, affordances, representations) described in section four have provided inspiration for the Dodlen (Dod game-piece).

Elements such as complexity of moving parts (polymagnets), environmental impact of materials, power supply requirement, size or variety of game piece (Hoberman sphere) are considered in the design adaptation.

During the original study, indicators for viable designs for a game-piece started to emerge in the artistic explorations of the Dod design. The Latch Dod is an example of this concept [10]. A spring latch was contained within each arm, which in turn was encased by an origami constructed, pentagonal frustrum, see Fig. 5a. At the top of the origami spring, a pentagonal facet was attached. This feature was to maintain the concept of the original Dod and arm rotation, as can be seen in Fig. 5b. Any of the 12 facets could be depressed in order to retract or in turn release the latch spring in order to extend the arm again. An interesting behaviour emerged when all the latches are depressed (in the retracted position) and the Latch Dod was dropped from a short height (e.g. 10 cm). The spring of the latch on which the Dod landed extended providing sufficient energy to propel the whole construction up and onto another latch. This essentially triggered a chain reaction causing the Dod to jump around an area until most latches had been activated.

Whilst similar in construct to toys such as 'Chuckle Ball' [55, 56], the appendages of these toys are stationary and the bounce or jiggle comes from within the spherical ball provided by an internal motor. In the instance of the Latch Dod there is no power source required, i.e. the energy for motion, bounce, topological and form change is provided by the potential energy contained in each of the 12 springs.

Fig. 5a – c. (a) Spring latches contained in the inner core, (b) single core-arm construction, (c) Final Latch Dod.

Another important quality in MAS to be able to build 3D structures, is the ability to self-assemble. This behaviour is simulated in the original Dod prototype through the use of permanent 3 mm ball magnets. As an alternative to using permanent magnets, the concept of polymagnets also proved to be of interest and as yet could be an avenue of future development. This relates to printing magnetic patterns thereby altering the magnetic field lines. The company Correlated Magnetics works on varying designs ranging from Latch, Align, Attach, Spring and even printing magnetic patterns onto non-linear surfaces. In their latest line of research are magnetic patterns that are encoded onto the required part so that it can be read by sensors [57]. Of interest to the Dodlen, among other future considerations, is the combination of an *Attract and Spring* mechanism. The pattern printed resembles a circular lock & key. Both magnets are restrained via a rod, which runs through the centre. When the latch is open the magnets repel each other and act like a spring, i.e. it cannot fully close and there is a specified distance between the magnets when at rest. When one magnet is rotated the magnetic pattern aligns and exhibits an attractive force essentially locking the magnets together and withstanding perpendicular outward forces [57]. There may be potential to print such patterns onto specific facets of the Dod and thereby automatically connecting a locking mechanism to the rotation-extension motion of the arm.

Considering these characteristics and possibilities again demonstrated the potential adaptability of the Dod design itself. For research purposes, ease of manufacturing and available resources, the Dod was developed as seen in Fig. 6 and is currently in production. It is currently still in the prototyping stage, with the aim to undergo user testing.

Fig. 6. Multiple Dodlens in various configurations.

Following the design principle described in section three (emulation versus replication), it is possible to see that inspiration was taken from the original Lego block mechanism. In order to facilitate space efficiency, the round nub fits into a pentagonal shaped hole. The Dodlen's arm are set in specific configurations ranging from 0 arms to all 12 arms being extended. The number of configurations versus the number of arms extended provide ample diversity with respect to the number of game-pieces available. For example, a Dodlen with 2 arms extended can have 4 configurations: Top and Bottom (creates straight lines), Top and near arm (creating an acute angle), Top and far arm (creating an obtuse angle) and two same hemisphere arms. There is also a degree of variance depending on whether the arms have nubs (can attach to another Dodlen) or whether they have holes (can be attached to). On each facet is either a nub or a hole and for each version of a Dodlen there is an inverted counterpart, i.e. if a Dodlen with all arms extended has nubs in each facet, then there is also a Dodlen, with all arms extended, that has a hole in each facet. It is possible to 3D print these pieces in PLA using a conventional hobbyist 3D printer, e.g. Ultimaker.

5.1 User Interaction

The Dodlens can be played with in two main ways, A) in the same manner as Lego blocks, i.e. as individual building blocks or B) as part of a game. This can initially prove challenging because it diverges from the familiar and traditional approach of building with cuboid blocks. The forms and shapes that are possible are not actively engaged with on a public level, in particular the additional consideration that spherical objects lack the ease of cohesion present in traditional cuboid building blocks. However, an interesting feature of the dodecahedron is the dual nature of its shape, i.e. it has flat faces enabling stable planes to exist, whilst at the same time embodying the essence of the curved form of a sphere. It can create straight lines by the extension of opposite arms as well as create curves along 2 axes. In this scenario it is possible for users to begin experimenting with shapes and constructs that can emerge from a semi-spherical building block. The overarching value of this interaction is fostering an engagement with unconventional results and ideally generating a new standard of acceptance. As mentioned previously, exploration and interaction through play is a useful and safe method of introducing novel ideas. The Dodlen takes inspiration from existing and strongly integrated games and toys, and has adapted 1 element: the shape. This ensures that users move from familiarity in concept (building -block) and interaction (stacking, connecting, building, etc.) and can focus on using the Dodlen rather than learning a new concept from scratch.

Mentally preparing the understanding for structures based on alternative building-blocks (or agents) gives shape-shifting technology more scope to define itself rather than be defined by existing computer concepts. The proposed Dodlen design highlights its affordances clearly and is intuitive to interact with. These qualities are important in the consideration of user interaction and engagement. It can easily be scaled to produce larger or smaller versions, and it can be constructed out of different materials, if necessary.

Implementing the Dodlen as part of game, a minimum of four playing boards that create the playing space are also envisioned. An additional 2 boards can be added to broaden the playing space. These playing boards are pentagonal in shape and connect at the same dihedral angle (116.57°) forming a larger dodecahedron. The boards range from having a plain to varied surface topology. A plain surface topology consists of a distribution of nubs and holes to which one or multiple Dod pieces can be fixed. This distribution can be a regular or random pattern. A varied surface topology will have certain structures already in place, e.g. half or full Dodlen affixed onto the surface in specific configurations. The purpose of these is to diversify the playing field and provide varying levels of difficulty.

5.2 Game Objectives

There are two fundamental objectives represented in this game format, which are as follows:

- Physical: Create lines or structures made up of Dodlens connecting two or more game boards.
- Interaction: Develop game strategies that enhance engagement with 3D thinking and manipulation

For the purposes of the prototype, different colours will represent the different levels of arm extension purely for identification purposes. However, colours can then also be considered in the development of game rules to indicate specific rules or behaviours, i.e. red Dodlen will prevent any player from connecting to that Dodlen - can be used as a blocking mechanism; a yellow Dodlen means a player can only connect to a specific hemisphere, etc. The mechanism by which a player's turn is indicated can be represented by a traditional die shape but with different symbols on its facets, see Fig. 7.

Fig. 7. A diagram dice from the game Coco Crazy by Ravensburger.

Applied to the overall game, it can define which colour Dodlen a player must use, or to turn the entire game-board, change connecting direction, connect to two different game boards, etc.

The variations in the game pieces include the size of the Dodlen pieces themselves, e.g. larger Dodlen pieces can have different rules associated with them. This would reflect the concept of a seed agent discussed in research into agent-to-agent communication [21, 58]. The final game strategies are currently being refined with the aim of undergoing usability testing in order to determine elements that require further adaptations or improvement. Whilst the aim is to create an engaging game, a strong underlying motivation is to support and foster 3D spatial manipulation and interaction.

6   Conclusion

In order to sustain research, it is necessary to explore avenues which help maintain its relevance. A project such as the Dod (MAS agent design) and on a larger scale, shape-shifting technology, due to its nature is primarily hypothetical. Research into individual aspects of such technology is necessary (e.g. self-assembly, communication, interaction). However, this paper has also highlighted that adapting design guidelines to provide support and scope for creativity and logic, is essential in projects whereby significant design parameters are still unknown. In order to bridge the gap between science-fiction and reality it is important to continuously evaluate research and maintain an overview of the context into which shape-shifting technology should orientate.

The second aspect of this paper describes the Dodlen – a Dod based game-piece. It relates to returning to a fundamental technique of exploration and experiential development: playing. Through this technique, it is possible to gradually influence 3D thinking, interaction techniques and structural possibilities of MAS. When the first computer graphical user interfaces (GUIs) aimed to digitally and conceptually represent a physical desktop (i.e. trashcan icon, filing system, individual applications - notepad, paint), it followed several design heuristics later defined by Nielson, e.g. recognition rather than recall [59]. Users were already familiar with the concept of a desktop and this concept was transferred into the digital realm. Similarly, MAS based shape-shifting technology has a diverse range of elements that require familiarity on behalf of the user: structural cohesion, AI learning frameworks, hive behaviour, agent communication, haptic dexterity, etc. Encouraging a longevity of engagement with research through whichever medium, ensures a deeper understanding as users will have had time to interact, think and engage with the physical output of research as well as the theories it aims to represent.

Acknowledgements. I would like to thank my family for their continued support and my supervisor, Dr. Mikael Fernström, for his guidance throughout my study. Thanks also go to the Irish Research Council for funding the first 3 years of this study (Project ID: GOIPG/2013/351).

References

1. Hasenfuss, H.: Emerging complexity: communication between agents in a mas for shape-shifting TUIs. In: 4th International Conference on Computer-Human Interaction Research and Applications2020: Online-Streaming (2020)
2. Lifton, J.H.: Pushpin computing: a platform for distributed sensor networks. In: School of Architecture and Planning2002, Massachusettes Institute of Technology
3. Rubenstein, M., Cornejo, A., Nagpal, R.: Programmable self-assembly in a thousand-robot swarm. Science **345**(6198), 795 (2014)
4. Werfel, J., Petersen, K., Nagpal, R.: Designing collective behavior in a termite-inspired robot construction team. Science **343**(6172), 754–758 (2014)
5. Roudaut, A., et al.: Cubimorph: designing modular interactive devices. In: 2016 IEEE International Conference on Robotics and Automation (ICRA) 2016
6. Romanishin, J.W., Gilpin, K., Rus, D.: M-blocks: momentum-driven, magnetic modular robots. In: 2013 IEEE/RSJ International Conference on Intelligent Robots and Systems (2013)
7. Gilpin, K., Knaian, A., Rus, D.: Robot pebbles: one centimeter modules for programmable matter through self-disassembly. In: 2010 IEEE International Conference on Robotics and Automation (2010)
8. Hasenfuss, H.: A design exploration of an agent template for multiagent systems (MAS) for shape shifting tangible user interfaces., in Computer Science and Information Systems, Univesity of Limerick: Unpublished (2018)
9. Hasenfuss, H.: Reinventing the cube: an alternative agent design for shape-shifting technology. In: 3rd International Conference on Computer-Human Interaction Research and Applications, pp. 15–27 Scitepress: Vienna (2019)
10. Hasenfuss, H.: *Through the Looking Glass: designing for MAS based shape-shifting technology using the STEAM approach*. In: Escalona, M.J., Ramirez, A.J., Silva, H.P., Constantine, L., Helfert, M., Holzinger, A. (eds.) Computer-Human Interaction Research and Applications. CHIRA CHIRA 2018 2019. *Communications is Computer and Information Science, vol. 1351*, p. 80–101 2021 Springer, Cham. https://doi.org/10.1007/978-3-030-67108-2_5
11. Saddik, A.E., et al.: *Haptics Technologies*. in *Bringing touch to multimedia*2011 Springer Berlin Heidelberg
12. Ishii, H., Ullmer, B.: *Tangible Bits: towards seamless interfaces between people, bits and atoms*. In: *Proceedings of the ACM SIGCHI Conference on Human factors in computing systems*, pp. 234–241, ACM: Atlanta, Georgia, USA (1997)
13. Butera, W.J.: *Painting the computer*, in *program in media arts and sciences*, p. 188 Massachusetts Institute of Technology (2002)
14. Horev, O.: *Talking to the hand. An exploration into shape shifting objects and morphing interfaces*, Interaction Design Institute Ivrea (2006)

15. Sutherland, I.: *The Ultimate Display*. In: *IFIP Congress* (1965)
16. Steinicke, F.: *The Science and Fiction of the Ultimate Display*. In: *Being Really Virtual*. Springer: Cham, pp. 19-32 (2016). https://doi.org/10.1007/978-3-319-43078-2_2
17. Memory Alpha. *Holodeck*. 2021 [cited 2021]. https://memory-alpha.fandom.com/wiki/Holodeck
18. Kann, S.V., Snoeijer, J.H., D.v.d. Meer *Phase diagram of vertically vibrated dense suspensions*, 27 (2013)
19. Lifton, J.H., Broxton, M., Paradiso, J.A.: Distributed sensor networks as sensate skin. BT Technol. J. **22**(4), 32–44 (2004)
20. Özgür, A., et al., *Cellulo: Versatile Handheld Robots for Education*, in *ACM/IEEE International Conference on Human-Robot Interaction* 2017: Vienna, Austria. p. pp. 119–127
21. Le Goc, M., et al.: Zooids: builidng blocks for swarm user interfaces. In: Proceedings of the Symposion on User Interface Software and Technology (UIST), New York (2016)
22. Gordon, D.M.: *Colonial Studies*. Boston Rev. pp. 59–62 (2010)
23. Thórisson, K.R.: *Communicative humanoids: a computational model of psychosocial dialogue skills*, in *school of architecture and planning*, Massachusetts Institute of Technology (1996)
24. Tero, A., Kobayashi, R., Nakagaki, T.: A mathematical model for adaptive transport network in path finding by true slime mold. J. Theor. Biol. **244**(4), 553–564 (2007)
25. Dallas, D.: *Richard Feynman the world from another point of view [HD]*, pp. 36(41): Yorkshire Public Television (2015)
26. Maindrivefailure, *BBC – Beautiful Equations*, BBC4, Editor 2012, Youtube
27. Ridden, P.: *Festo unveils robotic ants, butterflies and chameleon tongue gripper*. Gizmag 2015, 14 June 2016]. http://www.gizmag.com/festo-bionicants-flexshapegripper-emotionbutterflies/36765/
28. Festo. *Find out how Industry 4.0 can reach the next level*. 2018 Feb 2018]. https://www.festo.com/group/en/cms/11753.htm
29. Mlot, N.J., Tovey, C.A., Hu, D.L.: Fire ants self-assemble into waterproof rafts to survive floods. Proc. Natl. Acad. Sci. U.S.A. **108**(19), 7669–7673 (2011)
30. GeoBeats news, *ants can act like liquids as well as solids*, Youtube (2015)
31. Thaler, W.: *Ants: Nature's Secret Power*, 2004, ORF Enterprise. p. 54 mins
32. Poupyrev, I., et al.: *Lumen: interactive visual and shape display for calm computing*. In: *SIGGRAPH 2004 Emerging technologies*, New York, USA (2004)
33. Follmer, S., et al.: *inFORM: Dynamic Physical Affordances and Constraints through Shape and Object Actuation*, p. 10 ACM (2013)
34. Follmer, S., et al.: *deForm: an interactive malleable surface for capturing 2.5D arbitrary objects, tools and touch*. In: *Proceedings of the 24th Annual ACM Symposium on User Interface Software and Technology*, ACM, pp. 527–536 Santa Barbara, California, USA (2011)
35. Iwata, H., et al.: *Project FEELEX: adding haptic surface to graphics*. In: *Proceedings of the 28th Annual Conference on Computer Graphics and Interactive Techniques*, pp. 469–476, ACM (2001)
36. Marquardt, N., et al.: *The Haptic Tabletop Puck: tactile feedback for interactive tabletops*, in *Proceedings of the ACM International Conference on Interactive Tabletops and Surfaces* 2009, ACM: Banff, Alberta, Canada. p. 85 - 92
37. Leithinger, D. and H. Ishii. *Relief: A Scalable Actuated Shape Display*. in *Tangible, embedded and embodied interaction*. 2010. New York, NY, USA
38. Jansen, Y. Mudpad: fluid Haptics for multitouch surfaces. In: CHI 2010: Student Research Competition. Atlanta, GA, USA (2010)
39. Koh, J.T.K.V., et al.: Liquid interface: a malleable, transient, direct-touch interface. ACM Comput. Entertainment **2**(7), 8 (2011)

40. Kim, H. Lee, W.: *Kinetic tiles: modular construction units for interactive kinetic surfaces*. In: *Adjunct proceedings of the 23nd Annual ACM Symposium on User Interface Software and Technology*, pp. 431–432 ACM: New York, New York, USA (2010)

41. Raffle, H., Joachim, M.W., Tichenor, J.: *Super cilia skin: an interactive membrane*, in *CHI, short talk: tangible interfaces*, pp. 808–809. Lauderdale, Florida, USA (2003)

42. Cohrs, N.H., et al.: A soft total artificial heart—first concept evaluation on a hybrid mock circulation. Artif. Organs **41**, 948–958 (2017)

43. Kreigman, S., et al.: A scalable pipeline for designing reconfigurable organisms. Proc. Nat. Acad. Sci. **117**(4), 1853–1859 (2020)

44. Liu, X., et al.: *3D printing of living responsive materials and devices*. Advanced Materials, **30**, 1704821-n/a (2017)

45. Gupta, A.: *Toy Treasures*. 4th ed. 1999, New Delhi1: Arvind Gupta

46. Gupta, A.: *Little Toys*. 1st ed. 1997, New Delhi: National Book Trust

47. Gupta, A.: *Little Science*. 2nd ed. 1991, Bhopal: Eklavya

48. Khanna, S., Wolf, G., Ravishankar, A.: Toys and Tales with Everyday Material. Tara Publishing, Besant Nagar Chennai (2004)

49. Khanna, S.: *Joy of making Indian toys*. 2nd ed. 2000, New Delhi: National Book Trust

50. Raffle, H.S., Parkes, A.J., Ishii, H.: *Topobo: a constructive assembly system with kinetic memory*. In: *Computer Human Interaction*, ACM: Vienna, Austria (2004)

51. Sieden, L.S.: *Buckminster Fuller's universe: his life and work*. 1989, Cambridge, Mass, Perseus (1989)

52. Fuller, R.B.: *Synergetics : explorations in the geometry of thinking*, ed. E.J. Applewhite. 1975: New York, Macmillan, London, Collier Macmillan

53. Weiser, M.: *The computer for the 21st century*. In: *Scientific American Ubicomp* 1991

54. Memory Alpha. *Kal-toh*. Jan 2018] (2018). http://memory-alpha.wikia.com/wiki/Kal-toh

55. Lanard Toys Ltd. *Junior Jitter Ball*. 1994 12 Dec 2017]. https://www.amazon.co.uk/Lanard-Junior-Jitter-Ball-x/dp/B000WZCCJU

56. Chuckle Ball. *Chuckle Ball*. 2016 7 Dec 2017]. http://chucklechuckleball.com/

57. Polymagnet Correlated Magnetics. *About Polymagnets*. 2016 4 July 2016]. http://www.polymagnet.com/polymagnets/

58. Bojinov, H., Casal, A., Hogg, T.: Multiagent control of self-reconfigurable robots. Artif. Intell. **142**, 99–120 (2002)

59. Nielsen, J. *10 usability heuristics for user interface design*. 1995 3 November 2016]. https://www.nngroup.com/articles/ten-usability-heuristics/

60. BoardGameGeek. *3D Dominos* (2012). Accessed Jan 2018. https://boardgamegeek.com/boardgame/146135/3d-dominos

Learning Tonal Harmony Through Augmented Reality: Bridging the Gap Between Music Embodiment and Digital Experiences

Federico Avanzini[1], Adriano Baratè[1], Mauro Cottini[1],
Luca Andrea Ludovico[1(✉)], and Marcella Mandanici[2]

[1] Laboratorio di Informatica Musicale, Dipartimento di Informatica "Giovanni Degli Antoni", Università degli Studi di Milano, Via G. Celoria 18, Milano, Italy
{federico.avanzinim,adriano.barate,mauro.cottini,luca.ludovico}@unimi.it
[2] Dipartimento di Didattica della Musica, Conservatorio di Musica "Luca Marenzio", Piazza A. Benedetti Michelangeli 1, Brescia, Italy
marcella.mandanici@consbs.it
https://www.lim.di.unimi.it/, https://www.consbs.it/

Abstract. This paper aims to highlight how a technologically augmented approach can help developing tonal harmony awareness in young learners. The proposal is rooted in previous experiences conducted by the same research group and dealing, on one side, with the embodiment of music concepts, and, on the other, with a reenactment of the same activities in the digital domain. To the latter goal, a publicly-available web platform containing three types of exercises has been released. In order to bridge the gap between the physical experiences and their digital counterparts, we present a methodological approach based on the adoption of augmented-reality technologies. Such a vision has driven the design and implementation of an app for mobile devices that incorporates image recognition algorithms.

Keywords: Tonal harmony · Music education · Embodiment · Mobile devices · BYOD (bring your own device)

1 Introduction

Making young students acquire musical competences is not a trivial task. It involves motivation, engagement, experience sharing and the acquisition of motor and cognitive skills.

During the first part of the 20th Century, a vast movement of innovative theories and methods has developed in the field of music education. Among these, it is important to mention Carl Orff's *Schulwerk* (1950–1954), and particularly its American edition [17], where multiple movement games and bodily activities are proposed with the aim of acquiring motor skills and providing a better

© The Author(s), under exclusive license to Springer Nature Switzerland AG 2022
A. Holzinger et al. (Eds.): CHIRA 2020, CCIS 1609, pp. 54–73, 2022.
https://doi.org/10.1007/978-3-031-22015-9_4

understanding of the musical form. A similar approach was followed by the Swiss musician Émile Jaques-Dalcroze, who developed a method for training musical thought and expressiveness through coordinated movements and dance [34]. All these fundamental contributions have deeply influenced the way many instructors teach music, making games – and particularly movement-based ones – a well established practice. With these premises, the advent of personal digital devices and video games did not find music teachers completely unprepared. Nevertheless, much can be done to further encourage the use of digital games in order to increase the interest and the involvement of children in everyday classroom activities.

Many video games, and many music-oriented educational applications using game elements as well, are nowadays freely available on the web. Let us mention, e.g., the *Chrome Music Lab* suite,[1] which offers meaningful musical experiences using eye-catching graphics and intuitive responsiveness to user's interaction.

If, on the one side, the use of digital games can greatly enrich music teaching, on the other side a fundamental element is lacking: movement. Actually, there are systems and applications that are able to couple playful elements and movement. The *WizeFloor* system provides a rich choice of movement games through the use of motion tracking technologies and interactive floor projections.[2] The *SMALLab* system, a room-sized interactive environment where students are up out of their seats, moving as they learn, employs similar technologies, but integrates the learning platform with a web tool for the individual prosecution of learning activities.[3]

The mentioned solutions require to set up specific environments and present a non-trivial cost for their implementation in a formal learning space, such as a school. Despite the potential efficacy, their diffusion and usability is greatly biased by these limitations. Thus, every effort to combine the expressiveness of gestural or full-body interaction with the richness and versatility of the digital domain must be regarded with great interest. This is exactly the aim of *AREmbody*, a mobile application which extends the functionalities of *Harmonic Touch*, a web platform for the knowledge and practice of tonal harmony.

The present paper is the extension of a previous work focusing on the use of augmented reality on mobile devices to develop harmony awareness. That contribution was presented at the *4th International Conference on Computer-Human Interaction Research and Applications* (CHIRA 2020) [3]. In this article, we are going to generalize such an approach to different harmony-related experiences.

The rest of the paper is organized as follows: Sect. 2 explains the basic musical theory behind our proposal, Sect. 3 recalls the milestones in our background activities, Sect. 4 focuses on open research questions, Sect. 5 describes a technological platform to answer these questions, Sect. 6 presents a mobile-phone app that implements the technological solution, Sect. 7 discusses it, and, finally, Sect. 8 draws the conclusions.

---

[1] https://musiclab.chromeexperiments.com/.

[2] https://www.wizefloor.com/.

[3] https://www.smallablearning.com/.

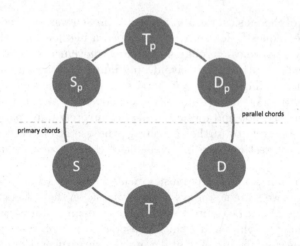

Fig. 1. Chord representation on a circle according to Riemann's theory.

2   A Spatial Approach to Develop Tonal Harmony Awareness

The basic idea we propose to foster tonal harmony awareness is the use of spatial representations for music relationships. According to the spatial schema introduced by the Swiss mathematician Leonard Euler in 1739 [16], chords can be seen as areas disposed on a surface crossed by three music intervals axes (fifths, major and minor thirds). This representation, called the *Tonnetz*, has been later revisited by Hugo Riemann, a German music theorist. In 1896, Riemann published his ideas about harmonic functions, subdividing the tonal space in primary chords and parallel chords [30]. The former category includes the tonic (T), subdominant (S), and dominant (D), built on the first, fourth, and fifth grade of the major scale respectively; the latter category embraces the parallel tonic (T_p), parallel subdominant (S_p), and parallel dominant (D_p), built on the sixth, second, and third grade of the major scale respectively. For the sake of clarity, in the key of C major, the pitches are C for T, F for S, G for D, A for T_p, D for S_p, and E for D_p. As a noticeable property, in a major tonality, all the primary chords are major triads and the parallel chords are minor triads.[4]

Following Riemann's theories, a graphical representation of the harmonic space can be mapped onto a circle (see Fig. 1), where:

- Primary chords are in the lower part, with T in the middle, S on the left, and D on the right;
- Parallel chords are above the corresponding primary chords in the upper part, with T_p in the middle, S_p on the left, and D_p on the right.

---

[4] A triad consists of three distinct notes: the so-called "root note", an interval of either minor or major third, and an interval of perfect fifth.

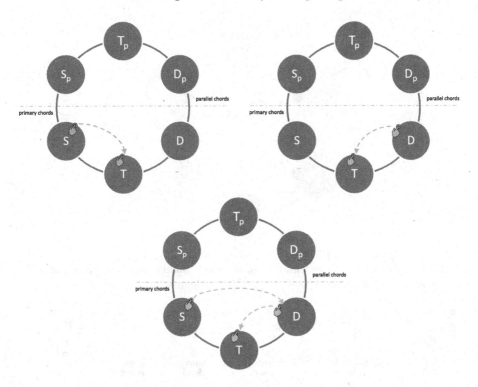

Fig. 2. Some standard harmonic cadences represented on the chord circle: in green a $S \rightarrow T$ cadence (top left), in pink a $D \rightarrow T$ cadence (top right), in orange a $S \rightarrow D \rightarrow T$ cadence (bottom). (Color figure online)

This layout greatly simplifies the possibilities offered by tonal harmony. For example, only triads are represented (thus excluding seventh chords or more complex note sets), chords are always in root position (i.e., no inversion is supported), the VII degree of the scale (i.e. the leading tone) is not present, there is no possibility to change from one tonality to another (modulation), and so on. Nevertheless, such a simplified layout turns to be useful to clarify basic tonal functions to a non-expert learner, since tonal centers and their harmonic function are easy to be identified. Please note that all locations can be reached without crossing other tonal areas.

Recalling the spatial approach, harmonic cadences[5] can be represented by paths connecting the nodes. Figure 2 shows a plagal cadence ($S \rightarrow T$), an authentic cadence ($D \rightarrow T$), and an extension of the authentic cadence including also the fourth degree ($S \rightarrow D \rightarrow T$). More complex patterns can be performed as well, covering the chord sequence of an unexpectedly wide range of popular tunes.

Anyway, this simplified schema can also be seen as the starting point towards more advanced representations of the harmonic space that may significantly

---

[5] A harmonic cadence is a progression of chords that concludes a section or a piece of music.

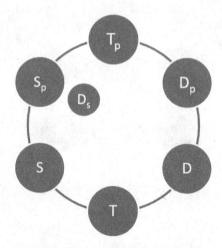

Fig. 3. A more complex representation of a major tonality harmonic space including also the secondary dominant D_s.

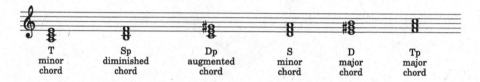

Fig. 4. The chords of the harmonic space in the A minor key.

improve its functionality. For example, the inclusion of secondary dominants could be evaluated by duplicating the sub-dominant parallel chord, as denoted by D_s in Fig. 3. The higher complexity introduced in the schema is counterbalanced by a lower degree of usability, or by higher requirements in terms of harmony-related competence from the user.

The representation of a minor tonality harmonic space could be experimented as well. As shown in Fig. 4, the subdivision between primary and parallel chords is less evident than in the major mode. Primary chords are not all minor triads, since D must always be a major chord. The case of parallel chords is even more complex, as only T_p is a major chord; S_p is a diminished chord, while the D_p is an augmented one. All these aspects of complexity, which clearly affect the usability of the chords circle, could be addressed in a more flexible way by employing different chord layouts to accommodate the music material.

3   Background Work

The space-based proposal to gain tonal harmony awareness has been developed by our research group along two directions, so far: i) harmony embodiment, namely the use of body and physical interactions to enact music-related concepts, and ii) computer-based activities, i.e. ad-hoc exercises to be performed on a personal computer or other digital device. In the former case, chords are represented in a physical space that the learner can bodily explore; in the latter case, the harmonic space is reconstructed through suitable graphical interfaces and user's movements can be mimicked through a pointing device (e.g., a mouse or the cursor of a touch screen).

Both the approaches have been explored in background research activities, resulting in two solutions already tested in educational environments: *Harmonic Walk* and *Harmonic Touch*. These applications will be shortly described in the next sections.

3.1 Harmonic Walk

A first attempt to apply embodiment to music harmony awareness led to the design of a system called *Harmonic Walk*. The goal of the initiative is to associate chord sequences to the movements of a user in a large-scale bi-dimensional environment. A free exploration of space should let the player acquire awareness of music chords and learn the paths referable to the most common harmonic progressions [26].

From a technical point of view, *Harmonic Walk* is made of a suitable combination of hardware and software components. The user's interface consists of a rectangular carpet positioned on the floor that virtually contains the chord circle. The visual reference for chord locations is provided via specific cue points, e.g., small crosses drawn on the carpet with duct tape (see Fig. 5).

Fig. 5. A young learner using *Harmonic Walk*. Image extracted from YouTube, https:// youtu.be/iQlYP5dztDY.

As it regards interaction, when the user steps on an interactive landmark, the corresponding chord sound is triggered. This activity could be performed also manually. For example, in a low-tech environment, a music teacher could evaluate the position of the learner on the floor by sight, and play a traditional instrument, like a piano or a guitar, accordingly. *Harmonic Walk*, conversely, implements an automatic evaluation of user's position over the sensitive area. To this end, the architecture include a software module aimed at video analysis. First, a video camera mounted on the ceiling and oriented perpendicular to the floor captures user's movements. Then, the video module analyzes the images provided by the camera in order to detect the user's position. Coordinates are sent via OSC[6] to the sound-synthesis module. Such a component, implemented in MAX,[7] aims to play the chords triggered by the user's movements detected on the floor.

The dimensions of the tracked area mainly depend on the camera-to-floor distance and the lens' field of view. As the system is designed for classroom activities, monitoring usually involves a limited area, about 3 m × 4 m. Bad lightning conditions and occlusions by other users are potential issues to consider during the activity.

Apart from these technicalities, the most relevant problem experienced with *Harmonic Walk* is the portability of the experience, that requires the availability of a suitable space, a non-trivial hardware setup, and fine-tuning operations.

3.2   Harmonic Touch

Harmonic Touch is a Web platform for the exploration and practice of tonal harmony. It was conceived as a step-by-step path that leads users towards the development of tonal harmony awareness by leveraging on chord perception, gestural interaction and gamification techniques. The platform is publicly and freely available at http://harmonictouch.lim.di.unimi.it/.

As explained in detail in [4], three groups of experiences are proposed to the user:

1. Experience ♯1 – "Recognition of the implicit harmony". The user is asked to match a short music tune with the single chord that best fits the whole melody [9]. The chord is picked from the set of primary and parallel chords introduced in Sect. 2. Chords are represented on a circle, randomly rotated and without any cue about scale degrees or tonal functions (see Fig. 6). The user can freely explore the chord layout during a pre-exercise training phase, so as to mentally build a map of the spatial relationship among chords. This activity can be seen as a digitally revised implementation of *Harmonic Walk*;
2. Experience ♯2 – "Timed recognition of harmonic changes". After listening to a complete piece (leading tune and chords together), the user is asked to

---

[6] Open Sound Control (OSC) is a protocol for networking sound and multimedia devices for purposes such as musical performance or show control. It was originally intended for sharing music performance data, such as gestures, parameters and note sequences, between digital musical instruments.

[7] https://cycling74.com/.

Fig. 6. The interface of *Harmonic Touch*, Experience ♯1.

Fig. 7. The interface of *Harmonic Touch*, Experience ♯2.

reconstruct it. Each tonal area is triggered by moving one step ahead over a map at the exact time when a new chord is expected. If the click does not occur at the right timing, music stops; if it is performed in advance, a part of the tune is skipped. This exercise focuses on the harmonic rhythm only, with no need to recognize tonal functions. An example of interface is shown in Fig. 7;

3. Experience ♯3 – "Melody harmonization". The final step invites the user to select the right chord at the right timing in order to accompany a known music tune. This exercise has been conceived as the natural evolution of the previous ones, being based on both the recognition of the best-fitting chord (Experience ♯1) and the occurrence of harmonic changes in time (Experience ♯2). The graphical interface, shown in Fig. 8, recalls the one of Experience ♯1:

Fig. 8. The interface of *Harmonic Touch*, Experience ♯3.

it adopts the same spatial relationship among chords, but tonal functions are made explicit by roman numerals.

Harmonic Touch extends the concept of tonal-harmony space exploration introduced by *Harmonic Walk*, bringing it into a Web environment. Physical movements in a bi-dimensional space are now translated onto a PC screen, without the hardware and software requirements and the space-related constraints described in Sect. 3.1. The Web framework embeds both the on-screen movement tracker and the sound synthesis module. Another advantage with respect to *Harmonic Walk* is the possibility to automatically assess and anonymously save user performances into a database [5].

An early experimentation was conducted in two Italian primary schools in February 2021, in the midst of the resurgence of the COVID-19 pandemic. Educational activities involved 46 children (29 females), aged 8 to 11, from 4th and 5th-grade classes. For further details, please refer to [6]. Other schools are currently using *Harmonic Touch*, but the experimentation is still running and results have not been analyzed yet.

4   Open Issues and Research Questions

Harmonic Walk and *Harmonic Touch* represented successful initiatives, tested in educational environments and documented in the scientific literature. Nevertheless, a critical analysis of both solutions makes some open issues emerge.

Harmonic Walk proved to be problematic to export to other contexts. For example, the required hardware and software equipment typically is not available at home, thus confining the educational activity to school time.

Concerning *Harmonic Touch*, out-of-school availability is guarantee by a suitable computer-based interface. Nevertheless, two key issues hamper its extensive adoption. The first problem is that exercise settings are fixed: chord layout and positions cannot be altered (e.g., being simplified for cognitively-impaired learners or changed in dimension, shape, and color for visually-impaired users); available chords are those listed in Riemann's theory (e.g., root notes are predefined, non-triadic chords are not supported, no modulation can be performed, etc.); and so on. Even if the platform lets authenticated users add new songs, thus supporting a certain degree of customization, exercise models are well defined and unchangeable.

The other issue of *Harmonic Touch* concerns the metaphor itself of moving in space, that is one of the pillars of our proposal. In this platform, the idea of embodiment is translated into the movement of a cursor in a screen through a pointing device. Such a solution presents a number of advantages, including the removal of physical-space constraints and the active participation by physically impaired users, but its didactic efficacy should be further investigated.

In conclusion, the activities taking place in the physical domain (*Harmonic Walk*) and in the digital one (*Harmonic Touch*) both offer pros and cons. What we are searching for is a technological solution capable of bridging the gap. The main research questions are:

RQ1. Is it possible to couple the efficacy of embodiment, intended as movements in a physical space, with the potential of a computer-based interface in order to foster tonal harmony awareness?

RQ2. What it the most suitable technology, also considering practical issues such as portability, affordability, accessibility?

RQ3. To what extent is the solution extensible, so as to respond to custom educational goals and accommodate user-tailored experiences?

5   The Technological Solution

In order to bridge the gap between the physical and the digital domain and positively answer RQ1, we designed and implemented an app for mobile devices that embeds real-time image tracking in a video stream and integrates augmented reality.

The first design choice regarded the expected user interaction. In order to selects a tonal area or trigger a new chord, we conceived a mechanism based on markers, namely physical objects carrying graphical information and univocally assigned to chords. In our opinion, the most intuitive way to interact with markers is to temporarily cover them in the frame captured by the device camera. Different strategies can be employed, depending on the characteristics of markers and the device position: a part of the body (e.g., a feet, a hand, etc.) or the whole body, a covering object (e.g., a paper sheet, a book, a paddle, etc.), a direct interaction with markers (such as flipping the sheet), and so on. The system is designed to promptly react to these events; moreover, when needed, the app can also record the timing of user actions. In detail, Experience ♯1 presents a fixed number of markers and simply fosters chord exploration, with no need to track timed events; Experience ♯2 supports a variable number of markers, but activation time is fundamental to assess user performances; finally, Experience ♯3 is based on a predefined set of markers and detects timed events.

Concerning the technological platform addressed by RQ2, the idea of releasing an app started from the analysis of some limitations in previous research. First, educational activities should be easily experienced out of the school. To this goal, as the reference technological platform, we identified an "all-in-one" portable device, equipped with a camera and able to reproduce sounds, with sufficient computational power to track images in a video stream and to synthesize sound. Mobile devices such as smart phones and tablets could do the trick.

As a side effect, this solution potentially facilitates also classroom activities, thanks to a BYOD[8] approach. Even if more common in higher education [1,14, 33] and sometimes criticized for its potential risks [2,10,32], BYOD has been experimented also in primary school [19,27,35] and appreciated for a number of aspects, including: educational continuity across school and home contexts, thus blurring boundaries between formal and informal learning spaces [22]; high levels of student engagement through interactive assignments [18], and parental engagement in their children's education [25]; personalized and self-regulated learning [29]; reduction of the cost pressure for one-to-one technology provision in schools [12]; relief for technology support [28].

As mentioned before, the app was designed to track markers representing tonal functions. Images are acquired from the device's camera and processed by ad-hoc recognition algorithms. The use of printable and movable graphical markers instead of a prepared physical space or a predefined computer interface presents many advantages. In this way, it is possible to customize, e.g., the number, size, position, graphical aspect, and intrinsic meaning of markers. An example of markers for Experience ♯3 is provided in Fig. 9.

A first noticeable effect consists in overcoming the limits of a 4 m × 4 m rectangular area (Experience ♯2) and of a circular layout (Experience ♯3). In these scenarios, markers can be placed in space according to any schema, in any desired number, and even moved during the educational activity to accomodate users with special needs. If space constraints are hindering the experience, markers can be printed in smaller size and disposed, e.g., on a table instead of the floor.

Thanks to the use of mobile devices and printed markers, the educational experience can occur in any place, also at home or outdoor. For example, Experiences ♯1 and ♯3 can be performed in the school gym or in the auditorium; and Experience ♯2, that adopts the metaphor of the treasure map, can be proposed in the open air, e.g., in the schoolyard or in a garden.

For Experiences ♯1 and ♯3, the layout made of 6 tonal areas could be initially simplified to meet the needs of beginners (e.g., including only T, S, and D) and incrementally extended, even beyond the diagram reported in Fig. 1.

The graphical representation of chords can be customized, too. In Experience ♯3, standard chord symbols can be replaced by pictograms, sheets with diversified

---

[8] BYOD stands for Bring Your Own Device.

Fig. 9. A possible graphic design of the markers for Experience ♯3.

colors and shapes, etc. to improve or reinforce the recognition by young learners. Linear barcodes, QR codes, and fiducials can be used as well.

Concerning accessibility, such a solution can help overcome visual, physical, and cognitive impairments. For example, it is possible to emphasize graphical differences between chord signs by stressing color contrast, increasing markers' sizes, using bigger or more readable fonts, etc. Moreover, visual markers can be associated with tangible cues for BVI[9] people. Concerning physical impairments, users are no more required to walk on a carpet or firmly hold a mouse, but they can, say, occlude markers on a table by hand or move the camera away; and these gestures still preserve the relationship between space and harmony. Finally, addressing cognitive impairments, the exercises can be suitably simplified, for example by reducing the number of choices or adopting other spatial layouts (e.g., linearizing and bringing together chord positions for Experiences ♯2 and ♯3).

---

[9] BVI stands for Blind or Visually Impaired.

Please note that all the mentioned aspects go in the direction of flexibility and customization of the user experience, as requested by RQ3.

The last piece of the puzzle consists in the adoption of an augmented reality (AR) approach. The capability of creating responsive environments where information may be superimposed to real objects, typical of AR, already proved to be extremely appealing in fields such as engineering analysis [24], maintenance [8], medical diagnosis [15] and many others.

The alignment of instructional design, system affordances, and didactic goals is the best way to fully exploit the learning potentials of AR environments. The fields of music perception and notation skills may benefit of AR applications. In [23], a melody composed of painted notes is filled by the children on paper and then recognized in real time by a mobile's camera; once the image is acquired and processed, the notes may be played and checked by the system. A similar application, called *Augmented Songbook*, is based on pre-printed music sheets [31]. These approaches are very engaging for children and, consequently, they represent effective tools for music education. The simplicity and ubiquity of mobile devices make them suitable for use in classroom and outdoor activities.

In this proposal, AR is employed to put virtual chord symbols over the corresponding markers in the app interface, as shown in Fig. 10. From a technical point of view, the use of AR mainly responds to three goals: i) making markers easily retrievable during the work session, ii) confirming that the tracking system is correctly managing their recognition, and iii) providing a graphical feedback when symbols are physically covered by the user, thus triggering a music event. In addition, the integration of AR can foster engagement [11] and even improve the app usability, when this issue is properly tackled [13, 20, 21].

6   *AREmbody*: An AR-Based App for Tonal Harmony

AREmbody is a freely-available iOS app for iPhone and iPad that currently implements only the most advanced activity, namely Experience ♯3. Born as a proof of concept in order to test the feasibility and the educational efficacy of the approach described in Sect. 5, it can be easily extended to the previous two steps.

At the moment of writing, the app is still at a prototype stage, and, for this reason, it is not available in Apple App Store, but it can be downloaded from http://harmonictouch.lim.di.unimi.it/app_download_ios.php. Due to the limitations imposed by Apple on the use of AR, *AREmbody* can be installed on models from iPhone 6s on and running iOS 13 or superior.

AREmbody was implemented in Swift, a programming language for macOS, iOS, watchOS, tvOS and other Apple platforms[10]. The user interface was realized in *SwiftUI*[11].

---

[10] https://developer.apple.com/swift/.
[11] https://developer.apple.com/xcode/swiftui/.

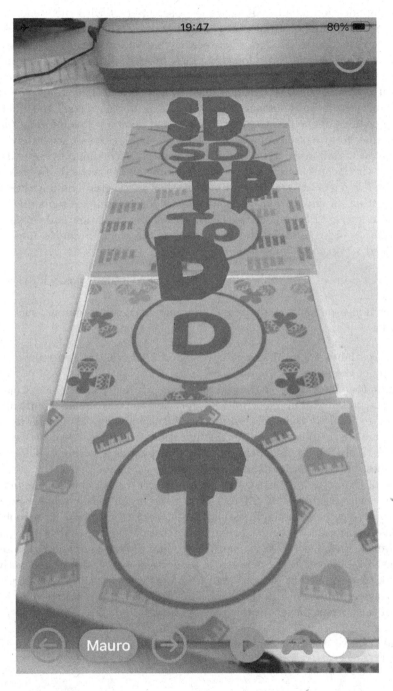

Fig. 10. Recognition of markers and superimposition of chord symbols in AR. Image taken from [3].

The application adopts AR to let the user interact with the scene. To this end, two frameworks by Apple, *ARKit* and *SceneKit*, have been used. *ARKit*[12] aims to create a correspondence between virtual and real spaces, thanks to the technique of visual-inertial odometry. This process combines the information coming from the sensors of the device (e.g., the accelerometer, the gyroscope, etc.) with the analysis of the scene framed by the camera. This framework is able to recognize the most important characteristics of the scene, track the differences in the positions of cue points across frames, and compare this information with that coming from motion sensors. In this way, the device can accurately model its orientation and position in space. As a result, *ARKit* connects the real world with the virtual space prepared by the developer to contain AR objects.

SceneKit[13] is a 3D graphics framework that lets the programmer create 3D scenes within an application. It combines a high-performance rendering engine with descriptive APIs that allow the ingestion, manipulation and rendering of 3D assets. In order to structure the content of the scene, *SceneKit* implements a so-called *scene graph*, consisting of:

- the root node of the graph, which defines the coordinate space for the whole scene;
- other nodes populating the scene and carrying visible content, such as 3D assets.

The spatial and logical structure of a *SceneKit* scene is determined by the hierarchy of the nodes it contains.

AREmbody integrates *ARKit* and *SceneKit* in order to analyze the scene, recognize the presence of markers, and suitably add the corresponding AR objects. In order to improve their recognition by *ARKit*, markers should be as different as possible. In this sense, the customization of graphical representations of chords not only represents an opportunity to exploit as a learning reinforcement techniques, but also responds to a precise technical goal.

One of the noticeable aspects of *AREmbody* is the possibility to manage on a single device a number of different users, also organized by school and class. In this way, a game session addressing a group of participants (e.g., schoolmates in a classroom) reduces the dead time for setting up the app and switch players. Moreover, a single app instance can trace, analyze and compare: i) the results obtained by different users in a single game session, ii) educational activities spanning across different sessions, and iii) an experimentation conducted in different classes and schools. In the lower part of Fig. 10, it is possible to notice the name of the current player (in this case, "Mauro") and the controls to switch to other players.

The app can run on a tripod-held and a hand-held device as well, as shown in Fig. 11.

---

[12] https://developer.apple.com/documentation/arkit/.
[13] https://developer.apple.com/documentation/scenekit/.

(a) Tripod-held device.   (b) Hand-held device.

Fig. 11. Different ways to hold the device while the app is running. Images taken from [3].

At the end of each session, results are stored in the device and can be exported in JSON[14] format, so as to feed a database or an external analysis module. The non-trivial problem of assessing these raw data has been investigated in [7].

7   Discussion

AREmbody is a portable solution that, in our intention, should bridge the gap between *Harmonic Walk* and *Harmonic Touch*. It shares with the other solutions the aim to make young learners acquire awareness in the field of tonal harmony, by adopting embodiment and a gamification approach. Anyway, the design goal was to simplify the setup requirements of *Harmonic Walk*, but preserve a kind of embodiment in a physical space that is lacking in *Harmonic Touch*.

AREmbody supports a personal user experience: educational activities can occur not only during school time in the classroom, but also out of the school. Many game aspects previously constrained by the setup can now be customized, ranging from the appearance of markers (graphical content, size, shape, etc.) to

---

[14] JSON, standing for JavaScript Object Notation, is a lightweight data-interchange format based on structured plain text.

their layout in the physical space (number of markers, relative position, distance, etc.) and the kind of interaction. Any learner equipped with a mobile device can play whenever and wherever, playing alone or with peers.

AREmbody has a great potential, but it needs to be further developed along different directions. First, it currently supports only the last type of experience, which is enough to appreciate its applicability to the full set of activities; nevertheless, a complete educational path based on *AREmbody* requires the implementation of all experiences in a unique framework.

Moreover, the AR component of the game play is still underused. In the current version of *ARembody*, the main purpose of AR is to enrich the user's experience, basically to highlight the recognition of markers, to reinforce their position, and to make the game play more appealing. In a future version, AR could support other customizable features. For example, colors, font types, text dimensions, etc. could fall under the user's control, thus improving the user's experience and helping impaired players. Besides, the app could adapt to specific environmental scenarios, such as poor lighting conditions or crowded scenes. Finally, the AR content itself could become more informative, providing alternative text or guidance in form of animations. For example, a visual hint could indicate the proximity of a chord change and suggest the right choice.

Finally, the app should be extensively tested in an educational scenario, and the results should be compared with both traditional classroom activities and those obtained with *Harmonic Touch* and *Harmonic Walk*. Unfortunately, two aspects have been affecting the experimentation so far: i) the COVID-19 pandemic, that has been hampering in-class activities throughout the last school year, and ii) the high requirements in terms of user device, a limitation that hopefully will be overcome by natural technological advances and the release of an Android version of *ARembody*.

8   Conclusions

In this paper we have discussed the use of embodiment to gain tonal harmony awareness, in accordance with theoretical approaches from the past and contemporary gamification strategies.

In order to demonstrate the feasibility and the educational valence of this approach, we have designed three kind of space-based musical activities, already implemented and tested in a web environment. Nevertheless, a critical analysis of our previous work has underlined the opportunity of bridging the gap between embodiment in the real world and the experiences proposed in the digital domain. To this end, we have designed and released *AREmbody*, an iOS app aiming to foster tonal harmony awareness in young students through embodiment. Its capabilities to analyze the real environment captured by the camera and add AR objects to the scene provide the user with a gamified approach to interact with the physical world. The app supports a number of customizable features that extend the original fixed layout of exercises as implemented in *Harmonic Walk* and *Harmonic Touch*. The app also improve performance assessment, ranging from the support to articulated game-play sessions (multi-player, multi-class, etc.) to the possibility to automatically collect, export, and analyze results.

Concerning future work, we hope that the school year 2021/22 will bring students back to school, giving them the possibility to test the prototype together and share their experiences. It will be an occasion to evaluate the efficacy of the proposed methodology with respect to traditional music learning and the fully digital alternative represented by *Harmonic Touch*. In the meanwhile, technological advancements in the field of portable devices and the implementation of the Android version are expected to foster also a personal and out-of-school use of *AREmbody*.

References

1. Afreen, R.: Bring your own device (BYOD) in higher education: opportunities and challenges. Int. J. Emerg. Trends Technol. Comput. Sci. **3**(1), 233–236 (2014)
2. Akeju, O., Butakov, S., Aghili, S.: Main factors and good practices for managing BYOD and IoT risks in a K-12 environment. Int. J. Internet Things Cyber-Assur. **1**(1), 22–39 (2018)
3. Avanzini, F., Baratè, A., Cottini, M., Ludovico, L.A., Mandanici, M.: Developing music harmony awareness in young students through an augmented reality approach. In: Constantine, L., Helfert, M., Holzinger, A., Silva, H.P. (eds.) Proceedings of the 4th International Conference on Computer-Human Interaction Research and Applications (CHIRA 2020), pp. 56–63. SCITEPRESS - Science and Technology Publications, Lda (2020). https://doi.org/10.5220/0010144700560063
4. Avanzini, F., Baratè, A., Ludovico, L.A., Mandanici, M.: A computer-based approach to teach tonal harmony to young students. In: Lane, H., Uhomoibhi, J., Zvacek, S. (eds.) Proceedings of the 11th International Conference on Computer Supported Education (CSEDU 2019), vol. 1, pp. 271–279. SCITEPRESS - Science and Technology Publications, Lda (2019)
5. Avanzini, F., Baratè, A., Ludovico, L.A., Mandanici, M.: Metrics for the automatic assessment of music harmony awareness in children. In: Barbancho, A.M., Barbancho, I., Peinado, A., Tardón, L.J. (eds.) Proceedings of the 16th Sound & Music Computing Conference (SMC 2019), pp. 372–379. SMC (2019)
6. Avanzini, F., Baratè, A., Ludovico, L.A., Mandanici, M.: Songs in music education: design and early experimentation of a web tool for the recognition of harmonic changes. In: Csapó, B., Uhomoibhi, J. (eds.) Proceedings of the 13th International Conference on Computer Supported Education (CSEDU 2021), vol. 1, pp. 709–720. SCITEPRESS - Science and Technology Publications, Lda (2021)
7. Avanzini, F., Baratè, A., Ludovico, L.A., Mandanici, M.: A web platform to foster and assess tonal harmony awareness. In: Lane, H.C., Zvacek, S., Uhomoibhi, J. (eds.) CSEDU 2019. CCIS, vol. 1220, pp. 398–417. Springer, Cham (2020). https://doi.org/10.1007/978-3-030-58459-7_19
8. Azuma, R.T.: A survey of augmented reality. Presence Teleoper. Virtual Environ. **6**(4), 355–385 (1997)
9. Bigand, E.: The influence of implicit harmony, rhythm and musical training on the abstraction of "tension-relaxation schemas" in tonal musical phrases. Contemp. Music Rev. **9**(1–2), 123–137 (1993)
10. Bruder, P.: Gadgets go to school: the benefits and risks of BYOD (bring your own device). Educ. Digest **80**(3), 15 (2014)

11. Cabiria, J.: Augmenting engagement: augmented reality in education. In: Increasing Student Engagement and Retention Using Immersive Interfaces: Virtual Worlds, Gaming, and Simulation. Emerald Group Publishing Limited (2012)
12. Cardoza, Y., Tunks, J.: The bring your own technology initiative: an examination of teachers' adoption. Comput. Sch. **31**(4), 293–315 (2014)
13. Chang, A., Paz, F., Arenas, J.J., Díaz, J.: Augmented reality and usability best practices: a systematic literature mapping for educational videogames. In: 2018 IEEE Sciences and Humanities International Research Conference (SHIRCON), pp. 1–5. IEEE (2018)
14. Cheng, G., Guan, Y., Chau, J.: An empirical study towards understanding user acceptance of bring your own device (BYOD) in higher education. Australas. J. Educ. Technol. **32**(4) (2016)
15. Douglas, D.B., Wilke, C.A., Gibson, J.D., Boone, J.M., Wintermark, M.: Augmented reality: advances in diagnostic imaging. Multimodal Technol. Interact. **1**(4), 29 (2017)
16. Euler, L.: Tentamen novae theoriae musicae ex certissismis harmoniae principiis dilucide expositae. Saint Petersburg Academy (1739)
17. Goodkin, D.: Orff-Schulwerk in the new millennium. Music. Educ. J. **88**(3), 17–23 (2001)
18. He, W., Zhao, L.: Exploring undergraduates' learning engagement via BYOD in the blended learning classroom. Int. J. Inf. Educ. Technol. **10**(2), 159–164 (2020)
19. Johnson, L., Adams Becker, S., Estrada, V., Freeman, A.: NMC Horizon Report: 2014 K-12 Edition. The New Media Consortium (2014)
20. Kaufmann, H., Dünser, A.: Summary of usability evaluations of an educational augmented reality application. In: Shumaker, R. (ed.) ICVR 2007. LNCS, vol. 4563, pp. 660–669. Springer, Heidelberg (2007). https://doi.org/10.1007/978-3-540-73335-5_71
21. Ko, S.M., Chang, W.S., Ji, Y.G.: Usability principles for augmented reality applications in a smartphone environment. Int. J. Hum.-Comput. Interact. **29**(8), 501–515 (2013)
22. Lai, K.W., Khaddage, F., Knezek, G.: Blending student technology experiences in formal and informal learning. J. Comput. Assist. Learn. **29**(5), 414–425 (2013)
23. Lemos, B., Correa, A., Nascimento, M., Lopes, R.: Augmented reality musical app to support children's musical education. J. Comput. Sci. Inf. Technol. **5**(4), 121–127 (2017)
24. Li, W., Nee, A., Ong, S.: A state-of-the-art review of augmented reality in engineering analysis and simulation. Multimodal Technol. Interact. **1**(3), 17 (2017)
25. Liao, C.C.Y., Cheng, H.N.H., Chang, W.-C., Chan, T.-W.: Supporting parental engagement in a BYOD (bring your own device) school. J. Comput. Educ. **4**(2), 107–125 (2017). https://doi.org/10.1007/s40692-017-0085-6
26. Mandanici, M., Rodà, A., Canazza, S.: The Harmonic Walk: an interactive physical environment to learn tonal melody accompaniment. Adv. Multimed. **2016** (2016)
27. McLean, K.J.: The implementation of bring your own device (BYOD) in primary [elementary] schools. Front. Psychol. **7**, 1739 (2016)
28. Nelson, D.: BYOD: an opportunity schools cannot afford to miss. Internet@schools **19**(5), 12–15 (2012)
29. Ng, W.: Mobile learning: BYOD and personalised learning. In: Ng, W. (ed.) New Digital Technology in Education, pp. 171–189. Springer, Cham (2015). https://doi.org/10.1007/978-3-319-05822-1_8
30. Riemann, H.: Harmony Simplified: Or the Theory of the Tonal Functions of Chords. Augener & Company (1895)

31. Rusiñol, M., Chazalon, J., Diaz-Chito, K.: Augmented songbook: an augmented reality educational application for raising music awareness. Multimed. Tools Appl. **77**(11), 13773–13798 (2018)
32. Saa, P., Moscoso-Zea, O., Lujan-Mora, S.: Bring your own device (BYOD): students perception - privacy issues: a new trend in education? In: 2017 16th International Conference on Information Technology Based Higher Education and Training (ITHET), pp. 1–5. IEEE (2017)
33. Safar, A.H.:. BYOD in higher education: a case study of Kuwait university. J. Educators Online **15**(2), n2 (2018)
34. Seitz, J.A.: Dalcroze, the body, movement and musicality. Psychol. Music **33**(4), 419–435 (2005)
35. Sweeny, J.: BYOD in Education. A Report for Australia and New Zealand: Nine Conversations for Successful BYOD Decision Making. Microsoft (2012)

The Telerobot Contact Hypothesis

Avner Peled[1]($\boxtimes$)(iD), Teemu Leinonen[1](iD), and Béatrice S. Hasler[2](iD)

[1] Department of Media, Aalto University, Espoo, Finland
`{avner.peled,teemu.leinonen}@aalto.fi`
[2] Sammy Ofer School of Communications, Reichman University, Herzliya, Israel
`hbeatrice@idc.ac.il`

Abstract. We propose using telerobots as a medium for intergroup contact, aiming to reduce prejudice between groups in conflict. Telerobots are located in the middle ground between the physical and the virtual realms, providing the flexibility of online communication and the depth of physical interactions. Combining research from intergroup contact theory, communication studies, and human-robot interaction, we present the telerobot contact hypothesis - a set of guidelines, recommendations, and caveats in robot interaction design that strive for the optimal intergroup contact result. The guidelines follow a consistent conceptual model and define the architecture of a telerobotic event, from the first encounter to the pursued reduction of prejudice. We end with recommendations and hopes for further empirical research.

Keywords: Intergroup contact · Human-robot interaction · Telepresence · Telerobots · Conflict resolution

1 Introduction

Considering the current state of human rights and ecological sustainability, it appears as if the bright future promised by globalization and technological advancement has, so far, not manifested as expected. On the one hand, an exponentially growing realization of the earth's finite resources [85] meets the human race's seemingly inept ability to navigate the market to morally favorable prospects [164]. On the other hand, the advent of a globally connected society has done little to alleviate hate, prejudice, and conflict between conflicting groups and nations. In some cases, the internet has even become a petri dish for disseminating prejudiced and violent dispositions [42,68,140,156]. At the same time, we are dealing with the global COVID-19 pandemic, which provides a blatant reminder of both the perils and importance of physical closeness and our reliance on technology to bridge physical gaps.

This research investigates how communication technology could nonetheless be a means for reconciliation and peacebuilding between groups that are plagued by a history of prejudice and racialized narratives. Standing by the proven principles of the *intergroup contact hypothesis*, outlined by Gordon Allport in the 1954 seminal work *The Nature of Prejudice* [3], we argue that with the right set of conditions, technologically mediated contact could reduce prejudice between groups in conflict. In an effort

Supported by The Kone Foundation.

to provide a more grounded and physical experience when face-to-face encounters are scant, we explore *telerobotics* (remotely operated robots) as a new medium that has the potential to facilitate positive intergroup contact.

We hypothesize that if designed equally, openly, and with cultural sensitivity, the physical presence of robots as a communication tool could address the intercorporeal lack that exists in virtual mediums. Telerobots live in the middle ground between physical and virtual [125]. They maintain the openness and accessibility of virtual spaces such as virtual reality (VR) and Social Networking Services (SNSes), yet they do not suffer from dissociations and confusions enacted by the dismissal of the body [32, 130, 157]. A more grounded interaction could also counteract tendencies for abstraction and reification of the other [1, 46, 137] and engage with the corporeality of identity [62]. Finally, by bringing online communication *Down to Earth* [86], we make it harder to dismiss the importance of the physical environment that enables sociality in the first place.

We have previously established the potentialities of telerobot-based contact and suggested basic guidelines and possible pitfalls [110]. In this chapter, we expound on this notion by conducting a more comprehensive literature review, integrating research on intergroup contact and Human-Robot-Interaction (HRI), and devising a complete *telerobot contact hypothesis*.

2   Taxonomy: Telepresence, Telerobots, and Avatars

Telerobots are often referred to as *telepresence robots*. Marvin Minsky and Patrick Gunkel used the term *telepresence* to describe their vision of a futuristic economy in which people perform manual, physical labor from remote locations [96]. While *teleoperation* refers to operating a robot remotely, telepresence describes an immersive experience of *being* in a remote environment, mediated by a physical sensing agent - a *telerobot* [33, 71, 134]. In phenomenology, the term *re-embodiment* is used to describe the experience of telepresence [43]. Today's telerobots go beyond industrial use and are deployed in social care [95], education [146], and interpersonal communication [107], utilizing the internet as a platform for teleoperation.

When a telerobot serves as a remote representation of a human operator, it is often referred to as its *avatar*. An avatar is an antonym for *agent*, a computer-controlled entity that acts autonomously without human intervention. A telerobot is usually, however, *semi-autonomous*; its actions are predominantly decided by the human operator, but supported by machine-controlled algorithms. While intergroup contact may as well take place against, or supported by, a fully simulated agent [54, 60, 70, 124, 133], we focus our attention on scenarios in which at least one of the group members is inhabiting a robotic avatar, thus forming mediated contact.

3 Conceptual Model

Allport's contact hypothesis specifies four conditions that support positive intergroup contact: equal status, having common goals, active cooperation, and institutional support. Decades of research that followed Allport's foundation verified the basic premise [115], problematizing it with further questions, exceptions, and specificities, as well as developing empirical models for prejudice reduction. A longitudinal model suggested by Pettigrew [114] outlines the timeline in which prejudice toward the outgroup is reduced: the ingroup member initially *decategorizes* the outgroup member from its group, seeing them as an individual. In due time, generalization occurs and prejudice toward the outgroup is reduced. Finally, the border between ingroup and outgroup completely dissolves, perceiving all as part of the same group. Other models predict and verify the link between common mediators such as anxiety and empathy, or moderators such as group salience to the outcome of the contact [28, 108, 152].

By integrating previous models from intergroup contact research and combining them with communication studies, and human-robot interaction studies, we suggest a conceptual model for telerobot-based contact (see Fig. 1). The generic model assumes a telerobotic contact in which the participants first form interpersonal impressions on one another and finally generalize their attitudes toward the outgroup. The interpersonal attitude is moderated by the general attitude toward robots and by the sense of *presence*. The type of presence depends on the type of telerobot interaction. For a person conversing with a telerobot, we hypothesize that the attitude toward the outgroup member (the teleoperator) is moderated by the perceived *co-presence* [47]. The term is used to describe the sense of cohabiting with another living person in both virtual [18, 36, 138] and physical [38, 64] spaces. Co-presence was found to mediate positive attitude and intimacy in social networking services [2].

For a person operating a telerobot, we look for a close and long-lasting social link between the operator and its avatar. Several models are used in the literature to describe these phenomena, including: Belk's *extended self* [17], the *proteus effect* [159], *parasociality* [67], and *self-presence* [15, 120]. Self-presence entails engagement and a lasting social effect and was shown to mediate intergroup friendship. Hence, the sense of self-presence is expected to moderate the effect of telerobot operation on attitudes towards the interaction partner.

How (positive) contact with an outgroup member generalizes to the outgroup as a whole remains an open and widely debated question [22, 94]. Nevertheless, longitudinal experiments in computer-mediated environments suggest that given enough time, interpersonal relations eventually do persist as generally improved attitudes toward the outgroup [99, 155]. Evidence suggests that at least some level of group salience (the presence of cues depicting the outgroup member's group affiliation) is required to achieve generalization [29, 35]. We, therefore, assume outgroup salience as a moderator in our model. However, the effect is highly volatile, especially in online settings [53], and requires elaborate contextualized experimentation. In this chapter, we begin to address some of the sub-factors which may play a role in how group identity may manifest in telerobotic encounters.

Another model, suggested by Gaertner and Dovido [44], is the *common ingroup identity model*. According to this model, priming the participants with the fact that they belong under a shared superordinate group helps to reduce intergroup bias. However, recent attempts to achieve this effect in avatar-mediated interactions have either failed to create a common ingroup [5,6] or have found that it had no significant impact [112]. This indicates that perhaps the model needs to be revised for computer-mediated contact.

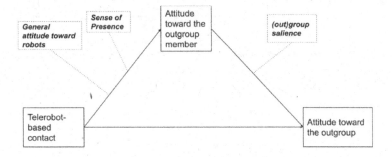

Fig. 1. Telepresence contact: conceptual model.

4   Design Hypotheses

The following sections present our hypotheses and design guidelines for telerobot interaction. We look into questions of robot appearance, voice, functionality, interaction modalities, and peacebuilding scenarios. A summary is available following the conclusions in Table 2.

4.1   System Architecture

A communication event mediated by telerobots could manifest in one of three different architectures that we identified as *telerobot systems* [110]. Figure 2 illustrates the three types. Utilizing concepts from Paynter's generalized systems theory [51,109], we describe two types of interactions: *signal*, and *physical*. *Physical* refers to real-world interactions between elements sharing a physical environment, such as a hand-shake or holding an object. *Signal* interactions occur on an abstract level, representing a unidirectional logical flow of cause and effect. For example, text that is typed on one end of online communication and appears on the other end.

In a symmetric unidirectional system, the participants are not physically interacting with a robot, but instead operate telerobots that interact with each other cooperatively. Although this system has its own merits, we focus here on the first two systems in which at least one participant is physically interacting with a robot.

Although harder to implement, symmetric telerobot systems such as in Nagendran et al. [100] provide the hardware foundation for equality - one of Allport's conditions for positive intergroup contact and a proven prompter of successful intergroup contact

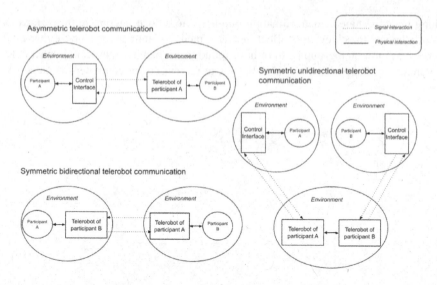

Fig. 2. Systems of telepresence communication.

projects in the context of the Israeli-Palestinian conflict [91]. Symmetric systems also assure that telerobot operation incorporates maximum self-presence and engagement since they form a seamless experience for the operator. In symmetric systems, the telerobot mirrors the actions of the operator without any need for intentional operation.

Asymmetric systems produce an experience that is different in nature on both ends. The participant operating the telerobot from a remote control interface is more aware of the interaction medium and may feel concealed behind it. In our previous experiment utilizing an asymmetric telerobotic system we have reported on possible benefits in empowering disadvantaged groups, but also on an incurred discomfort and resentment due to the unequal setting [111, p. 132], [110].

Teleoperators in asymmetric systems may exhibit behaviors that characterize anonymous computer-mediated communication (CMC). Research models have shown a varying effect of CMC on the outcome of intergroup contact and the reduction of prejudice [155]. The *deindividuation* model [163] warns that anonymity may release a person from social regulation and norms, leading to a negative effect on the conversation. The SIDE theory of deindividuation [139] provides a contrasting view, demonstrating that if group identity cues are present, anonymity further increases group salience, as it motivates individuals to act under a group context while pronouncing enhanced norms and tropes. Models such as SIP (social information theory) and *hyperpersonal* communication [154] advocate that more intimate interpersonal relations may form in online contact because of the need for the participants to make up for the lack of non-verbal cues.

Participants interacting with the robot on the other side of an asymmetric system are expected to experience stronger senses of agency, ownership, and identifiability [39,45] compared to their teleoperator counterparts. They are, therefore, expected to experience less deindividuation than the operators. However, insofar as the robot is perceived by the interlocutors as a mediating device (a sophisticated phone) rather than an avatar, the interlocutors may experience less co-presence and increased deindividuation.

To summarize, asymmetric telepresence systems may have some benefits associated with CMC and deindividuation, but may also induce a sense of inequality in communication. Symmetric systems provide the foundation for equal grounds and a high level of self-presence in operation.

4.2 Visual Appearance

The effect of a robot's appearance on attitude toward it has been studied extensively in the literature, predominantly in Human-Robot Interaction (HRI) and social robotics [50]. In relevance to intergroup contact, we discuss two considerations: anthropomorphism and avatar customization. We also note, however, two guiding principles: Firstly, as suggested in studies by Bremner et al. on personality perception of robot teleoperators [24,25], while a robotic avatar's appearance may project on the personality of its operator, the process is dependent on context and compliance with the speech and behavior of the operator. For example, a person conducting serious interviews using a stuffed bear avatar, as in Kuwamara's experiment [82], may invoke a sense of confusion and a low sense of co-presence within its users. However, a teleoperated animal puppet theater, as in Kawahara et al. [74], is likely to prompt more natural responses. In robot-mediated communication, we can place physical cues with the robot, such as setting props or clothing accessories. Those can include cues about the current context, or group identity cues using cultural or religious symbols, we expand on this later in this chapter.

Secondly, following Allport's condition of equality, a telerobot's appearance should consider its target audience and context so it would not seem overly powerful or weak in comparison. A study by Rae et al. found that the height of the robot affects the interlocutor's perception of the operator's persuasiveness [119]. We anticipate that if inequality is accentuated in characteristics of the robot such as height, power, speed, and volume, it may hamper positive intergroup encounters.

Anthropomorphism vs. Dehumanization. We have previously established the intricate relationship between human-likeness and the experience of the interlocutors in a telerobotic interaction [110]. While a non-anthropomorphic appearance may increase the operator's sense of self-presence and avoid the ever-present uncanny valley effect [104], it also incorporates the risk of *dehumanization* (seeing an outgroup member as nonhuman or less than human).

Dehumanization is both a marker and a driver of intergroup conflict [52,81]. Groups in conflict tend to view each other as either animal-like or mechanistic automata, both common forms for robots. Research shows that this can occur with virtual avatars as well when they are nonhuman [89], and may exacerbate in CMC [88]. However, dehumanization may also occur against human-like robots, especially when they convey racialized identities [13,142]. There are also intermediate approaches to anthropomorphism, such as *theomorphic robots* provided by Trovato [149]. Such robots attempt to portray a divine, non-anthropomorphic appearance without dehumanizing the avatar.

Ultimately, we believe that humanizing the other when mediated through a teler-obot is a gestalt effect that emerges from the experience and the associated narrative of the interaction. A nonhuman appearance could be justified and leveraged during contact while keeping the humanity of the operator in the foreground. That can be achieved sim-ply by placing identifying cues alongside the robot, but more importantly, by conversa-tion content that includes ostensibly human qualities such as empathy and vulnerability [49,73]. Table 1 provides a summary of the factors that correlate with anthropomor-phism.

Table 1. Anthropomorphism: summary table.

Level of anthro-pomorphism	Risk of the uncanny valley	Risk of dehumanization	Operator's sense of self-presence	Interlocutor's sense of co-presence
Low	Low	High	High	Low
High	High	Low	Low	High

Customization. The ability to customize an avatar is widespread in video games, virtual reality, and social media applications. It improves engagement with the plat-form [102] and primes the user's mindset to achieve certain goals [127]. In robotics, customizing an avatar is a more complex task than in a virtual environment. Design options are constrained by the hardware platform of the robot, requiring co-design between the robot engineers and the user. Assembling the robot takes physical effort and requires basic knowledge in mechatronics. Nevertheless, involving users in the design and assembly process of their robotic avatar may have benefits. Groom et al. showed that operators had a greater sense of self-extension to a robot that was assembled by them, rather than by another [48]. Robots were also successfully co-designed with chil-dren as the target users. The YOLO robot focused on creativity and storytelling, allow-ing children to design behaviors and movements [4], while the PAL robot involved chil-dren in designs for diabetes self-management [57]. Co-design methods also improved the general attitude of students toward robots in educational settings [121].

In the context of intergroup contact, and especially in situations of conflict, co-designing avatars may have even greater virtues. Participants could control their rep-resentation and its behavior, considering how they wish to be seen by the other side. The assembly work in itself may be therapeutic, both as a tactile experience [135] and as a self-expressive art form [98]. Finally, a participatory approach for robot-building has the potential to empower oppressed groups and minorities by providing meaningful education in modern communication technologies.

Highly anthropomorphic robotic avatars could also be modeled to resemble their operator. The most notable example is *Geminoid* from Ishiguru laboratories.[1] In a small-scale survey among visitors in Ars Electronica, their impression of Geminoid was a combination of amusement and fear due to the uncanny valley effect [14]. Additionally, as noted in a study by Peña et al., self-resembling avatars could have mixed results on

---

[1] http://www.geminoid.jp/projects/kibans/resources.html.

the result of intergroup contact [112]. On the one hand, the priming effect mentioned earlier may strengthen one's beliefs and ideologies which in turn amplifies the social distance to the outgroup. On the other hand, customizing an avatar to resemble oneself increased the sense of identifiability which reduced the negative effects of deindividuation (mostly relevant to asymmetric systems). Finally, the study by Alvidrez and Peña found that self-resembling avatars decreased the operator's engagement presence (feeling of involvement in the remote environment [129]) because the avatars were perceived to have their own agency [5]. These findings are in line with the research by Groom et al. [48], which concluded that for the same reason robot operators have a lesser sense of *self-extension* [16] to their robotic avatar when it is human (Fig. 3).

Fig. 3. Geminoid and Professor Hisroshi Ishiguro. Retrieved from http://www.geminoid.jp/.

4.3 Use of an Embedded Display

The telepresence robot market is growing rapidly, and is predicted to accelerate even more in the upcoming years due to increased demand for advanced technological solutions to support remote working and social services.[2] Telerobot forms are continuously branching into new directions but the dominant form remains that of a tablet device attached or embedded in a motor vehicle [80]. The tablet typically displays the talking head of the operator, as in a video call. Examples from market leaders include *Double Robotics,*[3] *Mantaro*[4] and Revolve Robotics.[5] Telepresence robots in this form are primarily geared toward remote offices and public environments, such as hospitals or schools, or conferences. Recently, in Japan, such robots allowed students to attend their graduation ceremony despite the COVID-19 restrictions[6].

The question of using a flat face display on a robot, vis-à-vis an embodied, mechatronic face, has been troubling the HRI community since the early days of personal service robots [147]. More recently, the sense of inconsistency felt when interacting with a 2D display on a telepresence robot was verbalized by Choi and Kwak as the *dual*

---

[2] https://www.marketwatch.com/press-release/telepresence-robots-market-size-2020-to-showing-impressive-growth-by-2024-industry-trends-share-size-top-key-players-analysis-and-forecast-research-2020-04-20.

[3] https://www.doublerobotics.com/.

[4] http://www.mantarobot.com/products/teleme-2/index.htm.

[5] https://telepresencerobots.com/robots/kubi.

[6] https://www.euronews.com/2021/01/04/how-japan-is-using-technology-to-make-us-feel-closer-during-the-covid-19-pandemic.

Fig. 4. The Avatar Graduation Ceremony at BBT University, Tokyo. Retrieved from https://prtimes.jp/main/html/rd/p/000000002.000055410.html.

ecologies problem [37]. In their study, the perceived presence of a user in a tablet-based video call was higher when it was disembodied (tablet only) than when the tablet was attached to a wheeled robotic body. The authors explain this by referring to the different ecologies present in the same robot; one is a 2D projection of the remote location, and another is the physical presence of the robotic body in a shared space. The authors suggest that the receiver of communication experiences confusion, having to interact simultaneously with the immediate environment, and with the depiction of the remote environment (Fig. 4).

An initial intergroup telerobotic experiment performed by Peled [111] between national citizens and immigrants showed similar results: the use of a display on the body of a telerobot was disruptive to the participants' perceived sense of co-presence. Participants reported reverting to the experience of using a phone-like device while they were interacting with the display, despite having to touch the robot to initiate actions in the virtual interface. We, therefore, recommend the use of a display to be planned carefully for intergroup contact. Preferably, the robot could be designed without an external display, maintaining uniformity and consistency.

4.4   Voice

In a telerobot-based contact, an operator may choose to use their voice or a synthetic voice that does not disclose their personality, gender, and culture. They may also use a synthetically cloned voice that is highly similar to their natural voice [66]. A synthetic voice adds modalities for speech augmentation and language translation, as we discuss in the section on interaction modalities.

Research on effect of an avatar's voice on user attitude shows that as with visual appearance, one must strike a balance between relatedness and consistency. Lee and Nass studied the sense of social presence of e-commerce agents with machine-generated voices [87] concerning their personality (introvert or extrovert). When the voice personality of an agent is closer to that of the interlocutor, the perceived sense of social presence increased. However, the consistency of the voice with its personality is essential. Social presence drops if a voice's style is incongruent with its textual character (the content of the speech). Another study by Mitchel et al. [97] found that a mismatch between the voice and face of a talking head generated an uncanny sensation. A human with a synthetic voice felt as uncanny as a robot with a human voice. Therefore, the optimal synthetic voice (if one wishes to use the benefits of speech augmentation) would take the human teleoperator into account, without diverging abruptly the physical form of the avatar.

4.5 Materiality

The choice of materials has considerable implications for robot design. In industrial robots, materials are chosen *functionally* following the task at hand. In robots designated for human interaction, we examine *materiality* - the physical qualities of material as we sense them [56]. Materiality is exhibited through two main aspects of a robot's constitution: 1) The outer skin: the part of the robot that touches and is touched, and 2) Actuation: the material that actuates, generating the robot's movements. With the former, we place materials on a scale of firmness and rigidness; how soft they feel to the touch. With the latter, we define materials on a scale of flexibility and linearity that describes the nature of the material's movement.

Previous research in social robotics supports the use of soft materials for the outer skin of robots, especially in interaction with children [79] and in elderly care [26,78]. Soft materials contribute to a sense of *affective touch* between the robot and humans [77,141]. The human body and other natural forms are inherently soft, favoring coexistence with other soft materials [40]. However, carrying an object closer to the realm of the living risks invoking an uncanny feeling as with an anthropomorphic appearance. For example, touching a smooth, soft material that is also cold evokes the uncanny [103,158].

A soft touch on the surface doesn't necessarily imply a softness as a whole. For example, a gripping robotic hand made from powerful servo motors wrapped in a soft skin could still easily, and inadvertently, crush soft tissue. *Soft Robotics* is a rapidly developing research field for robots that operate on soft materials down the level of actuation [12]. Commonly used materials are fabrics and silicone rubbers, while the most typical form of actuation is pneumatic: applying air pressure or vacuum. Presently, the largest consumers of soft robotics are the medical industry, utilizing soft materials for invasive and surgical procedures. The use of soft robots for human interaction is nonetheless being actively researched and has so far exhibited positive results [20,69,153]. In our test of soft robotic telepresence, we have reached similarly promising conclusions [111].

Designers using soft robotics for interaction should nevertheless take special note of some idiosyncratic features of soft actuators. Due to the highly organic style of soft-robotic actuation, the risk of falling into the uncanny valley is increasing as the robot moves like a living creature. Additionally, pneumatic soft robots are often tethered (connected by a cable), restricting their ability to move around the space [122]. Nevertheless, a soft approach deems viable for telerobotic contact. Soft movement and touch may increase empathy and intimacy between the participants, which are key mediators of a positive intergroup contact [28]. Softness also instills a notion of safety; an inability to cause harm. That is a desirable climate in situations of intergroup conflict.

5   Interaction Modalities

5.1   Movement in Space

The ability to move a body in space distinguishes robots from other interactive technologies. However, not all robots have the same degrees of freedom and granularity when it comes to movement. In the field of social robots, *mobile robots* typically travel around using wheeled motion. Examples include service robots, such as Pepper[7] and Samsung bots[8], and telepresence robots such as Double Robotics[9] and Beam[10]. Other robots only move their body while remaining stationary in place; for example, care robots such as PARO,[11] and telepresence robots from Ishiguro laboratories.[12] Due to the complexity of maintaining both modalities in interaction, mobile robots often keep a physical distance from the user, interacting using voice and visuals as they travel around the space. Stationary robots, on the other hand, tend to rely more on haptic interaction, allowing the user to hold and touch them. Only a few robots attempt to combine both modalities, such as Teo [23].

Touch-based human-robot interactions have an affective value [7,77] that may be beneficial for intergroup contact and should hold a high priority in the design process. Furthermore, in the case of symmetric telepresence, moving around is in itself limited since the operator does not have a dedicated control interface for traveling, and movement relies only on body tracking. In asymmetric systems, camera navigation is possible but may divert the attention of the operator from interpersonal interactions.

Movement in space may nonetheless prove beneficial in intergroup conflict scenarios when groups are not allowed to travel to the opposing group's location. In such cases, there may be a political value in the ability to move around a forbidden area. Moreover, in asymmetric conflicts where the oppressed group suffers from tight movement restrictions in their day-to-day life, as is the situation in Palestine [27], an operator may feel empowered by having the ability to travel with their avatar. That, in turn, may contribute to a greater sense of equality and confidence within the conversation.

5.2   Nonverbal Communication and Emotional Expression

Nonverbal communication (NVC) signals such as facial expressions, eye gaze, and bodily gestures play a substantial role in our day-to-day interactions. In telerobot-based

---

[7] https://www.softbankrobotics.com/emea/en/pepper.

[8] https://research.samsung.com/robot.

[9] https://www.doublerobotics.com/.

[10] https://suitabletech.com/.

[11] http://www.parorobots.com/.

[12] http://www.geminoid.jp/en/robots.html.

contact, those signals need to be accurately picked up from the operator and portrayed using the telerobot's body without losing or changing the meaning.

In a pioneering work by Argyle [9], nonverbal signals were enumerated and categorized according to their level of awareness. The majority of them, as defined by Argyle, are *mostly unaware* on the part of the sender and *mostly aware* on the receiver side [9, p. 5]. For example, we are seldom aware that we are smiling during a conversation, but the sentiment is registered much more attentively with our conversation partner.

Since NVCs communicate emotion, we should handle them with great care in intergroup contact. While unaware emotional signals from the operator could be detected using facial recognition, prosodics, and body tracking, deep learning systems are still subjected to noise and error [63, 162]. A mistake in communicating an emotional state could lead to confusion and frustration in the conversation. Therefore, it may be safer to rely strictly on explicit gestures made by the operator with full awareness. Expression of emotions in an asymmetric system could be invoked by the operator using emojis [75] or other dedicated buttons that activate an emotional gesture in the robot. In body-tracking systems, explicit body gestures could be used (such as a thumbs-up, or a sign-language symbol), or touch-based interactions, such as a pat or a stroke on the robot's body, a high-five, or a hug.

Even if body signals and facial expressions are accurately detected, their meaning is not guaranteed to preserve across cultures [65]. Some gestures require translation in intercultural interactions in order to prevent misunderstandings or misinterpretation by the target culture [55]. The problem further exacerbates in non-anthropomorphic avatars that do not have eyebrows and cannot exhibit granular gaze motion as in the humanoid SEER robot [148].

A possible solution could be to use the *flow* and *rhythm* of body movements to express emotions instead of explicitly formed gestures [59]. Dance is recognized as cross-culturally universal [136], and much of our emotional states are expressed through the body rather than facial expressions [11]. Successful attempts that use movement as a mechanism for expression in robots have made use of existing frameworks and tools, including Laban's movement analysis (LMA) [83, 132] in [92, 101] and the PAD emotional state model [93] in [8, 105].

Some signals, such as shifts in gaze and body orientation, are performed unconsciously during the conversation, yet they have an impact on turn-taking and attention signaling [76, 123]. A smooth turn-taking flow can promote the sense of equality in contact, and was demonstrated to benefit human-robot interaction [84, 150]. Turn-taking signals cannot be explicitly pronounced by the operator, without impairing the flow of the conversation. Instead, they should be a part of the robot's semi-autonomous functionality. In symmetric systems, the end-of-turn could be predicted using several tracking modalities [41], while an asymmetric interface can infer the end-of-turn using typing and clicking indicators.

5.3 Verbal Communication

Language is often the best tool to convey layered and abstract information, as required during peacebuilding efforts. Previously we have outlined the risks and benefits of using machine translation for verbal communication [110]. Despite the benefit of enabling dialogue between speakers that do not speak the same language, caution is required when using automatic interfaces. Minute mistakes in translation could impair participants' confidence and trust in the process.

Some mitigating steps could be taken to improve the experience of the participants when using machine translation. First, when using speech recognition, feedback of the result in the operator's native tongue should be provided, perhaps at the cost of delaying the flow of conversation. Second, when possible, the interface may display the confidence level of the translation before it gets sent to the other side. Finally, in case a mistake was realized by the operator only after submitting, there can be a quick "oops" button that has the robot express an apologizing gesture. If used according to those principles of design and interaction, real-time language translation could be an important facilitator for telerobot-based contact.

5.4 Synchrony, Reciprocity, and Feedback

Synchrony and reciprocity facilitate interpersonal and intergroup sympathy and empathy across all communication modalities [19,31,54,131,144]. The process is referred to as "social entrainment" [117,143]. It includes interactions such as rhythmic movements (e.g., clapping, jumping), a smooth conversation beat, synchronized dance, give-and-receive interactions, gaze synchrony, affective matching, and mimicry. Positive effects are also observed in human-robot interaction scenarios, particularly in cases of care and therapy robots for children and the elderly [10,90].

Achieving interpersonal synchrony over mediated communication stumbles upon the problem of *latency* [34]. The unavoidable time delay due to physical distance between the participants can instill confusion and frustration when performing rhythmic and simultaneous tasks. Research in online music performance is at the forefront of tackling such issues [106] and can be used as an inspiration. Semi-autonomous methods in the likes of action prediction, lag compensation, and global metronomes enable musicians to collaborate in jam sessions from different locations around the globe. The same methods can assist in synchronizing robot-mediated activities. In symmetric systems, the participants would be coordinating the exact same action, for example, clapping together. In asymmetric systems, one participant would use a control interface, for example, by tapping or shaking a mobile phone, while another would act in front of the telerobot.

Some reciprocal actions do not require real-time synchrony between the participants. For example, a hand-shake and a "high five" could be performed in a turn-based flow, where one participant reaches out first, and then the other reciprocates. Such actions may not have the same valence as real-time synchronization, but could still benefit the conversation due to their reciprocal nature. Additionally, people tend to be forgiving toward the sluggishness of robots, which may lower the sense of awkwardness that might occur during the use of reciprocal actions in a face-to-face encounter.

In asymmetric systems where the robot's operator is using a control interface, having instant feedback to the control actions provides a sense of reciprocity with the control medium and can increase perceived agency and ownership within the operator [43]. At the high-end of the spectrum, advanced control systems, such as the ones for 'Robonauts' at the Johnson Space Center [39], mix virtual reality and haptic feedback. As a bare minimum, an operator should have visual feedback on how the robot acts in response to control commands.

In an initial test of this novel telerobotic contact paradigm [111], participants expressed concern over their inability to see the facial expressions they were invoking with the robot, or their avatar's arm when it was being touched. When designing an asymmetric control interface, it is necessary to provide maximum visibility of the telerobot's body to the operator to increase the sense of self-presence. If one camera is not enough, multiple camera angles could be utilized. Additionally, placing mirrors on-site could allow the operators to examine their re-embodied appearance. Finally, practicing the use of the telerobot ahead of the encounter could help operators get comfortable with the new interface without the pressure of the ensuing intergroup contact.

5.5   Semi-autonomous Functions

The conversation between the participants can be guided using the robot's semi-autonomous functions. Modern types of interaction may include cooperative games and simulations that engage the participant toward a common goal, in line with the principles set by Allport. Games have shown potential for peacebuilding in face-to-face meetings [30] and co-located cooperative gameplay sessions [72]. When interacting with a robot, its body parts may be appropriated as game controllers, for example, by squeezing the arms of the robot; thus, indirectly forming touch interactions between the participants. However, when integrating interactive visuals, it is necessary to embed a 2D display within the telerobot or place one beside it. In such cases, the interface design should carefully manage the attention of the user to avoid the dual ecologies problem [37].

Intergroup conflict resolution may also benefit from active robotic mediation. Automated mediation devices by Zanacarno et al. [160, 161] support 'controlled' means for escalation and de-escalation of the process and were found beneficial. At the forefront, machine learning is sought as a tool for peacebuilding that can understand complex sentiments and situations [61], predict conflict escalation before it occurs [113], and offer help to resolve issues [145]. Nevertheless, machine learning tools should be used with transparency to avoid issues of trust and suspected bias in the process. Active mediation may also decrease the sense of co-presence, as the robot is perceived more like a middle-agent rather than an avatar.

6   Public Space Interventions

Robotic avatars are an excellent communication tool for organized intergroup encounters where participants are unable to meet face-to-face. While it is possible to use robots privately at home or in a discreetly organized session, the physical nature of telerobots makes them exceptionally suitable for public space interventions. Robots can transcend national borders and roam public spaces, having the potential to reach individuals that wouldn't normally engage in intergroup contact. In symmetric systems, robots could be placed in public urban areas on both sides and facilitate bi-directional contact. In asymmetric systems, one robot is placed in a public spot while operators inhabit the avatar from their home or a dedicated control spot. An advantage of public space interventions is that any form of intergroup contact which is observed by a public audience manifests as *Viacrious Contact* [125]: an indirect contact with the outgroup member supported by the imagination of the audience. Vicarious contact has been shown to improve attitude between groups [151], even if it is watched on television [118]. When planning a public space intervention, the designated site and its demographics should be considered along with the design of the robot and interaction content. Tailoring the contact experience to its local context may increase the likelihood of public engagement and improve the outcome of the encounter. We elaborate on two types of public space interventions: dyadic and performative.

6.1 Dyadic Intervention

In a dyadic intervention, a telerobotic avatar appears in a public space, ready to engage in a one-on-one conversation with passersby. The group identity of the telerobot's operator could be widely exposed to passersby via physical cues, allowing them to make a voluntary decision to make contact, or they could first approach the robot and only then realize its group identity during the conversation. According to a meta-analysis by Pettigrew et al. [116] contact that begins voluntarily is less likely to exacerbate intergroup attitudes.

A robot that emerges in the middle of a public space might be intriguing enough for some people to approach, particularly those who generally have positive attitudes towards robots. One method to get even more public interest would be to equip the telerobot with some actions designed to draw a crowd. For example, play a sound, a musical theme, or perform an inviting gesture. In an asymmetric system, an operator has more control over the robot's interaction with the environment. They may look around by moving a camera or even drive around using wheeled motion.

6.2 Performative Intervention

A performative type of intervention is oriented toward an audience and typically consists of remotely controlled storytelling rather than direct dialogue. For example, a theatrical performance by a member of an oppressed group as a form of political activism (see Boal's *theatre of the oppressed* [21]). An advantage of this type of intervention is that it does not portray the telerobots as avatars of the operator, but rather as *puppets*, thus avoiding the risk of dehumanization and confusion (at the cost of a lower co-presence). To remind the audience that a human outgroup member is operating the show, physical cues could be added. The performance could be an asymmetric single-performer show in front of an audience or a symmetric collaboration with a performer at another location.

Table 2. Summary table.

Aspect	Hypothesis	Implementation considerations
System architecture	• Asymmetric systems invoke deindividuation effects in one side of the conversation • Symmetric systems provide a more equal foundation • Symmetric systems increase self-presence in operation	• Asymmetric systems are easier to implement and disseminate • Symmetric systems require a seamless/transparent control interface
Visual appearance	• Anthropomorphism has both advantages and disadvantages (refer to Table 1) • Robot self-customization increases engagement • Avatar self-resemblance increases prejudice/social distance • Maintain context congruency	
Embedded display	Decreases co-presence	Required for some semi-autonomous functions
Voice	A synthetic voice that maintains a human tone and is consistent with the appearance of the telerobot increases co-presence	A synthetic voice is required for language translation
Materiality	Soft materials and actuators increase intimacy and empathy	• Soft actuators restrict movement • Soft actuators and skin increase the risk of the uncanny
Movement in space	Stationary robots encourage the use of affective touch	A symmetric system restricts mobility
Nonverbal communication	• Turn-taking and attention signals promote the sense of equality • Movement-based emotional expression increases reliability and trust	• Turn-taking signals could be performed autonomously
Verbal communication	Automatic language translation could assist in communication	AI is prone to error. Should be used with sensitivity and transparency
Synchrony, reciprocity and feedback	• Rhythmic synchronization promotes empathy • Reciprocal actions promote empathy • Operation feedback reduces anxiety and increases self-presence	• Internet latency is a challenge for telepresence synchronization • Symmetric systems have a transparent interface and do not require teleoperation feedback
Semi-autonomous functions	• Could engage participants • But agency decreases co-presence	
Public space interventions	• Public audience undergoes vicarious contact • Voluntary approach results in a more positive attitude • Performative interventions are less restricted, but decrease co-presence	

7   Conclusions and Future Research

Our theoretical framework outlines both potential benefits and risks of using telerobots for intergroup contact, and aims to serve as a research agenda and guideline for future empirical studies. The hypotheses, derived from existing literature in the fields of inter-group contact, communication and human-robot interaction, require a careful empir-ical investigation. Such future empirical studies will provide crucial insights on how the variables discussed in the current chapter influence the process or outcome of a telerobot-based intergroup encounter. Future empirical research on the telerobot con-tact hypothesis will also further establish what sets telerobotics apart from other forms of online communication, and provide an empirical basis for the practical implementa-tion of this novel approach to intergroup contact.

While the proposed telerobotic contact approach may be applied in any intergroup context, we see the greatest potential in the context of intergroup conflicts in which the involved societies are physically separated and have difficulties meeting face-to-face. One such case is the Israeli-Palestinian conflict that we mentioned in this chapter. However, it is important to distinguish in future research which factors might be suitable for which type of intergroup context. What might work for more mild intergroup contexts, might not work or even lead to negative consequences in contexts of violent long-term conflicts.

Toward any organized attempt for intergroup contact, one should always consider the broader context, the long-term effects, and the ethics of research. That is espe-cially true in the context of violent, asymmetric conflicts, where one group is a domi-nant majority, and another is an oppressed minority; even more so, when technology is involved, along with its inherent biases and connotations of power. A common concern is that the act of leveling the play-field, treating both groups as equals, will dissolve the real-world injustices and reduce the motivation for social change [58, 126]. That is reflected in the Israeli-Palestinian setting by the "Anti-Normalization" movement [128]. The movement rejects attempts for normalizing relations between Israel and Palestine that are not predated by an overall restoration of justice in the area.

We have suggested some ways to tackle this concern by recognizing power relations and injustices from within the system architecture, the design of the telerobot, and the practice of participatory co-design. Finally, we stress that complete transparency should accompany any attempt to insert technology into a conflicted scenario. That includes disclosing any source of funding for resources, the identity of the platform designers, and the location and maintainers of the internet servers. Teleoperation software and hardware should be open-sourced and training sets for any machine learning models used should be disclosed, opting for open-source datasets instead of data owned by commercial companies.

Finally, the guidelines presented here, while being tailored for use in intergroup scenarios, may also apply to other contexts of robot-mediated communication, including interpersonal and intercultural interactions. Our design considerations focus on empathy, equality, understanding, and mutual respect, essential values in any human-to-human interaction. In an era where communication is becoming increasingly remote, robots present an opportunity to bring back material and tangible aspects to our communications. We are excited to further evaluate the use of telerobots as a means of prejudice reduction and conflict resolution, and as a positive social tool in our daily lives.

References

1. Ahmed, S.: Strange Encounters: Embodied Others in Post-Coloniality. Routledge, London (2000)
2. Al-Ghaith, W.: Understanding social network usage: impact of co-presence, intimacy, and immediacy. Int. J. Adv. Comput. Sci. Appl. **6**(8) (2015). https://doi.org/10.14569/IJACSA. 2015.060813
3. Allport, G.W.: The Nature of Prejudice. Addison-Wesley, Oxford (1954)
4. Alves-Oliveira, P., Arriaga, P., Paiva, A., Hoffman, G.: YOLO, a robot for creativity: a co-design study with children. In: Proceedings of the 2017 Conference on Interaction Design and Children, Stanford, California, USA, pp. 423–429. ACM (2017). https://doi.org/10. 1145/3078072.3084304
5. Alvidrez, S., Peña, J.: Contact in VR: testing avatar customisation and common ingroup identity cues on outgroup bias reduction. Ann. Rev. Cybertherapy Telemed. (2020)
6. Alvidrez, S., Peña, J.: Verbal mimicry predicts social distance and social attraction to an outgroup member in virtual reality. In: 2020 IEEE International Conference on Artificial Intelligence and Virtual Reality (AIVR), pp. 68–73 (2020). https://doi.org/10.1109/AIVR50618. 2020.00023
7. Andreasson, R., Alenljung, B., Billing, E., Lowe, R.: Affective touch in human–robot interaction: conveying emotion to the Nao robot. Int. J. Soc. Robot. **10**(4), 473–491 (2017). https://doi.org/10.1007/s12369-017-0446-3
8. Ardila, L.R., Coronado, E., Hendra, H., Phan, J., Zainalkefli, Z., Venture, G.: Adaptive fuzzy and predictive controllers for expressive robot arm movement during human and environment interaction. Int. J. Mech. Eng. Robot. Res. 207–219 (2019). https://doi.org/10. 18178/ijmerr.8.2.207-219
9. Argyle, M.: Bodily Communication. Routledge, London (2013)
10. Aucouturier, J.J., et al.: Cheek to chip: dancing robots and AI's future. IEEE Intell. Syst. **23**(2), 74–84 (2008). https://doi.org/10.1109/MIS.2008.22
11. Aviezer, H., Trope, Y., Todorov, A.: Body cues, not facial expressions, discriminate between intense positive and negative emotions. Science **338**(6111), 1225–1229 (2012). https://doi. org/10.1126/science.1224313
12. Bao, G., et al.: Soft robotics: academic insights and perspectives through bibliometric analysis. Soft Rob. **5**(3), 229–241 (2018)
13. Bartneck, C., et al.: Robots and racism. In: Proceedings of the 2018 ACM/IEEE International Conference on Human-Robot Interaction, Chicago, IL, USA, pp. 196–204. ACM (2018). https://doi.org/10.1145/3171221.3171260
14. Becker-Asano, C., Ogawa, K., Nishio, S., Ishiguro, H.: Exploring the Uncanny Valley with Geminoid HI-1 in a Real-World Application, p. 9 (2010)
15. Behm-Morawitz, E.: Mirrored selves: the influence of self-presence in a virtual world on health, appearance, and well-being. Comput. Hum. Behav. **29**(1), 119–128 (2013). https:// doi.org/10.1016/j.chb.2012.07.023
16. Belk, R.W.: Possessions and the extended self. J. Consum. Res. **15**(2), 139 (1988). https:// doi.org/10.1086/209154
17. Belk, R.W.: Extended self in a digital world. J. Consum. Res. **40**(3), 477–500 (2013). https:// doi.org/10.1086/671052
18. Bente, G., Rüggenberg, S., Krämer, N.C., Eschenburg, F.: Avatar-mediated networking: increasing social presence and interpersonal trust in net-based collaborations. Hum. Commun. Res. **34**(2), 287–318 (2008). https://doi.org/10.1111/j.1468-2958.2008.00322.x
19. Bernieri, F.J., Rosenthal, R.: Interpersonal coordination: behavior matching and interactional synchrony (1991)

20. Bewley, H., Boer, L.: Designing Blo-nut: design principles, choreography and otherness in an expressive social robot. In: Proceedings of the 2018 on Designing Interactive Systems Conference 2018, DIS 2018, Hong Kong, China, pp. 1069–1080. ACM Press (2018). https://doi.org/10.1145/3196709.3196817

21. Boal, A.: Theatre of the Oppressed. Get Political, no. 6, New edn. Pluto Press, London (2008)

22. Boin, J., Rupar, M., Graf, S., Neji, S., Spiegler, O., Swart, H.: The generalization of intergroup contact effects: emerging research, policy relevance, and future directions. J. Soc. Issues **77**(1), 105–131 (2021). https://doi.org/10.1111/josi.12419

23. Bonarini, A., Garzotto, F., Gelsomini, M., Romero, M., Clasadonte, F., Yilmaz, A.N.Ç.: A huggable, mobile robot for developmental disorder interventions in a multi-modal interaction space. In: 2016 25th IEEE International Symposium on Robot and Human Interactive Communication (RO-MAN), pp. 823–830 (2016). https://doi.org/10.1109/ROMAN.2016.7745214

24. Bremner, P., Celiktutan, O., Gunes, H.: Personality perception of robot avatar tele-operators. In: 2016 11th ACM/IEEE International Conference on Human-Robot Interaction (HRI), pp. 141–148 (2016). https://doi.org/10.1109/HRI.2016.7451745

25. Bremner, P.A., Celiktutan, O., Gunes, H.: Personality perception of robot avatar teleoperators in solo and dyadic tasks. Front. Robot. AI **4**, 16 (2017). https://doi.org/10.3389/frobt.2017.00016

26. Broekens, J., Heerink, M., Rosendal, H.: Assistive social robots in elderly care: a review. Gerontechnology **8**(2), 94–103 (2009). https://doi.org/10.4017/gt.2009.08.02.002.00

27. Brown, A.P.: The immobile mass: movement restrictions in the west bank. Soc. Legal Stud. **13**(4), 501–521 (2004). https://doi.org/10.1177/0964663904047331

28. Brown, R., Hewstone, M.: An integrative theory of intergroup contact. Adv. Exp. Soc. Psychol. **37**(37), 255–343 (2005)

29. Brown, R., Vivian, J., Hewstone, M.: Changing attitudes through intergroup contact: the effects of group membership salience. Eur. J. Soc. Psychol. **29**(5–6), 741–764 (1999)

30. Brynen, R., Milante, G.: Peacebuilding with games and simulations. Simul. Gaming **44**(1), 27–35 (2013). https://doi.org/10.1177/1046878112455485

31. Burgoon, J.K., Dillman, L., Stem, L.A.: Adaptation in dyadic interaction: defining and operationalizing patterns of reciprocity and compensation. Commun. Theory **3**(4), 295–316 (1993). https://doi.org/10.1111/j.1468-2885.1993.tb00076.x

32. Burgoon, J.K., Hoobler, G.D.: Nonverbal signals. Handb. Interpers. Commun. **2**, 229–285 (1994)

33. Campanella, T.: Eden by wire: webcameras and the telepresent landscape, pp. 22–46 (2000)

34. Campbell, J.: Interpersonal coordination in computer-mediated communication. In: Encyclopedia of Information Science and Technology, 3rd edn., pp. 2079–2088. IGI Global (2015)

35. Cao, B., Lin, W.Y.: Revisiting the contact hypothesis: effects of different modes of computer-mediated communication on intergroup relationships. Int. J. Intercult. Relat. **58**, 23–30 (2017). https://doi.org/10.1016/j.ijintrel.2017.03.003

36. Casanueva, J., Blake, E.: The effects of avatars on co-presence in a collaborative virtual environment (2001)

37. Choi, J.J., Kwak, S.S.: Can you feel me?: how embodiment levels of telepresence systems affect presence. In: 2016 25th IEEE International Symposium on Robot and Human Interactive Communication (RO-MAN), New York, NY, USA, pp. 606–611. IEEE (2016). https://doi.org/10.1109/ROMAN.2016.7745180

38. Choi, J.J., Kwak, S.S.: Who is this?: identity and presence in robot-mediated communication. Cogn. Syst. Res. **43**, 174–189 (2017). https://doi.org/10.1016/j.cogsys.2016.07.006

39. Cole, J., Sacks, O., Waterman, I.: On the immunity principle: a view from a robot. Trends Cogn. Sci. **4**(5), 167 (2000). https://doi.org/10.1016/S1364-6613(00)01459-5

40. Danese, E.: Soft machine. In: Machines That Become Us: The Social Context of Personal Communication Technology, pp. 267–276 (2003)

41. de Kok, I., Heylen, D.: Multimodal end-of-turn prediction in multi-party meetings. In: Proceedings of the 2009 International Conference on Multimodal Interfaces, ICMI-MLMI 2009, Cambridge, Massachusetts, USA, p. 91. ACM Press (2009). https://doi.org/10.1145/1647314.1647332

42. Del Vicario, M., et al.: Echo chambers: emotional contagion and group polarization on Facebook. Sci. Rep. **6**, 37825 (2016)

43. Dolezal, L.: The remote body: the phenomenology of telepresence and re-embodiment. Hum. Technol. **5**, 208–226 (2009)

44. Gaertner, S.L., Dovidio, J.F., Anastasio, P.A., Bachman, B.A., Rust, M.C.: The common ingroup identity model: recategorization and the reduction of intergroup bias. Eur. Rev. Soc. Psychol. **4**(1), 1–26 (1993). https://doi.org/10.1080/14792779343000004

45. Gallagher, S.: Philosophical conceptions of the self: implications for cognitive science. Trends Cogn. Sci. **4**(1), 14–21 (2000)

46. Gallagher, S.: How the Body Shapes the Mind. Clarendon Press (2006)

47. Goffman, E.: Behavior in Public Places. Simon and Schuster (2008)

48. Groom, V., Takayama, L., Ochi, P., Nass, C.: I am my robot: the impact of robot-building and robot form on operators. In: Proceedings of the 4th ACM/IEEE International Conference on Human Robot Interaction, HRI 2009, La Jolla, California, USA, p. 31. ACM Press (2009). https://doi.org/10.1145/1514095.1514104

49. Gubler, J.R., Halperin, E., Hirschberger, G.: Humanizing the outgroup in contexts of protracted intergroup conflict. J. Exp. Polit. Sci. **2**(1), 36–46 (2015). https://doi.org/10.1017/xps.2014.20

50. Hancock, P.A., Billings, D.R., Schaefer, K.E., Chen, J.Y.C., de Visser, E.J., Parasuraman, R.: A meta-analysis of factors affecting trust in human-robot interaction. Hum. Factors J. Hum. Factors Ergon. Soc. **53**(5), 517–527 (2011). https://doi.org/10.1177/0018720811417254

51. Hannaford, B.: Feeling is Believing: A History of Telerobotics. The Robot in the Garden: Telerobotics and Telepistemology in the Age of the Internet. Edited by Ken Goldberg. The MIT Press (2000)

52. Haslam, N.: Dehumanization: an integrative review. Pers. Soc. Psychol. Rev. **10**(3), 252–264 (2006)

53. Hasler, B.S., Amichai-Hamburger, Y.: Online intergroup contact. In: Amichai-Hamburger, Y. (ed.) The Social Net, pp. 220–252. Oxford University Press (2013). https://doi.org/10.1093/acprof:oso/9780199639540.003.0012

54. Hasler, B.S., Hirschberger, G., Shani-Sherman, T., Friedman, D.A.: Virtual peacemakers: mimicry increases empathy in simulated contact with virtual outgroup members. Cyberpsychol. Behav. Soc. Netw. **17**(12), 766–771 (2014). https://doi.org/10.1089/cyber.2014.0213

55. Hasler, B.S., Salomon, O., Tuchman, P., Lev-Tov, A., Friedman, D.: Real-time gesture translation in intercultural communication. AI Soc. **32**(1), 25–35 (2014). https://doi.org/10.1007/s00146-014-0573-4

56. Hayles, N.K.: Speculative aesthetics and object-oriented inquiry (OOI). Speculations J. Speculative Realism **5**, 158–179 (2014)

57. Henkemans, O.B., et al.: Co-Design of the Pal Robot and Avatar That Perform Joint Activities with Children for Improved Diabetes Self-management. IEEE Press, New York (2016)

58. Hewstone, M.: Living apart, living together? The role of intergroup contact in social integration. In: Proceedings of the British Academy, vol. 162, pp. 243–300 (2009)

59. Hoffman, G., Ju, W.: Designing robots with movement in mind. J. Hum.-Robot Interact. **3**(1), 89–122 (2014). https://doi.org/10.5898/JHRI.3.1.Hoffman

60. Hoffman, G., Zuckerman, O., Hirschberger, G., Luria, M., Shani-Sherman, T.: Design and evaluation of a peripheral robotic conversation companion. In: 2015 10th ACM/IEEE International Conference on Human-Robot Interaction (HRI), pp. 3–10 (2015)

61. Honkela, T.: Rauhankone: Tekoälytutkijan testamentti (2017)

62. Hook, D.: The 'real' of racializing embodiment. J. Commun. Appl. Soc. Psychol. **18**(2), 140–152 (2008). https://doi.org/10.1002/casp.963

63. Hossain, M.S., Muhammad, G.: Emotion recognition using deep learning approach from audio–visual emotional big data. Inf. Fusion **49**, 69–78 (2019). https://doi.org/10.1016/j.inffus.2018.09.008

64. Hwang, J., Lee, S., Ahn, S.C., Kim, H.: Augmented robot agent: enhancing co-presence of the remote participant. In: 2008 7th IEEE/ACM International Symposium on Mixed and Augmented Reality, Cambridge, UK, pp. 161–162. IEEE (2008). https://doi.org/10.1109/ISMAR.2008.4637346

65. Jack, R.E., Garrod, O.G., Yu, H., Caldara, R., Schyns, P.G.: Facial expressions of emotion are not culturally universal. Proc. Natl. Acad. Sci. **109**(19), 7241–7244 (2012)

66. Jia, Y., et al.: Transfer learning from speaker verification to multispeaker text-to-speech synthesis. arXiv:1806.04558 [cs, eess] (2019)

67. Jin, S.A.A., Park, N.: Parasocial interaction with my avatar: effects of interdependent self-construal and the mediating role of self-presence in an avatar-based console game, Wii. CyberPsychol. Behav. **12**(6), 723–727 (2009). https://doi.org/10.1089/cpb.2008.0289

68. Johnson, N.A., Cooper, R.B., Chin, W.W.: Anger and flaming in computer-mediated negotiation among strangers. Decis. Support Syst. **46**(3), 660–672 (2009). https://doi.org/10.1016/j.dss.2008.10.008

69. Jørgensen, J.: Appeal and perceived naturalness of a soft robotic tentacle. In: Companion of the 2018 ACM/IEEE International Conference on Human-Robot Interaction, Chicago, IL, USA, pp. 139–140. ACM (2018). https://doi.org/10.1145/3173386.3176985

70. Jung, M.F., Martelaro, N., Hinds, P.J.: Using robots to moderate team conflict: the case of repairing violations. In: Proceedings of the Tenth Annual ACM/IEEE International Conference on Human-Robot Interaction, HRI 2015, pp. 229–236. Association for Computing Machinery, New York (2015). https://doi.org/10.1145/2696454.2696460

71. Kac, E.: Telepresence and Bio Art: Networking Humans, Rabbits and Robots. University of Michigan Press, Ann Arbor (2005)

72. Kampf, R.: Are two better than one? Playing singly, playing in dyads in a computerized simulation of the Israeli-Palestinian conflict. Comput. Hum. Behav. **32**, 9–14 (2014). https://doi.org/10.1016/j.chb.2013.11.005

73. Kashian, N., Jang, J., Shin, S.Y., Dai, Y., Walther, J.B.: Self-disclosure and liking in computer-mediated communication. Comput. Hum. Behav. **71**, 275–283 (2017). https://doi.org/10.1016/j.chb.2017.01.041

74. Kawahara, K., Sakashita, M., Koike, A., Suzuki, I., Suzuki, K., Ochiai, Y.: Transformed human presence for puppetry. In: Proceedings of the 13th International Conference on Advances in Computer Entertainment Technology, ACE 2016, pp. 1–6. Association for Computing Machinery, New York (2016). https://doi.org/10.1145/3001773.3001813

75. Kaye, L.K., Malone, S.A., Wall, H.J.: Emojis: insights, affordances, and possibilities for psychological science. Trends Cogn. Sci. **21**(2), 66–68 (2017). https://doi.org/10.1016/j.tics.2016.10.007

76. Kendon, A.: Conducting Interaction: Patterns of Behavior in Focused Encounters, vol. 7. CUP Archive (1990)

77. Kerruish, E.: Affective touch in social robots. Transformations (14443775) (29) (2017)

78. Kidd, C., Taggart, W., Turkle, S.: A sociable robot to encourage social interaction among the elderly. In: Proceedings 2006 IEEE International Conference on Robotics and Automation, ICRA 2006, Orlando, FL, USA, pp. 3972–3976. IEEE (2006). https://doi.org/10.1109/ROBOT.2006.1642311

79. Kozima, H., Nakagawa, C.: Social robots for children: practice in communication-care. In: 9th IEEE International Workshop on Advanced Motion Control, Istanbul, Turkey, pp. 768–773. IEEE (2006). https://doi.org/10.1109/AMC.2006.1631756

80. Kristoffersson, A., Coradeschi, S., Loutfi, A.: A review of mobile robotic telepresence. Adv. Hum.-Comput. Interact. **2013**, 1–17 (2013). https://doi.org/10.1155/2013/902316

81. Kteily, N., Hodson, G., Bruneau, E.: They see us as less than human: metadehumanization predicts intergroup conflict via reciprocal dehumanization. J. Pers. Soc. Psychol. **110**(3), 343–370 (2016). https://doi.org/10.1037/pspa0000044

82. Kuwamura, K., Minato, T., Nishio, S., Ishiguro, H.: Personality distortion in communication through teleoperated robots. In: 2012 IEEE RO-MAN: The 21st IEEE International Symposium on Robot and Human Interactive Communication, Paris, France, pp. 49–54. IEEE (2012). https://doi.org/10.1109/ROMAN.2012.6343730

83. Laban, R., Ullmann, L.: The Mastery of Movement (1971)

84. Lala, D., Inoue, K., Kawahara, T.: Smooth turn-taking by a robot using an online continuous model to generate turn-taking cues. In: 2019 International Conference on Multimodal Interaction, ICMI 2019, Suzhou, China, pp. 226–234. Association for Computing Machinery (2019). https://doi.org/10.1145/3340555.3353727

85. Latour, B.: We Have Never Been Modern. Harvard University Press (2012)

86. Latour, B.: Down to Earth: Politics in the New Climatic Regime. Wiley, Hoboken (2018)

87. Lee, K.M., Nass, C.: Social-psychological origins of feelings of presence: creating social presence with machine-generated voices. Media Psychol. **7**(1), 31–45 (2005)

88. Lee, M.K., Fruchter, N., Dabbish, L.: Making decisions from a distance: the impact of technological mediation on riskiness and dehumanization. In: Proceedings of the 18th ACM Conference on Computer Supported Cooperative Work & Social Computing, CSCW 2015, Vancouver, BC, Canada, pp. 1576–1589. ACM Press (2015). https://doi.org/10.1145/2675133.2675288

89. Lin, S.F.: Effect of opponent type on moral emotions and responses to video game play. Cyberpsychol. Behav. Soc. Netw. **14**(11), 695–698 (2011). https://doi.org/10.1089/cyber.2010.0523

90. Lorenz, T., Weiss, A., Hirche, S.: Synchrony and reciprocity: key mechanisms for social companion robots in therapy and care. Int. J. Soc. Robot. **8**(1), 125–143 (2015). https://doi.org/10.1007/s12369-015-0325-8

91. Maoz, I.: Evaluating the communication between groups in dispute: equality in contact interventions between Jews and Arabs in Israel. Negot. J. **21**(1), 131–146 (2005). https://doi.org/10.1111/j.1571-9979.2005.00050.x

92. Masuda, M., Kato, S.: Motion rendering system for emotion expression of human form robots based on Laban movement analysis. In: 19th International Symposium in Robot and Human Interactive Communication, Viareggio, Italy, pp. 324–329. IEEE (2010). https://doi.org/10.1109/ROMAN.2010.5598692

93. Mehrabian, A., Russell, J.A.: An Approach to Environmental Psychology. The MIT Press (1974)

94. Meleady, R., Crisp, R.J., Hodson, G., Earle, M.: On the generalization of intergroup contact: a taxonomy of transfer effects. Curr. Dir. Psychol. Sci. **28**(5), 430–435 (2019). https://doi.org/10.1177/0963721419848682

95. Michaud, F., et al.: Telepresence robot for home care assistance. In: AAAI Spring Symposium: Multidisciplinary Collaboration for Socially Assistive Robotics, California, USA, pp. 50–55 (2007)

96. Minsky, M.: Telepresence (1980)
97. Mitchell, W.J., Szerszen, K.A., Lu, A.S., Schermerhorn, P.W., Scheutz, M., MacDorman, K.F.: A mismatch in the human realism of face and voice produces an uncanny valley. i-Perception **2**(1), 10–12 (2011). https://doi.org/10.1068/i0415
98. Muri, S.A.: Beyond the face: art therapy and self-portraiture. Arts Psychother. **34**(4), 331–339 (2007). https://doi.org/10.1016/j.aip.2007.05.002
99. Nagar, I., Hoter, E., Hasler, B.S.: Intergroup attitudes and interpersonal relationships in online contact between groups in conflict. J. Glob. Inf. Technol. Manag. 1–16 (2021). https://doi.org/10.1080/1097198X.2021.1953318
100. Nagendran, A., Steed, A., Kelly, B., Pan, Y.: Symmetric telepresence using robotic humanoid surrogates: robotic symmetric telepresence. Comput. Animation Virtual Worlds **26**(3–4), 271–280 (2015). https://doi.org/10.1002/cav.1638
101. Nakata, T., Sato, T., Mori, T., Mizoguchi, H.: Expression of emotion and intention by robot body movement. In: Proceedings of the 5th International Conference on Autonomous Systems (1998)
102. Ng, R., Lindgren, R.: Examining the effects of avatar customization and narrative on engagement and learning in video games. In: Proceedings of CGAMES 2013, USA, pp. 87–90 (2013). https://doi.org/10.1109/CGames.2013.6632611
103. Nie, J., Pak, M., Marin, A.L., Sundar, S.S.: Can you hold my hand?: physical warmth in human-robot interaction. In: Proceedings of the Seventh Annual ACM/IEEE International Conference on Human-Robot Interaction, HRI 2012, Boston, Massachusetts, USA, p. 201. ACM Press (2012). https://doi.org/10.1145/2157689.2157755
104. Nissen, A., Jahn, K.: Between anthropomorphism, trust, and the uncanny valley: a dual-processing perspective on perceived trustworthiness and its mediating effects on use intentions of social robots. In: Hawaii International Conference on System Sciences (2021). https://doi.org/10.24251/HICSS.2021.043
105. Noguchi, Y., Tanaka, F.: OMOY: a handheld robotic gadget that shifts its weight to express emotions and intentions. In: Proceedings of the 2020 CHI Conference on Human Factors in Computing Systems, Honolulu, HI, USA, pp. 1–13. ACM (2020). https://doi.org/10.1145/3313831.3376775
106. Oda, R.K.: Tools and techniques for rhythmic synchronization in networked musical performance. Ph.D. thesis, Princeton University (2017)
107. Ogawa, K., et al.: Telenoid: tele-presence Android for communication. In: ACM SIGGRAPH 2011 Emerging Technologies on SIGGRAPH 2011, Vancouver, British Columbia, Canada, p. 1. ACM Press (2011). https://doi.org/10.1145/2048259.2048274
108. Pagotto, L., Voci, A., Maculan, V.: The effectiveness of intergroup contact at work: Mediators and moderators of hospital workers' prejudice towards immigrants. J. Commun. Appl. Soc. Psychol. **20**(4), 317–330 (2010). https://doi.org/10.1002/casp.1038
109. Paynter, H.M.: Analysis and Design of Engineering Systems. MIT Press (1961)
110. Peled, A., Leinonen, T., Hasler, B.: The potential of telepresence robots for intergroup contact. In: Proceedings of the 4th International Conference on Computer-Human Interaction Research and Applications, CHIRA, pp. 210–217, no. 2184–3244 (2020). https://doi.org/10.5220/0010148102100217
111. Peled, A.: Soft Robotic Incarnation (2019)
112. Peña, J., Wolff, G., Wojcieszak, M.: Virtual reality and political outgroup contact: can avatar customization and common ingroup identity reduce social distance? Soc. Media + Soc. **7**(1), 2056305121993765 (2021). https://doi.org/10.1177/2056305121993765
113. Perry, C.: Machine learning and conflict prediction: a use case. Stab. Int. J. Secur. Dev. **2**(3), 56 (2013)
114. Pettigrew, T.F.: Intergroup contact theory. Annu. Rev. Psychol. **49**(1), 65–85 (1998)

115. Pettigrew, T.F., Tropp, L.R.: A meta-analytic test of intergroup contact theory. J. Pers. Soc. Psychol. **90**(5), 751–783 (2006). https://doi.org/10.1037/0022-3514.90.5.751

116. Pettigrew, T.F., Tropp, L.R., Wagner, U., Christ, O.: Recent advances in intergroup contact theory. Int. J. Intercult. Relat. **35**(3), 271–280 (2011). https://doi.org/10.1016/j.ijintrel.2011.03.001

117. Phillips-Silver, J., Aktipis, C.A., A. Bryant, G.: The ecology of entrainment: foundations of coordinated rhythmic movement. Music Percept. **28**(1), 3–14 (2010). https://doi.org/10.1525/mp.2010.28.1.3

118. Preuß, S., Steffens, M.C.: A video intervention for every straight man: the role of preattitudes and emotions in vicarious-contact effects. Group Process. Intergroup Relations 1368430220910462 (2020). https://doi.org/10.1177/1368430220910462

119. Rae, I., Takayama, L., Mutlu, B.: The influence of height in robot-mediated communication. In: 2013 8th ACM/IEEE International Conference on Human-Robot Interaction (HRI), pp. 1–8 (2013). https://doi.org/10.1109/HRI.2013.6483495

120. Ratan, R.A., Hasler, B.: Self-presence standardized: introducing the self-presence questionnaire (SPQ). In: Proceedings of the 12th Annual International Workshop on Presence, vol. 81 (2009)

121. Reich-Stiebert, N., Eyssel, F., Hohnemann, C.: Involve the user! Changing attitudes toward robots by user participation in a robot prototyping process. Comput. Hum. Behav. **91**, 290–296 (2019). https://doi.org/10.1016/j.chb.2018.09.041

122. Rich, S.I., Wood, R.J., Majidi, C.: Untethered soft robotics. Nat. Electron. **1**(2), 102–112 (2018). https://doi.org/10.1038/s41928-018-0024-1

123. Richardson, D.C., Dale, R., Tomlinson, J.M.: Conversation, gaze coordination, and beliefs about visual context. Cogn. Sci. **33**(8), 1468–1482 (2009). https://doi.org/10.1111/j.1551-6709.2009.01057.x

124. Rifinski, D., Erel, H., Feiner, A., Hoffman, G., Zuckerman, O.: Human-human-robot interaction: robotic object's responsive gestures improve interpersonal evaluation in human interaction. Hum.-Comput. Interact. 1–27 (2020). https://doi.org/10.1080/07370024.2020.1719839

125. Robertson, N.: Robot avatars and the vicarious realm, p. 14 (2020)

126. Saguy, T., Tausch, N., Dovidio, J.F., Pratto, F.: The irony of harmony: intergroup contact can produce false expectations for equality. Psychol. Sci. **20**(1), 114–121 (2009). https://doi.org/10.1111/j.1467-9280.2008.02261.x

127. Sah, Y.J., Ratan, R., Tsai, H.Y.S., Peng, W., Sarinopoulos, I.: Are you what your avatar eats? Health-behavior effects of avatar-manifested self-concept. Media Psychol. **20**(4), 632–657 (2017). https://doi.org/10.1080/15213269.2016.1234397

128. Salem, W.: The anti-normalization discourse in the context of Israeli-Palestinian peacebuilding. Palestine-Israel J. Polit. Econ. Cult. **12**(1), 100 (2005)

129. Schubert, T., Friedmann, F., Regenbrecht, H.: The experience of presence: factor analytic insights. Presence Teleoper. Virtual Environ. **10**(3), 266–281 (2001). https://doi.org/10.1162/105474601300343603

130. Schumann, S., Klein, O., Douglas, K., Hewstone, M.: When is computer-mediated intergroup contact most promising? Examining the effect of out-group members' anonymity on prejudice. Comput. Hum. Behav. **77**, 198–210 (2017). https://doi.org/10.1016/j.chb.2017.08.006

131. Sevdalis, V., Keller, P.E.: Captured by motion: dance, action understanding, and social cognition. Brain Cogn. **77**(2), 231–236 (2011). https://doi.org/10.1016/j.bandc.2011.08.005

132. Shafir, T., Tsachor, R.P., Welch, K.B.: Emotion regulation through movement: unique sets of movement characteristics are associated with and enhance basic emotions. Front. Psychol. **6** (2016). https://doi.org/10.3389/fpsyg.2015.02030

133. Shen, S., Slovak, P., Jung, M.F.: "Stop. I See a Conflict Happening.": a robot mediator for young children's interpersonal conflict resolution. In: Proceedings of the 2018 ACM/IEEE International Conference on Human-Robot Interaction, Chicago, IL, USA, pp. 69–77. ACM (2018). https://doi.org/10.1145/3171221.3171248

134. Sheridan, T.B.: Teleoperation, telerobotics and telepresence: a progress report. Control. Eng. Pract. 3(2), 205–214 (1995). https://doi.org/10.1016/0967-0661(94)00078-U

135. Sholt, M., Gavron, T.: Therapeutic qualities of clay-work in art therapy and psychotherapy: a review. Art Ther. 23(2), 66–72 (2006). https://doi.org/10.1080/07421656.2006.10129647

136. Sievers, B., Polansky, L., Casey, M., Wheatley, T.: Music and movement share a dynamic structure that supports universal expressions of emotion. Proc. Natl. Acad. Sci. 110(1), 70–75 (2013). https://doi.org/10.1073/pnas.1209023110

137. Silva, S.: Reification and fetishism: processes of transformation. Theory Cult. Soc. 30(1), 79–98 (2013). https://doi.org/10.1177/0263276412452892

138. Söeffner, J., Nam, C.S.: Co-presence in shared virtual environments: avatars beyond the opposition of presence and representation. In: Jacko, J.A. (ed.) HCI 2007. LNCS, vol. 4550, pp. 949–958. Springer, Heidelberg (2007). https://doi.org/10.1007/978-3-540-73105-4_104

139. Spears, R., Postmes, T., Lea, M., Wolbert, A.: When are net effects gross products? Commun. J. Soc. Issues 58(1), 91–107 (2002)

140. STANO, S.: The Internet and the Spread of Conspiracy Content (2020)

141. Stiehl, W., Lieberman, J., Breazeal, C., Basel, L., Lalla, L., Wolf, M.: Design of a therapeutic robotic companion for relational, affective touch. In: IEEE International Workshop on Robot and Human Interactive Communication, ROMAN 2005, Nashville, TN, USA, pp. 408–415. IEEE (2005). https://doi.org/10.1109/ROMAN.2005.1513813

142. Strait, M., Ramos, A.S., Contreras, V., Garcia, N.: Robots racialized in the likeness of marginalized social identities are subject to greater dehumanization than those racialized as white. In: 2018 27th IEEE International Symposium on Robot and Human Interactive Communication (RO-MAN), pp. 452–457 (2018). https://doi.org/10.1109/ROMAN.2018.8525610

143. Stupacher, J., Wood, G., Witte, M.: Synchrony and sympathy: social entrainment with music compared to a metronome. Psychomusicology Music Mind Brain 27(3), 158–166 (2017). https://doi.org/10.1037/pmu0000181

144. Sullivan, P., Rickers, K.: The effect of behavioral synchrony in groups of teammates and strangers. Int. J. Sport Exercise Psychol. 11(3), 286–291 (2013). https://doi.org/10.1080/1612197X.2013.750139

145. Sycara, K.P.: Machine learning for intelligent support of conflict resolution. Decis. Support Syst. 10(2), 121–136 (1993). https://doi.org/10.1016/0167-9236(93)90034-Z

146. Tanaka, F., Takahashi, T., Matsuzoe, S., Tazawa, N., Morita, M.: Telepresence robot helps children in communicating with teachers who speak a different language. In: Proceedings of the 2014 ACM/IEEE International Conference on Human-robot Interaction, HRI 2014, Bielefeld, Germany, pp. 399–406. ACM Press (2014). https://doi.org/10.1145/2559636.2559654

147. Thrun, S.: Toward a framework for human-robot interaction. Hum.-Comput. Interact. 19(1–2), 9–24 (2004). https://doi.org/10.1080/07370024.2004.9667338

148. Todo, T.: SEER: simulative emotional expression robot. In: ACM SIGGRAPH 2018 Emerging Technologies, Vancouver, British Columbia, Canada, pp. 1–2. ACM (2018). https://doi.org/10.1145/3214907.3214921

149. Trovato, G., Cuellar, F., Nishimura, M.: Introducing 'theomorphic robots'. In: 2016 IEEE-RAS 16th International Conference on Humanoid Robots (Humanoids), pp. 1245–1250 (2016). https://doi.org/10.1109/HUMANOIDS.2016.7803429

150. Vázquez, M., Carter, E.J., McDorman, B., Forlizzi, J., Steinfeld, A., Hudson, S.E.: Towards robot autonomy in group conversations: understanding the effects of body orientation and gaze. In: 2017 12th ACM/IEEE International Conference on Human-Robot Interaction, HRI, pp. 42–52 (2017)
151. Vezzali, L., Hewstone, M., Capozza, D., Giovannini, D., Wölfer, R.: Improving intergroup relations with extended and vicarious forms of indirect contact. Eur. Rev. Soc. Psychol. **25**(1), 314–389 (2014). https://doi.org/10.1080/10463283.2014.982948
152. Voci, A., Hewstone, M.: Intergroup contact and prejudice toward immigrants in Italy: the mediational role of anxiety and the moderational role of group salience. Group Process. Intergroup Relations **6**(1), 37–54 (2003). https://doi.org/10.1177/1368430203006001011
153. Walker, C.Y.Z.K.: Soft grippers not only grasp fruits: from affective to psychotropic HRI. Louis-Philippe Demers's keynote talk 'Experiencing the Machine Alterity' offered unique insights into situated bodies in motion and how we perceive their agency beyond morphological mimicry. Demers is Director of the Creative Lab at QUT, p. 15 (2019)
154. Walther, J.B.: Computer-mediated communication: impersonal, interpersonal, and hyperpersonal interaction. Commun. Res. **23**(1), 3–43 (1996)
155. Walther, J.B., Hoter, E., Ganayem, A., Shonfeld, M.: Computer-mediated communication and the reduction of prejudice: a controlled longitudinal field experiment among Jews and Arabs in Israel. Comput. Hum. Behav. **52**, 550–558 (2015). https://doi.org/10.1016/j.chb.2014.08.004
156. Waqas, A., Salminen, J., Jung, S., Almerekhi, H., Jansen, B.J.: Mapping online hate: a scientometric analysis on research trends and hotspots in research on online hate. PLOS ONE **14**(9), e0222194 (2019). https://doi.org/10.1371/journal.pone.0222194
157. White, F.A., Harvey, L.J., Abu-Rayya, H.M.: Improving intergroup relations in the internet age: a critical review. Rev. Gen. Psychol. **19**(2), 129–139 (2015). https://doi.org/10.1037/gpr0000036
158. Willemse, C.J.A.M., Toet, A., van Erp, J.B.F.: Affective and behavioral responses to robot-initiated social touch: toward understanding the opportunities and limitations of physical contact in human-robot interaction. Front. ICT **4**, 12 (2017). https://doi.org/10.3389/fict.2017.00012
159. Yee, N., Bailenson, J.N., Ducheneaut, N.: The Proteus effect: implications of transformed digital self-representation on online and offline behavior. Commun. Res. **36**(2), 285–312 (2009). https://doi.org/10.1177/0093650208330254
160. Zancanaro, M., Stock, O., Eisikovits, Z., Koren, C., Weiss, P.L.: Co-narrating a conflict: an interactive tabletop to facilitate attitudinal shifts. ACM Trans. Comput.-Hum. Interact. **19**(3), 24:1–24:30 (2012). https://doi.org/10.1145/2362364.2362372
161. Zancanaro, M., et al.: Evaluating an automated mediator for joint narratives in a conflict situation. Behav. Inf. Technol. **39**(9), 1022–1037 (2020). https://doi.org/10.1080/0144929X.2019.1637940
162. Zhang, Š., Zhang, S., Huang, T., Gao, W.: Multimodal deep convolutional neural network for audio-visual emotion recognition. In: Proceedings of the 2016 ACM on International Conference on Multimedia Retrieval, ICMR 2016, pp. 281–284. ACM Press, New York (2016). https://doi.org/10.1145/2911996.2912051
163. Zimbardo, P.G.: The human choice: individuation, reason, and order versus deindividuation, impulse, and chaos. Nebr. Symp. Motiv. **17**, 237–307 (1969)
164. Žižek, S.: First as Tragedy, Then as Farce. Verso (2009)

Boggle: An SSVEP-Based BCI Web Browser

Alison Camilleri[1]([✉])(iD), Chris Porter[2](iD), and Tracey Camilleri[3](iD)

[1] Department of Computer Information Systems, c/o Chris Porter, 1A22, Faculty of ICT,
University of Malta, Msida MSD2080, Malta
`alison.camilleri.15@um.edu.mt`
[2] Department of Computer Information Systems, 1A22, Faculty of ICT, University of Malta,
Msida MSD2080, Malta
`chris.porter@um.edu.mt`
[3] Department of Systems and Control Engineering, 411, Faculty of Engineering,
University of Malta, Msida MSD2080, Malta
`tracey.camilleri@um.edu.mt`

Abstract. Brain-Computer Interfaces (BCIs) have led to significant enhancements in the lives of physically-restricted individuals. BCIs based on Steady State Visually Evoked Potentials (SSVEPs) are robust and rely on a neuronal response evoked when a person focuses attention onto a flickering visual stimulus. Our first study [5], which provided empirical insights on web technologies' applicability for SSVEP stimuli-generation, demonstrated that both Cascading Style Sheets (CSS) and Web Graphics Library (WebGL) can produce effective stimuli via square wave approximations, using Google Chrome and Mozilla Firefox. Building upon these findings, this work explores the feasibility of adopting these technologies to implement an SSVEP-driven web browser, supporting online and asynchronous BCI-based control. Informed by a systematic review of literature and a succession of user-centred studies, this paper discusses results produced throughout the development of Boggle - a novel SSVEP-based BCI web-browser. As for in-browser stimuli-generation, enhanced stimuli efficacy was observed when adopting a custom-developed CSS-based stimuli-generator on Chrome, particularly in high-load rendering conditions. In turn, this contributed to increased classification accuracy and Information Transfer Rates (ITRs), compared to other BCI-based browsers. When evaluated within an online, asynchronous BCI context, participants achieved a global mean classification accuracy and ITR of 90.98% and 29.58 Bits Per Minute (BPM) respectively. Moreover, various usability tests were adopted to gauge progress throughout the different iterations. Boggle is the first cross-platform, SSVEP-based BCI browser that is fully developed using web-native technologies, and which exploits approximation techniques for stimuli-generation. Feedback provided by domain experts further highlights Boggle's suitability as a primary assistive technology.

Keywords: Brain-Computer Interface (BCI) · Steady State Visually Evoked Potential (SSVEP) · SSVEP-based BCI web browser

A. Holzinger et al. (Eds.): CHIRA 2020, CCIS 1609, pp. 100–123, 2022.
https://doi.org/10.1007/978-3-031-22015-9_6

1   Introduction

World Wide Web (WWW) ubiquity has permitted instantaneous, global communication, greatly revolutionizing the ways in which humans interact with one another
[8]. Notwithstanding this, millions of physically-restricted individuals face accessibility barriers, which hinder their ability to exploit a wide range of online services [32].
Assistive Technology (AT), such as that based on eye-tracking or brain control [4], can
support web interaction for people with limited mobility, enabling their participation in
employment, education and other sectors.

A Brain-Computer Interface (BCI) is a form of high-tech AT which operates independently of the body's standard output channels of the peripheral nerves and muscles
[43]. BCIs often rely on electroencephalography (EEG), which offers a non-invasive
approach to capture brain activity [5].

BCIs based on Steady State Visually Evoked Potentials (SSVEPs) are robust and
necessitate negligible amounts of user training to operate. Humans produce SSVEPs
in response to visual stimuli flickering at frequencies greater than 5 Hz [5]. During
periods of SSVEP stimulation, scalp electrodes, positioned over the brain's occipital
region, detect brain responses oscillating at the same frequency as the stimulus being
attended to by the user [42]. BCI classification algorithms can identify which stimulus
is being targeted and, based on this, trigger some corresponding action [5].

Within a BCI environment, stimuli stability and accuracy are key to robust SSVEP
response generation. Literature shows that monitor-based stimulation is currently preva-
lent, with the adoption of technologies like C++, OpenGL and Psychtoolbox to reliably
render visual flickers. Consequently, the applicability of web technologies for building highly flexible, accurate and portable SSVEP stimulation tools has been scarcely
researched [5].

Although web browser interaction has been previously explored within the context
of an SSVEP-based BCI [44,45], none of these attempts have focused on web-based
stimuli-generation. In fact, solely a few initial works have considered in-browser stimuli, namely through the development of two online SSVEP spellers using Graphics
Interchange Format (GIF) files [34] and Cascading Style Sheets (CSS) [33]. Rezazadeh
et al. [31] have also succeeded at navigating a virtual home environment by means of
browser-generated SSVEP stimuli.

Despite these studies' favourable outcomes, minimal empirical evidence exists on
the feasibility of different web technologies and underlying browser engines for rendering effective in-browser SSVEP stimuli. Furthermore, stimuli approximation techniques, which permit enhanced user interaction efficiency, have not been investigated
within a web environment [5].

Our previously published work [5] initially sought to address these two research
gaps, by empirically evaluating web-based SSVEP stimuli's stability and accuracy, as
well as their adequacy for BCI adoption.

This paper augments our first study [5], by building upon its findings to assess the
viability of building a specialized, evidence-based, SSVEP-driven BCI web browser,
via cross-platform and web-native technologies, for providing physically-restricted
individuals with a reliable, alternative means of web access.

2   Research Background

BCIs facilitate interaction through the establishment of a direct communication pathway between a human's brain and a machine. BCIs can either function in synchronous or asynchronous modes, whereby interaction timings are fully controlled by the system or user respectively. When opting for synchronous approaches, brain activity is processed at predefined, regular intervals, and it is constantly assumed that the user wishes to trigger a specific BCI command. On the contrary, asynchronous systems provide a greater degree of independence to users, enabling them to proceed with system interactions at will [29].

The functioning of a synchronous or an asynchronous BCI can be summarized into four key, sequential phases, specifically: (a) signal capture, (b) feature extraction, (c) feature classification and (d) command execution. The procedure is initiated by the real-time processing of captured EEG signals, through which features are extracted to reliably classify the subject's intent. Based on this, an automatic control function is produced [5] and optionally, auditory or visual feedback is provided to the user. BCI performance is typically reported using a range of different metrics, with classification accuracy and Information Transfer Rate (ITR) (reported in Bits Per Minute (BPM)) being among some of the most widely adopted measures in literature [36].

SSVEP-based BCIs are this study's prime focus, given their minimal training times [11], high Signal-to-Noise Ratios (SNRs) [14], as well as their capacity to reach high ITRs [28]. Upon focusing visual attention onto an SSVEP stimulus, non-invasive scalp electrodes, located over the subject's visual cortex, record oscillations at the target stimulus' fundamental and harmonic/sub-harmonic frequency components [5]. SSVEP stimulation is typically presented using Liquid Crystal Displays (LCDs), although some efforts have also focused on visual stimuli-rendering via Light-Emitting Diode (LED) panels and Cathode-Ray Tubes (CRTs) [25].

Conventional constant-period techniques of stimuli-generation, as well as the relatively novel square wave approximation method are thoroughly discussed in our previous work [5], along with the benefits and limitations of each approach. The next section focuses on advancements in BCI-based web browsing, through which the current state of the art is also highlighted.

2.1   BCI-Based Web Browsing

WWW access is vital for individuals who live with some form of physical disability. Through the review of existing literature, several efforts aimed at providing an entirely BCI-based browsing experience were identified [2,3,21,26,27,40,44,45] (see Table 1). These systems depend on a range of input modalities, including Slow Cortical Potentials (SCPs), Sensorimotor Rhythms (SMRs) and P300 evoked potentials, and each have their own benefits and limitations.

Based on the conducted review, it is evident that the majority of BCI browsers lack support for core functionality [2,3,21,26,40,45], while some necessitate lengthy command detection times [21,27,44,45] or training periods [2,21], making them less than ideal for day-to-day use. Furthermore, some of the implemented tools have not been evaluated with actual users [40], or else have not reported any BCI performance evaluation results [2,3,26,45], which means that their viability is currently unknown.

Considering Mankoff et al. [26] and Mugler et al.'s [27] 'true web access' criteria for

Table 1. Table providing a brief overview of all BCI browsers identified through the review of literature [2,3,21,26,27,40,44,45], alongside their development dates and interaction paradigms.

BCI browser	Date	Paradigm(s)	Brief overview
Descartes	1999	SCPs	• Supports back navigation, link selection and typing; • The tool's major drawbacks are its limitations in the representation of different links, lengthy training/selection times, as well as restrictions in web pages that can be navigated to; • Descartes was tested by a single participant, who achieved a mean classification accuracy of 80%.
Mankoff et al.	2002	Neural signal modulation	• Supports history tracking, bookmarking, in-page element selections and back/forward navigation; • Web navigation is solely limited to a set of predefined web pages.
Nessi	2003	SCPs/SMRs	• Extends the Mozilla browser; • Supports typing, bookmarking, in-page element selections and interactions with a custom, in-built email interface; • Requires prior training for successful operation.
BrainBrowser	2003	Neural signal modulation	• Developed using JavaSwing; • Supports home/back navigation, page reloading, link selection and printing; • Not yet evaluated with actual users.
Yin et al.	2009	SSVEP	• Implemented using .Net C#; • Limited information is provided, yet it is understood that the browser supports page scrolling; • The browser has slow recognition speeds and lacks support for complex browser functionality.
Mugler et al.	2010	P300	• Supports typing, link selection, URL entry, page reloading, back/forward/home navigation, form element input and page scrolling; • Based on provided user feedback, web surfing via the P300 browser takes too long; • Healthy participants achieved satisfactory performance results, with a mean classification accuracy and ITR of 90% and 13.4 BPM respectively.
Bose et al.	2016	Attention level modulation	• Built as an Android-based tool; • Supports home/back/forward navigation and in-page element selections.
WeBB	2017	SSVEP	• Developed as an Eclipse plugin and uses constant-period designs for stimuli-generation; • Supports typing, scrolling, history traversal, link navigation, page previewing and bookmarking; • Command detection times for WeBB are lengthy and interaction with complex in-page elements is unsupported; • Globally, participants achieved a mean classification accuracy of 86.08%, while their ITRs fell between 3.39 BPM and 4.68 BPM.

low bandwidth input systems (refer to [26, 27] for full web accessibility guidelines), it is worth noting that the SSVEP-based BCI browser, WeBB [27], may be considered as the most compliant, with the satisfaction of 80% of the proposed criteria. Despite WeBB's high accessibility ranking, the browser achieved low ITRs (3.39 BPM–4.68 BPM) in comparison to other studies, where the highest mean ITR reached 13.4 BPM [27]. Additionally, the browser's reliance on constant-period designs restricts stimuli frequency selection, and in certain screens, necessitates the use of multi-step selection techniques, which entail users to perform a greater number of steps to trigger the desired action.

Yin et al.'s [45] browser also operates via SSVEPs, however, is characterized by slow recognition speeds and a lack of support for complex browser functionality. Moreover, insufficient information is available on its performance and feature support.

3   Research Aims

This work's prime goal is to bring the WWW closer to individuals whose physical condition prevents them from gaining access via standard means of input.

Prompted by the various benefits of web-based SSVEP stimulation, in terms of portability, flexibility and cross-platform compatibility, the initial phase of our work [5] sought to deduce the viability of constant-period and square wave approximated in-browser SSVEP stimuli. To reach these objectives, standard web graphics and animation rendering technologies were considered, namely CSS and Web Graphics Library (WebGL), whose stimuli-rendering capacity was studied on Google Chrome and Mozilla Firefox, which are supported across major operating systems. Encouragingly, it was found that all studied browser-technology pairs can produce reliable and efficacious SSVEP stimulation via square wave approximations. These findings were evidenced by the consistent stability and accuracy of produced stimuli, as well as the minimal performance discrepancies noted between different stimuli-rendering scenarios [5].

Building upon our previous work's outcomes [5], this paper investigates the feasibility of adopting web technologies to build Boggle, a cross-platform, online and asynchronous SSVEP-based BCI web browser, and assesses its efficacy over a series of development and design stages (specifically **Stages 1–4**).

4   Methodology

Since the initial research phase demonstrated that multiple browser engines and web technologies are valid for stimuli-generation [5], the developed SSVEP stimuli approximation libraries (arising from [5]) were further studied under high-load rendering conditions, to re-confirm their applicability for rendering large quantities of concurrent on-screen stimuli (e.g. for the browser's keyboard menu) and to inform the choice of stimulation technologies for Boggle. Boggle's development was also based on a review process, which was conducted for features supported by most accessible web browsers, giving rise to a succession of iterative design cycles, as well as offline and online BCI experiments. Ultimately, feedback from domain experts was also gathered on the developed tool.

The methodological approach adopted for Boggle's multi-stage design process is further discussed in subsequent sections.

4.1   Stage 1 - Initial Prototype Design

Stage 1 of this study initiates Boggle's design process, and is targeted towards the development of an initial browser prototype, for which, design decisions are based on reviewed literature and empirical evidence, arising from both the first research phase [5], as well as high-load performance trials.

Specifically, a thorough review of literature was first conducted on existing accessible web browsers and alternative tools (such as browser-based accessibility plugins), operable through various alternative input modalities, including eye-trackers and BCIs. Information extracted through this review was collated in the form of a ranking table, listing widely-adopted browsing features in order of their adoption rates, to guide initial design decisions on Boggle's feature support.

Additionally, high-load stimulation trials were executed on a single machine to re-confirm the applicability of the developed CSS and WebGL approximation libraries [5] for rendering a large number of stimuli simultaneously on-screen, as was required for Boggle's keyboard screen. During experimental sessions, the stimulators were configured to run 40 concurrent on-screen stimuli, while maintaining horizontal and vertical inter-stimuli distances of 0.55 cm (see Fig. 1). A similar methodology to that applied in [5] was re-adopted such that, for each stimulus, tachometer readings were gathered over three separate test runs, for frequencies 8 Hz, 9.6 Hz, 10.8 Hz, 11.6 Hz, 12.8 Hz, 13 Hz, 14.4 Hz and 15.6 Hz. Frequencies for stimuli rendered via CSS and WebGL were recorded on both Chrome and Firefox, for a total of four minutes each. Considerations relating to each library's hardware resource consumption were also taken into account at this stage. These results, in turn, informed the choice of stimulation technologies for Boggle.

4.2   Stage 2 - Design Iterations

Stage 2 of this study iteratively improves upon the implemented browser prototype, in direct collaboration with potential users, following a User-Centred Design (UCD) methodology. A total of 7 participants were recruited for this phase of study (4 males, 3 females), none of whom had any prior experience with Boggle. This research stage's

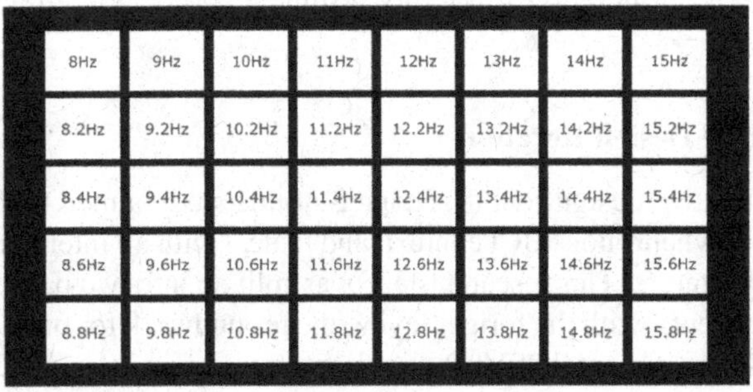

8Hz	9Hz	10Hz	11Hz	12Hz	13Hz	14Hz	15Hz
8.2Hz	9.2Hz	10.2Hz	11.2Hz	12.2Hz	13.2Hz	14.2Hz	15.2Hz
8.4Hz	9.4Hz	10.4Hz	11.4Hz	12.4Hz	13.4Hz	14.4Hz	15.4Hz
8.6Hz	9.6Hz	10.6Hz	11.6Hz	12.6Hz	13.6Hz	14.6Hz	15.6Hz
8.8Hz	9.8Hz	10.8Hz	11.8Hz	12.8Hz	13.8Hz	14.8Hz	15.8Hz

Fig. 1. The web-based approximation libraries' interface during the presentation of 40 concurrent on-screen stimuli, indicating the frequencies assigned to each stimulus.

iterative approach enabled the identification of usability issues within the browser, through a combination of methods, including usability metrics and feedback gathering techniques.

A within-subject study was designed, such that the same user group participated in usability testing sessions across different iterations, with the aim of minimizing subject-to-subject variability [37]. In total, two design rounds were conducted for Boggle, approximately four weeks apart, to 'wash out' learning effects from the previous run [37]. Each iteration involved the execution of a set of browsing tasks, which were executed via mouse clicks (performed on interface stimuli), without any form of guidance or feedback. Although Boggle is intended for BCI control, the use of mouse clicks ensured that this research stage's focus remained entirely on the browser's usability, without introducing the additional complexity of interfacing with a BCI. Usability insights, captured through the first iteration, led to the enhancement of certain browser components and features, whose impact was later evaluated as part of the second design round.

Throughout the first iteration, all 7 participants were assigned 11 browsing tasks, which were kept consistent between different subjects and also covered all of Boggle's supported functionality. These involved typing, scrolling, page reloading, back navigation, video playing, the use of read mode, link/input field/button selections, the triggering of Google searches (using an in-built menu), zooming in/out or resetting the page zoom levels, as well as visiting/adding and deleting bookmarks (individually or in bulk). As for the second design round, 6 participants (1 of the initial 7 participants was later unavailable) were given a total of 8 browsing tasks, which were focused on newly updated features within Boggle.

At each iteration, qualitative user feedback was collected through the think-aloud protocol and semi-structured discussions (held after the completion of each task or session), and later thematically analyzed. Gathered insights were either directly observed/noted during the session, or else extracted from transcripts of audio-visual clips recorded throughout the entire session. Additionally, each iteration involved the capture of a range of task-level metrics, namely the Single Ease Question (SEQ), completion rates, confidence ratings and error rates, which were applied for each executed task. With regards to study-level metrics, the System Usability Scale (SUS) was administered at the end of each browser evaluation session, to assess the entire system's usability. Overall, each iteration's usability testing sessions took around 1 to 1.5 h to complete.

4.3 Stage 3 - BCI Design Iteration

Following two iterative design rounds, **Stage 3** of this study aimed to evaluate Boggle within an online, asynchronous BCI context, and to deal with all intermediary steps necessary to reach this target. This research stage was split up into two parts, namely offline and online experiments, with the former laying the groundwork for online BCI sessions. Throughout both experiments, SSVEP detection was performed via the unsupervised, state-of-the-art Filter Bank Canonical Correlation Analysis (FBCCA) algorithm, which requires no prior training to operate, and is also capable of reaching high classification accuracies [6].

Web browsing activities within Boggle are facilitated through the browser's support for both non-control and intentional-control states [24]. Non-control states correspond to instances during which users are deliberately not focusing onto any SSVEP stimuli, for example while reading a web page, while intentional-control states refer to periods during which users are focusing onto SSVEP stimuli of interest, to trigger some browser function, such as the opening of a browser menu [24].

The EEG hardware setup, as well as the methods adopted for the conducted offline and online BCI experiments, are further discussed below.

EEG Data Acquisition. To capture brain signal data, participants were fitted with an electrode cap (g.GAMMACAP[1]) and 8 channels (PO3, PO4, PO7, PO8, POz, O1, O2, Oz), positioned over the brain's occipital and parietal regions, were used to record brain activity. Cz (ground electrode) and an ear lobe electrode clip were chosen as a means of referencing during EEG data collection. All electrodes were positioned in accordance with the International 10–20 electrode placement system.

Before attaching non-invasive g.SCARABEO (see footnote 1) electrodes to the corresponding g.GAMMACAP (see footnote 1) holder rings, conductive electrolyte gel was used to minimize impedance contact with the skin [39]. Electrodes were connected to the g.GAMMAbox (see footnote 1), which interfaces with the g.USBAMP (see footnote 1) amplifier, configured to run at a sampling rate of 256 Hz. Highpass and lowpass filters were applied at 0.5 Hz and 100 Hz respectively, while a 50 Hz notch filter was used to suppress power line interference.

Offline BCI Experiments. Offline BCI sessions involved EEG data collection with participants from **Stage 2** of this study, over a specific number of trials. During offline experiments, Boggle was run in a cue-based mode for complex (>10 stimuli) and non-complex (<10 stimuli) interfaces. Throughout these sessions (each one lasting roughly 1 to 2 h in duration), both intentional-control and non-control state EEG data was gathered from participants.

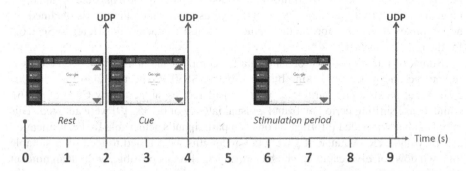

Fig. 2. Timing scheme for a single offline trial conducted within Boggle's home screen.

For intentional-control state EEG data collection, cues were shown in random order as a coloured stimulus border. A single stimulus trial (refer to Fig. 2) lasted 9.185 s

---
[1] Products developed by g.tec [13].

and for each participant, a maximum of 10 trials per stimulus were conducted. A trial commenced with a 2 s rest period, during which all SSVEP stimuli were inactive. In the next 2 s, a cue was shown around one randomly selected stimulus, to direct the subject's gaze to the target stimulus. At the fourth second, the cue was hidden and all on-screen SSVEP stimuli flickered simultaneously at unique frequencies, for a period of 5.185 s. A single run was completed once a single trial per stimulus within the interface was collected. Participants were also allowed several minutes of rest in-between two consecutive runs to minimize visual fatigue.

To facilitate EEG data segmentation, indicator values were transmitted from Boggle's client application to the implemented Simulink data processing module (via User Datagram Protocol (UDP) packets), at time points corresponding to the onset of cue presentation, start of SSVEP stimulation, end of each trial and completion of every run. All values transmitted via UDP were synchronized with captured EEG data and were stored in a separate file for further analysis.

Intentional-control state EEG data was initially collected for non-complex interfaces, namely Boggle's home screen, which consists of 8 stimuli. Data was collected from 5 participants over 10 runs, such that a total of 10 trials per stimulus were collected for each participant. Three stimuli conditions were considered, specifically (a) blue and magenta stimuli with non-flickering content[2], (b) blue and magenta stimuli with flickering content (see footnote 2) and (c) white stimuli with flickering content (see footnote 2), all of which were shown over a black background. Thus, a total of 2204.4 s' worth (9.185 s × 8 stimuli × 10 trials × 3 stimuli conditions) of EEG data was gathered for each participant. All subjects were exposed to the three different conditions in random sequence [37], so that the stimuli which yielded the highest classification performance and ITR could be adopted for subsequent data collection sessions, as well as online experiments.

A similar procedure was used to capture intentional-control state EEG data for complex interfaces, specifically for the keyboard menu, which contains 18 stimuli. A total of 4 participants were involved in data collection, with each session lasting approximately 1653.3 s (9.185 s × 18 stimuli × 10 trials) per participant. This time round, blue-magenta stimuli (with flickering contents) were used, based on the results obtained for non-complex interfaces, for the three studied stimuli characteristics (refer to Sect. 6.3 for the relative results).

Subjects' intentional-control state data for complex and non-complex screens, was segmented and processed offline by the FBCCA SSVEP detection algorithm. In this case, 5 sub-bands and 5 harmonics were considered, as suggested by Chen et al. [6], while a gaze shifting period of 1s and a visual latency of 0.135 s [9] were adopted. This initial analysis provided information on each participant's achievable BCI classification accuracy and ITR. A range of gaze window lengths were tested to identify a suitable time window for EEG capture, which is ideally as short as possible, without significant detriment to BCI performance.

Non-control state EEG data was also captured during the process of reading a web page within Boggle (with read mode enabled), to assess typical brain activity during idle

---

[2] Stimulus content refers to text/images contained within a stimulus, which could either be non-flickering or else flickering at the same rate as the stimulus' background.

browsing periods. This data was ultimately used to determine a reasonable classification threshold for FBCCA, which can discriminate between non-control and intentional-control states, thus satisfying this study's requirement for an asynchronous BCI.

Online BCI Experiments. The results of the offline study were subsequently used to assess Boggle's usability, when operated within an online, asynchronous BCI context. In this case, numeric identifiers were transmitted from Boggle's client application (via UDP packets) on every menu transition or stimulus state update, enabling the classifier to maintain an updated list of classifiable stimuli frequencies.

All 6 participants from Boggle's final design iteration (**Stage 2**) were involved in the BCI evaluation phase. Similar to offline sessions, EEG data was recorded over 8 channels, while the FBCCA algorithm was used with the previous parameter settings, for SSVEP detection and classification. Stimuli frequencies (6 Hz–14.5 Hz in 0.5 Hz steps) were common to all subjects, with the entire frequency range, or subsets of it, being reused across Boggle's various screens, depending on the required number of stimuli. Blue-magenta stimuli (with flickering contents) were also adopted, based on results achieved for offline analyses (see Sect. 6.3), conducted for non-complex interfaces, for the range of studied stimuli characteristics.

As opposed to the implemented offline system, the online BCI is constantly active and continually outputting a classification response every 4 s, corresponding to the specified gaze window length parameter (set based on offline evaluation results, discussed in Sect. 6.3). Users' EEG is continuously captured and processed in chunks of 1024 data points, that are either labelled as a particular stimulus frequency (intentional-control state) or a non-control state by the FBCCA classifier. The output label is sent to Boggle and, on its receipt, some corresponding action is executed and system feedback shown to the user, in the form of a coloured border around the selected stimulus.

For online experiments, participants carried out 5 web browsing tasks (chosen from the final design iteration for **Stage 2** of the study) through BCI control (see Fig. 3), with these tasks being read out once verbally, to ensure that users were confident with the task requirements.

Throughout online sessions, a range of usability/performance metrics, namely the Samn-Perelli Fatigue Scale (SPS), Raw Task Load Index (RTLX), Time on Task (TOT), completion rates, as well as classification accuracy and ITR measures, were adopted as task-level metrics. As for study-level metrics, the SUS was applied to holistically evaluate the entire BCI system's usability. Sources of data collection also included semi-structured post-study discussions, direct observations and audio-visual capture, which altogether, enabled a comprehensive understanding of Boggle's usability from different perspectives.

4.4 Stage 4 - Domain Expert Feedback

Boggle's design process was concluded with in-depth discussions on Boggle's usability, which were held with two senior occupational therapists (employed with a national agency), who often work with individuals from this study's target user group. A remote, semi-structured interview was set up, prior to which interviewees were also given a set

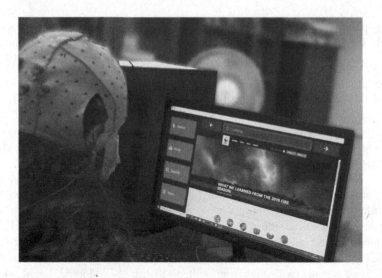

Fig. 3. User interacting with Boggle via asynchronous, BCI-based control.

of resources to familiarize themselves with Boggle. The resource pack included (a) a video of a participant interacting with Boggle via BCI, (b) detailed documentation on all features supported by Boggle and (c) screen capture of various browsing actions being executed via Boggle using mouse-clicks.

All captured interview details were transcribed based on audio-visual recordings and later thematically analyzed. In this way, present-day challenges in assisting motor-impaired individuals could be further understood, while gaining insight into Boggle's real-world applicability and possible enhancements that could address target users and carers' needs more accurately.

5   Boggle - Implementation Details

This section focuses on Boggle's final browser design (emerging from **Stage 3** of this study), which operates through various hardware and software tools (refer to Fig. 4), functioning in tandem with one another, to capture and process users' neuronal signals, and to convert them into browser commands or non-control state executions.

Boggle's operation (see Fig. 4) starts off with EEG acquisition (see Sect. 4.3 for EEG hardware setup) and is directly followed by signal processing, at which point a classification response is output by the FBCCA algorithm. The classification output is sent to the SSVEP hub (a Node.js server) via an HTTP POST request. In turn, the hub employs the publish/subscribe (pub/sub) communication model to publish classification labels, which are ultimately received by the Boggle engine (i.e. the client web browsing application) over a WebSocket connection. On the label's receipt, some corresponding action is triggered, resulting in User Interface (UI) updates, feedback provision and potentially, changes to Boggle's state (maintained via the state manager and an underlying SQLite database). Given the asynchronous nature of the adopted architecture, EEG classification may also lead to non-control state instructions.

5.1 Signal Processing Module

During online operation, Boggle's Simulink-based signal processing module processes EEG data in real-time, and handles incoming data from two main sources: (a) the amplifier's EEG signals and (b) numeric identifiers sent out by the Boggle engine (via UDP packets).

EEG data is received in batches of 256 data points per second and is held in a buffer until the data point count equals that required for a specified gaze length. For instance, in the case of this study, a 4 s gaze length was considered, thus, at most, 1024 data points (4 s × 256 data points) can be stored within the buffer. On collection of 1024 data points, the data block is released for further processing, only if the recorded menu scenario identifiers (received over UDP) are valid. These indicate the state of Boggle's UI to the signal processing module, such that classifications are solely performed between frequencies of interest, resulting in reduced error rates.

Additionally, a threshold-based approach [46] is adopted for non-control state detection within Boggle. The FBCCA algorithm's classification process involves the computation of correlation coefficients between SSVEP sub-band components and pregenerated sinusoidal reference signals, for all stimuli frequencies. Thus, a reference signal frequency having maximal correlation with multi-channel SSVEPs is deemed as the actual target stimulus frequency [6], only if its maximal correlation coefficient exceeds a predefined threshold. Otherwise, the signal is labelled as a non-control state and a classification label is output accordingly.

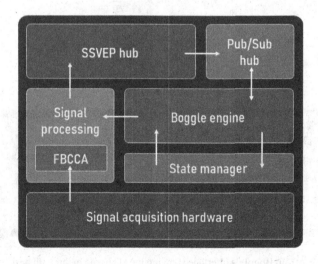

Fig. 4. Architectural overview of Boggle's online, asynchronous BCI framework.

5.2   Boggle Engine

The Boggle engine, which refers to the client web browsing application, was built using the Chromium-based Electron framework, which permits cross-platform desktop application development [10] via web-native technologies. The technologies chosen to implement the engine, as well as decisions on its feature support, were based on results arising from our first study [5] and **Stage 1** of this research (see Sect. 6.1).

The client application is responsible for (a) setting up a customized browsing experience, (b) transmitting numeric indicators to the signal processing module, (c) handling classification responses, (d) providing user feedback, as well as for (e) rendering Boggle's UI, using the initial research phase's [5] CSS stimuli approximation library, which was deemed as the most performant stimulator, based on the results of the conducted high-load performance trials (results for **Stage 1** of this study are available in Sect. 6.1).

Fig. 5. Screenshots from Boggle's interface showing the (1) home menu with basic navigation and reading controls, (2) an 18-target keyboard interface with auto-completion facilities, (3) on-page region selection control (to activate links/buttons/text fields in a particular region), (4) on-page link/button/text field selection control (numbered), (5) in-built Google search menu, as well as (6) page and bookmark management facilities.

Boggle's final interface design also includes several aspects, such as link selection functionality and bookmark management support, as outlined in Fig. 5.

6 Results

This section documents the findings of the high-load performance tests, as well as the results of a review process, which was conducted for features supported by various accessible web browsers and tools. Subsequent sections also highlight the usability results achieved for the iterative design process, as well as for Boggle's offline and online BCI experiments. Feedback provided by domain experts is also thoroughly discussed in upcoming sections.

6.1 Stage 1 - Initial Prototype Design

This section discusses the findings of the review, compiled for existing accessible web browsers/tools, as well as the outcomes of the high-load stimulation trials, conducted for the implemented web-based stimuli approximation libraries [5].

All identified web browsing functionality, arising from reviewed literature, was summarized in table form and ordered by popularity, based on each feature's adoption rate (computed as a percentage across all reviewed accessibility tools). It was noted that highly-ranked browsing functionality was common to both accessible browsers and alternative tools, hence **Stage 1** of this study focused on equipping Boggle with features that are widely supported by various accessible web browsers [1–3, 20–23, 26, 27, 30, 40, 41, 44, 45], as shown in Table 2.

In high-load stimulation conditions, an increased number of inaccuracies/instabilities were noted across all rendering scenarios, which were previously studied for the initial research phase [5]. Considering all stimuli-generation combinations [5], CSS and Chrome achieved the highest performance levels, with an overall mean bias of 0.0207 ($\sigma = 0.2708$) for all tested stimulation frequencies (refer to [5] for a definition of the 'bias'). On the other hand, the poorest performance was recorded for WebGL and Firefox, with an average bias of 0.0404 ($\sigma = 0.3963$) across all studied stimuli frequencies. With regards to hardware usage, all logged CPU, GPU and memory consumption values were in close proximity to one another, across all technology-browser setups.

Based on these outcomes, a performance advantage was noted for CSS and Chrome-based SSVEP stimuli as these showed the least inaccuracies and instabilities in high-load rendering scenarios. The adoption of Chromium (a core aspect of Google Chrome) and CSS was thus identified as the most plausible way forward, for the implementation of a highly performant and reliable SSVEP-based BCI browser. Altogether these results shaped Boggle's initial prototype design.

6.2 Stage 2 - Design Iterations

Quantitative/qualitative usability data, gathered over two design iterations, was crucial to the enhancement of Boggle's initial prototype design. This section goes over the

Table 2. Accessible web browsers' functionality listed in order of popularity. This table also indicates whether or not each browser feature is supported by Boggle's first design.

Browser feature	Adoption rate (%)	Supported by Boggle
Link navigation	85.71%	✔
Back/forward navigation	78.57%	✔
Scrolling	78.57%	✔
Home navigation	64.29%	✗
Page reload	64.29%	✔
Bookmarks	57.14%	✔
Web searches	50%	✔
Typing	42.86%	✔
Form elements	42.86%	✔
Menu navigation	35.71%	✔
Browsing history	28.57%	✗
Automatic scrolling	14.29%	✗
Multimedia content	14.29%	✔
Zoom in/out	14.29%	✔
Text selection	7.14%	✗
Tab management	7.14%	✗
Word prediction	7.14%	✔
Cut, copy and paste	0%	✗
Boggle's feature coverage (%)	—	**66.67%**

adopted evaluation strategies and the final usability results for Boggle's two-phase iterative design process.

A brief overview of results obtained for the final iteration's usability metrics, namely the SEQ, confidence ratings, task completion rates, error rates and the SUS is provided in Table 3. Task completion was measured based on the following Successful Completion Criteria (SCC): (a) users had to fully achieve task aims, (b) specified sub-tasks had to be followed to accomplish tasks and (c) no more than 3 erroneous selections could be performed during the task's execution.

As for task error rates, these were quantified using Eq. 1 [35], whereby participants' error counts were divided by the total number of browsing actions executed during the specific task. Resultant values were subsequently multiplied by 100 for conversion into percentage form. Additional error rectification steps were also considered as correct commands for all error rate computations.

$$ErrorRate = \left(\frac{ErrorCount}{TotalActions} \right) \times 100 \tag{1}$$

Table 3. Table portraying the 6 participants' global mean usability scores, benchmark values, and the least/most desirable scores for each metric applied during Boggle's final design iteration.

Usability measure	Participants' global mean score	Benchmark comparison score	Least desirable score	Most desirable score
SEQ	6.88	5.5 (based on research conducted by Sauro [16])	1	7
Error rate	1.82%	—	100%	0%
Completion rate	97.92%	78% (based on research conducted by Sauro [19])	0%	100%
Confidence	6.9	5.75 (based on research conducted by Sauro [18])	1	7
SUS	90.42	68 (based on research conducted by Sauro [17])	0	100

Statistical analyses were conducted using 95% Confidence Intervals (CIs), to estimate the uncertainty in participants' global mean usability scores [7]. Wherever possible, mean usability/performance measures were also compared against established benchmarks, either using the non-parametric Binomial test or its parametric alternative (the One Sample t-test). Furthermore, comparisons between participants' mean scores across design iterations were performed using the Paired Samples t-test (parametric) or Wilcoxon Signed-Rank test (non-parametric), to identify potential improvements in mean usability measures for the final iteration. An alpha level of .05 was also assumed for all statistical tests.

The final results of the iterative design process demonstrate Boggle's usability through the high task completion rates attained (95% CI [93.73%,100%]), in combination with the satisfactory SEQ (95% CI [6.78,6.97]) and confidence scores (95% CI [6.81,6.99]) given out by participants, for all browsing tasks executed via Boggle. Encouragingly, users also maintained low error rate levels throughout (95% CI [0.28%,3.37%]). Participants' SUS ratings (95% CI [81.89,98.95]) also complement these findings and evidence that, globally, the system was perceived as highly usable. Additionally, Binomial test/One Sample t-test results showed that, where applicable, participants' mean usability scores were all significantly higher ($p < .05$) than the specified benchmark values (see Table 3). A significant improvement ($p < .05$) in participants' mean SEQ scores was also noted for the final iteration, while discrepancies for confidence ratings ($p = .08$), completion rates ($p = .655$) and the SUS ($p = .699$) were found to be marginal, when using either the Wilcoxon Signed-Rank test or Paired Samples t-test as applicable.

Participants' feedback supplements these results, with the web browsing experience being described as "very positive" and most users perceiving the system as memorable [15]. Some participants also remarked on the effectiveness of newly implemented enhancements.

6.3   Stage 3 - BCI Design Iteration

This section highlights the evaluation techniques and results achieved for offline and online BCI studies, which were both conducted with potential target users, to gauge Boggle's usability in the context of brain control.

Offline BCI Experiments - Intentional-Control States. Offline BCI experiments started off with intentional-control state EEG data gathering for the browser's home interface (non-complex screen), with stimuli characteristics being set as described in Sect. 4.3. EEG data corresponding to SSVEP stimulation periods was segmented into 5.135 s time windows, which included an initial visual latency of 0.135 s. A total of 8 EEG stimulation segments (one segment per stimulus), for each of the 10 data collection runs, were passed to the FBCCA algorithm. Performance was measured through classification accuracy, via Eq. 2, and ITR, using both Eqs. 3 and 4.

$$ClassificationAccuracy = \left(\frac{CorrectClassifications}{TotalClassifications} \right) \times 100 \qquad (2)$$

Eq. 3, introduced by Wolpaw et al. [36,43], provides an average measure of the quantity of bits transferred per selection (bits/trial) [38], where N refers to the total number of selection options available within the screen (in the home menu's case this is equal to 8), while p denotes the classification accuracy.

$$BitsPerTrial = \log_2 N + P \log_2 P + (1 - P) \log_2 \left(\frac{1 - P}{N - 1} \right) \qquad (3)$$

$$ITR = BitsPerTrial \times \frac{60}{SelectionTime} \qquad (4)$$

To convert ITR from bits/trial (result of Eq. 3) to BPM, Eq. 4 [38] is applied where *selection time* refers to the total classification time in seconds. For the purpose of offline experiments, selection time incorporates both periods of gaze focus (duration varied across tests, such that values between 0.5 s and 5 s were considered in 0.5 s increments) and gaze shifting (fixed at 1 s).

Across all gaze length parameters, participants' averaged performance scores indicate that the highest mean classification accuracies and ITRs were consistently obtained for blue-magenta stimuli with flickering contents. Given participants' overall higher performance, stimuli with these characteristics were deemed as the most effective SSVEP stimulation source out of all three studied options. Overall, the highest mean classification accuracies and ITRs amount to 97.75% and 40.51 BPM respectively, and correspond to data lengths of 5 and 2.5 s (see Table 4).

Table 4. Table depicting subjects' mean offline classification accuracies and ITRs, along with standard deviations, considering blue-magenta stimuli (with flickering content) across different gaze lengths, for the home menu (non-complex interface).

Data length (s)	Mean acc. (%)	Acc. std. dev. (%)	Mean ITR (BPM)	ITR std. dev. (BPM)
0.5	33.25	8.6	11.34	5.91
1	51	13.87	22.34	11.47
1.5	72	17.08	36.79	16.08
2	82.25	13.45	40.29	12.56
2.5	89.25	10.77	**40.51**	10.05
3	93	5.97	38.8	5.49
3.5	95.5	5.63	36.25	4.94
4	96.5	4.09	33.38	3.38
4.5	97	2.88	30.68	2.1
5	**97.75**	2.24	28.58	1.5

Since complex screens are likely to yield some level of performance degradation [12], attainable accuracy and ITR in such conditions were also investigated prior to selecting a gaze length parameter value. Thus, a similar analysis strategy to that described for non-complex interfaces was also employed for the complex keyboard screen, consisting of 18 stimuli. Based on the FBCCA algorithm's classification output, the highest mean accuracy and ITR for the keyboard menu amounted to 87.09% and 36.34 BPM respectively, corresponding to data lengths of 4.5 and 4 s (see Table 5), for blue-magenta stimuli with flickering contents. Based on these results, a 4 s gaze length was selected, which should permit for the maintenance of reasonable performance levels in complex screens, while giving a reasonable tradeoff between ITR and classification accuracy.

Offline BCI Experiments - Non-Control States. Given the asynchronous nature of this study's implemented BCI, offline studies also sought to determine a suitable subject-independent classification threshold, to discriminate between non-control and intentional-control states in a web browsing scenario.

The maximal correlation coefficients, recorded for different subjects for correctly classified intentional-control state trials, were occasionally as low as ≈0.8, going up to at most ≈1.6, whereas those of non-control states were found to range between ≈0.6 and ≈1. Based on this, a subject-independent correlation threshold of 0.85 was chosen for online BCI studies, which is expected to minimize false non-control state classifications and unnecessary delays during BCI-based interaction.

Table 5. Table depicting subjects' mean offline classification accuracies and ITRs, along with standard deviations, considering blue-magenta stimuli (with flickering content) across different gaze lengths, for the keyboard menu (complex interface).

Data length (s)	Mean acc. (%)	Acc. std. dev. (%)	Mean ITR (BPM)	ITR std. dev. (BPM)
0.5	4.86	0.83	0.23	0.13
1	6.39	0.96	0.68	0.52
1.5	19.86	9.12	6.01	4.63
2	46.53	20.43	22.87	15.77
2.5	65.42	19.89	33.89	16.39
3	72.5	21.35	35.74	16.05
3.5	79.17	16.81	36.29	12.74
4	84.58	11.72	**36.34**	8.85
4.5	**87.09**	10.64	34.63	7.65
5	86.94	9.32	31.53	6.02

It's worth noting that although classification threshold selection was required to satisfy this study's requirement for an asynchronous BCI, the system's effectiveness at discriminating between the two control states was not directly tested during subsequent online studies. Having said this, incorrect non-control state classifications still occurred throughout task executions, thus influencing the time taken to trigger a specific command and the achievable ITR.

Online BCI Experiments. This section discusses the adopted evaluation strategies and results obtained for online BCI experiments, which cover a range of standard usability/BCI performance metrics, and shed light onto insights gained through users' own feedback.

Table 6 depicts the various usability metrics applied throughout Boggle's BCI design iteration, including SPS, RTLX, SUS, task completion rates, as well as BCI classification accuracy and ITR measures. The global mean scores achieved by participants, the benchmark values considered for this study, as well as the least and most desirable usability score values, are shown alongside each metric.

Once more, task completion was measured by means of the three SCC defined for Boggle's iterative design study (Sect. 6.2). As for classification accuracy, Eq. 2 was applied, for which the *total classifications* and *correct classifications* values were specified based on actions executed across the different menus throughout a specific task. For the purpose of this analysis, and similar to the approach adopted in [34], any steps executed to rectify erroneous actions were considered as correct commands. Incorrect non-control state classifications were also excluded from accuracy measures, as these only result in classification delays [46], and were thus solely considered for ITR as discussed below.

ITRs were measured in BPM, using Eqs. 3 and 4 for individual browser menus, while for task executions across different menus, Eq. 5 (gives results in BPM) was used, where t_{tot} refers to the time taken to complete the entire task in seconds, N_m equals

Table 6. Table portraying the 6 participants' global mean usability scores, benchmark values, as well as the least/most desirable scores, for each metric applied during online BCI sessions.

Usability measure	Participants' global mean score	Benchmark comparison score(s)	Least desirable score	Most desirable score
SPS	3.1	—	7	1
RTLX	28.03	—	100	0
Completion rate	90%	78% (based on research conducted by Sauro [19])	0%	100%
SUS	77.08	68 (based on research conducted by Sauro [17])	0	100
Classification accuracy	90.98%	70% (based on criteria specified by Mugler et al. [27])	0%	100%
ITR	29.58 BPM	Equal to the maximum achievable ITR (ITR_{max}) per task: • $Task1_{ITR_{max}}$ = 33.703 BPM • $Task2_{ITR_{max}}$ = 31.005 BPM • $Task3_{ITR_{max}}$ = 37.359 BPM • $Task4_{ITR_{max}}$ = 36.784 BPM • $Task5_{ITR_{max}}$ = 43.610 BPM *Note:* ITR_{max} was computed by using optimal values for Eq. 5, including for t_{tot}, which assumed a 4.25-s detection time per command (4 s gaze focus + 0.25 s feedback provision)	0 BPM	—

the total number of commands executed within menu m, B_m is the ITR in bits/trial for menu m, and M refers to the total number of menus used to accomplish the specified task goal.

$$ITR_{overall} = \frac{60}{t_{tot}} \sum_{m=1}^{M} N_m B_m \qquad (5)$$

Although incorrect non-control state classifications did not result in any accuracy penalties, the average command detection time increased, leading to ITR drops.

For the most part, the adopted statistical evaluation technique was similar to that outlined in Sect. 6.2 (**Stage 2**). This involved the computation of 95% CIs, to approximate a range of plausible values for participants' true global mean usability results. Moreover, depending on the data distribution, the Binomial test or One Sample t-test were used to compare participants' mean usability scores against established benchmarks, permitting for a more accurate understanding of Boggle's true usability levels. Across all statistical test runs, an alpha level of $\alpha = .05$ was also assumed.

Boggle's usability is evidenced by participants' low SPS (95% CI [2.69,3.51]) and RTLX scores (95% CI [20.35,35.71]) throughout most task executions. Furthermore, high task completion rate scores (95% CI [78.61%,100%]) were achieved, with a global mean classification accuracy and ITR amounting to 90.98% (95% CI [86.52%,95.44%]) and 29.58 BPM (95% CI [27.05 BPM,32.11 BPM]) respectively. Considering all tasks executed by the different subjects, accuracies ranged between 61.29% and 100%, while ITRs fell between 11.589 BPM and 43.255 BPM. A total of 4 subjects had mean classification accuracies which were significantly higher ($p <.05$) than the benchmark score of 70% [27], yet each task's mean ITR was found to be remarkably lower ($p <.05$) than its corresponding ITR_{max} value (see Table 6). Additionally, it was noted that for the majority of tasks executed via Boggle, the achieved ITRs surpassed 13.4 BPM [27], which corresponds to the highest mean ITR reported for any of the other reviewed BCI-based browsers.

Although 4 of the 5 assigned tasks resulted in mean completion rates which were higher than the benchmark score of 78% (refer to Table 6), the 6 subjects' individual mean completion rates did not differ significantly from this benchmark ($p > .05$). Obtained SUS scores (95% CI [68.24,85.93]) are also encouraging, with One Sample t-test results indicating that subjects' global mean SUS rating is significantly higher ($p < .05$) than the established benchmark (refer to Table 6). Overall, user feedback was also quite positive and reflects Boggle's usability, with some issues and areas of potential improvements being discussed.

6.4   Stage 4 - Domain Expert Feedback

As indicated earlier, Boggle was discussed with two domain experts (E1 and E2), who provided insightful feedback on Boggle's utility as an assistive BCI-based browser. Based on their experiences, E1 and E2 asserted that the web has the capacity to "open up the world" for motor-impaired individuals. E2 added that, to date, a sizeable portion of target users are excluded from Internet access, either because "no suitable access method is available to them" or because they are unable to handle the "increased complexity of web browsing".

As for the implemented BCI browser, the experts found the continuous stimuli flickering to be quite tedious, yet thought Boggle included all core functionality and also had a "very good response time". E1 particularly liked the browser's "simplification aspect", which makes it "ideal for individuals with limited cognitive abilities". All in all, both E1 and E2 believe that Boggle could positively impact target users' lives, giving them a sense of independence, which would ultimately translate to a "reduced reliance on caregivers".

7   Conclusion

Motivated by the pervasiveness of existing web accessibility barriers, especially those faced by individuals living with severe motor impairments, this work builds upon our initial study's findings [5], to investigate the applicability of web-native technologies for developing an SSVEP-driven BCI-based browser.

Stage 1 of this work re-confirmed the outcomes of our first study [5], and demonstrated web technologies' applicability for generating SSVEP stimuli, with a slight performance edge being observed for CSS and Chrome in high-load rendering conditions. Based on this, and a thorough review of literature to shortlist features necessary for building an accessible web browser, Boggle's initial prototype was designed and developed. Using this first design as a starting point, insights into the most adequate browser interaction patterns were primarily gained via usability metrics and participants' feedback throughout **Stage 2**, which involved a two-phased iterative UCD process. At this point, insights into interaction issues were gleaned, leading to further browser enhancements, which altogether shaped Boggle into a more usable tool. Results indicate that, when operated via asynchronous BCI-based control (**Stage 3**), in most cases, users found Boggle to be highly usable, as shown by the relatively high usability scores attained. All six subjects also maintained satisfactory online BCI performance, with mean accuracies and ITRs ranging between 84.93%–98.33% and 25.36 BPM–34.94 BPM respectively. Domain experts' feedback also complements these findings and demonstrates Boggle's potential for use by target users in a real-world context (**Stage 4**).

Overall, obtained results are very promising as they show that Boggle fared better than existing SSVEP-based BCI browsers, namely WeBB, whose maximum accuracy amounted to 90.7%, while the highest recorded ITR was as low as 4.68 BPM. Boggle's global mean ITR (29.58 BPM) also surpasses that of the reviewed BCI-based browsers, for which the highest reported mean ITR amounted to 13.4 BPM. In contrast to WeBB, Boggle is flexible and portable, since it is built using a web-native and cross-platform framework (Electron) that can be installed across major operating systems. Boggle also introduces other important advances over existing browsers, including its support for stimuli approximations, which permit enhanced user interaction efficiency, through the presentation of an increased number of SSVEP targets.

Based on these encouraging outcomes, one can conclude that Boggle, a cross-platform SSVEP-driven web browser, can serve as a suitable assistive technology for individuals with severe motor impairments, affording unrestricted web access through online and asynchronous BCI-based interaction.

References

1. Abe, K., Owada, K., Ohi, S., Ohyama, M.: A system for web browsing by eye-gaze input. Electron. Commun. Jpn. **91**(5), 11–18 (2008)
2. Bensch, M., et al.: Nessi: an EEG-controlled web browser for severely paralyzed patients. Comput. Intell. Neurosci. **2007** (2007)
3. Bose, J., Singhai, A., Patankar, A.A., Kumar, A.: Attention sensitive web browsing. In: Proceedings of the 9th Annual ACM India Conference, pp. 147–152 (2016)
4. Brumberg, J.S., Pitt, K.M., Mantie-Kozlowski, A., Burnison, J.D.: Brain-computer interfaces for augmentative and alternative communication: a tutorial. Am. J. Speech Lang. Pathol. **27**(1), 1–12 (2018)
5. Camilleri, A., Porter, C., Camilleri, T.: Towards accurate browser-based SSVEP stimuli generation. In: Proceedings of the 4th International Conference on Computer-Human Interaction Research and Applications, vol. 1, pp. 74–83. CHIRA. INSTICC, SciTePress (2020). https://doi.org/10.5220/0010159400740083
6. Chen, X., Wang, Y., Gao, S., Jung, T.P., Gao, X.: Filter bank canonical correlation analysis for implementing a high-speed SSVEP-based brain-computer interface. J. Neural Eng. **12**(4), 046008 (2015)
7. Ci, B., Rule, R.O.: Confidence intervals. Lancet **1**(8531), 494–497 (1987)
8. Dentzel, Z.: How the internet has changed everyday life. Change: 19 Key Essays on How the Internet is Changing Our Lives (2013)
9. Di Russo, F., Spinelli, D.: Electrophysiological evidence for an early attentional mechanism in visual processing in humans. Vision. Res. **39**(18), 2975–2985 (1999)
10. Electron: Electron. https://www.electronjs.org/. Accessed 24 June 2021
11. Friman, O., Volosyak, I., Graser, A.: Multiple channel detection of steady-state visual evoked potentials for brain-computer interfaces. IEEE Trans. Biomed. Eng. **54**(4), 742–750 (2007)
12. Gembler, F., Stawicki, P., Volosyak, I.: Suitable number of visual stimuli for SSVEP-based BCI spelling applications. In: Rojas, I., Joya, G., Catala, A. (eds.) IWANN 2017. LNCS, vol. 10306, pp. 441–452. Springer, Cham (2017). https://doi.org/10.1007/978-3-319-59147-6_38

13. Guger Technologies: g.tec. https://www.gtec.at/. Accessed 26 June 2021
14. İşcan, Z., Nikulin, V.V.: Steady state visual evoked potential (SSVEP) based brain-computer interface (BCI) performance under different perturbations. PLoS ONE **13**(1), e0191673 (2018)
15. Nielsen, J.: Usability 101: introduction to usability. https://www.nngroup.com/articles/usability-101-introduction-to-usability/. Accessed 28 June 2021
16. Sauro, J.: 10 things to know about the single ease question (SEQ). https://measuringu.com/seq10/. Accessed 15 July 2021
17. Sauro, J.: Measuring usability with the system usability scale (SUS). https://measuringu.com/sus/. Accessed 11 July 2021
18. Sauro, J.: Measuring user confidence in usability tests. https://measuringu.com/measuring-confidence/. Accessed 12 July 2021
19. Sauro, J.: What is a good task-completion rate? https://measuringu.com/task-completion/. Accessed 17 July 2021
20. Juang, K., Jasen, F., Katrekar, A., Ahn, J., Duchowski, A.T.: Use of eye movement gestures for web browsing. Computer Science Department, Clemson University, p. 7 (2005). Available as early as Jan 1
21. Karim, A.A., et al.: Neural internet: web surfing with brain potentials for the completely paralyzed. Neurorehabil. Neural Repair **20**(4), 508–515 (2006)
22. King, A., Evans, G., Blenkhorn, P.: WebbIE: a web browser for visually impaired people. In: Proceedings of the 2nd Cambridge Workshop on Universal Access and Assistive Technology, Springer-Verlag, London, UK, pp. 35–44. Citeseer (2004)
23. Kumar, C., Menges, R., Müller, D., Staab, S.: Chromium based framework to include gaze interaction in web browser. In: Proceedings of the 26th International Conference on World Wide Web Companion, pp. 219–223 (2017)
24. Leeb, R., Friedman, D., Müller-Putz, G.R., Scherer, R., Slater, M., Pfurtscheller, G.: Self-paced (asynchronous) BCI control of a wheelchair in virtual environments: a case study with a tetraplegic. Comput. Intell. Neurosci. **2007** (2007)
25. Liu, Y., et al.: Implementation of SSVEP based BCI with Emotiv EPOC. In: 2012 IEEE International Conference on Virtual Environments Human-Computer Interfaces and Measurement Systems (VECIMS), pp. 34–37. IEEE (2012)
26. Mankoff, J., Dey, A., Batra, U., Moore, M.: Web accessibility for low bandwidth input. In: Proceedings of the Fifth International ACM Conference on Assistive Technologies, pp. 17–24 (2002)
27. Mugler, E.M., Ruf, C.A., Halder, S., Bensch, M., Kubler, A.: Design and implementation of a P300-based brain-computer interface for controlling an internet browser. IEEE Trans. Neural Syst. Rehabil. Eng. **18**(6), 599–609 (2010)
28. Nicolas-Alonso, L.F., Gomez-Gil, J.: Brain computer interfaces, a review. Sensors **12**(2), 1211–1279 (2012)
29. Nooh, A.A., Yunus, J., Daud, S.M.: A review of asynchronous electroencephalogram-based brain computer interface systems. In: International Conference on Biomedical Engineering and Technology IPCBEE, vol. 11, pp. 55–59 (2011)
30. Porta, M., Ravelli, A.: WeyeB, an eye-controlled web browser for hands-free navigation. In: 2009 2nd Conference on Human System Interactions, pp. 210–215. IEEE (2009)
31. Rezazadeh, Z., Sheikhani, A.: An SSVEP-based brain-computer interface to navigate in a virtual home. In: Proceedings of the 7th International Conference on Bioscience, Biochemistry and Bioinformatics, pp. 22–27 (2017)
32. Rutter, R., et al.: Web Accessibility: Web Standards and Regulatory Compliance. Apress, Berkeley (2007)

33. Saboor, A., Benda, M., Gembler, F., Volosyak, I.: Word prediction support model for SSVEP-based BCI web speller. In: Rojas, I., Joya, G., Catala, A. (eds.) IWANN 2019. LNCS, vol. 11506, pp. 430–441. Springer, Cham (2019). https://doi.org/10.1007/978-3-030-20521-8_36

34. Saboor, A., et al.: A browser-driven SSVEP-based BCI web speller. In: 2018 IEEE International Conference on Systems, Man, and Cybernetics (SMC), pp. 625–630. IEEE (2018)

35. Salkind, N.J.: Encyclopedia of Research Design, vol. 1. Sage (2010)

36. Schlogl, A., Kronegg, J., Huggins, J., Mason, S.: 19 evaluation criteria for BCI research. Toward Brain-Comput. Interfacing **327** (2007)

37. Seltman, H.J.: Experimental design and analysis (2012)

38. Speier, W., Arnold, C., Pouratian, N.: Evaluating true BCI communication rate through mutual information and language models. PLoS ONE **8**(10), e78432 (2013)

39. Teplan, M., et al.: Fundamentals of EEG measurement. Meas. Sci. Rev. **2**(2), 1–11 (2002)

40. Tomori, O., Moore, M.: The neurally controllable internet browser (BrainBrowser). In: CHI 2003 Extended Abstracts on Human Factors in Computing Systems, pp. 796–797 (2003)

41. Vella, D.: Investigating gaze interaction usability for web browsing. B.S. thesis, University of Malta (2019)

42. Walter, S., Quigley, C., Andersen, S.K., Mueller, M.M.: Effects of overt and covert attention on the steady-state visual evoked potential. Neurosci. Lett. **519**(1), 37–41 (2012)

43. Wolpaw, J.R., et al.: Brain-computer interface technology: a review of the first international meeting. IEEE Trans. Rehabil. Eng. **8**(2), 164–173 (2000)

44. Yehia, A.G., Eldawlatly, S., Taher, M.: WeBB: a brain-computer interface web browser based on steady-state visual evoked potentials. In: 2017 12th International Conference on Computer Engineering and Systems (ICCES), pp. 52–57. IEEE (2017)

45. Yin, J., Jiang, D., Hu, J.: Design and application of brain-computer interface web browser based on VEP. In: International Conference on Future BioMedical Information Engineering. FBIE 2009, pp. 77–80. IEEE (2009)

46. Zerafa, R., Camilleri, T., Bartolo, K., Camilleri, K.P., Falzon, O.: Reducing the training time for the SSVEP-based music player application. Biomed. Phys. Eng. Express **3**(3), 034001 (2017)

Exploring a Cognitive Interface to Support Trust and Acceptability of Future Users of Autonomous Vehicles

Benjamin Chateau[1]([⊠]), Hélène Unrein[2], and Jean-Marc André[2]

[1] CATIE, 1 avenue Dr Albert Schweitzer, 33400 Talence, France
`bc@uxit.fr`
[2] IM UMR 5218, ENSC-BDX INP, 33400 Talence, France
`{hunrei910e,jean-marc.andre}@ensc.fr`

Abstract. The lack of acceptability of future autonomous vehicles (AVs) is a challenge for investing in their design. Driving simulators offer opportunities to imagine and test possible solutions to achieve acceptability. The solution studied here is a cognitive interface based on theories of mental representation, under the assumption that they are the basis of acceptability and trust. A first interface was designed and then tested by users on board a simulator. The interviews carried out at the end of the tests allowed characterization of user fears regarding self-driving vehicles and identification of ways of improving the initial concept. In particular, there is a need for information on the functioning and decisions of the AV. This information is essential for the construction of a mental representation that is sufficiently rich to establish a satisfactory level of confidence. However, information about AV functioning is not an end in itself, but a necessity to help in decision making processes according to the situation. For this reason, the second version of the interface will be connected to an empathic function in order to inform and reassure the user when his cognitive and emotional states require it.

Keywords: Autonomous vehicle · Acceptability · Trust · Situational awareness · Empathetic interface · Mental representation

1 Theorical Background

1.1 Context of the Study

Most car manufacturers have started to integrate self-driving functions into their vehicles. Some have already reached a fairly high level, where the vehicle is able to drive autonomously under the active supervision of the driver [1]. Some countries have already paved the way for this practice. In Europe, road users (motorists, pedestrians, cyclists, etc.) are increasingly open to autonomous vehicles, but there is still a long way to go to completely convince the population [2]. European countries are focusing on autonomous vehicules through various research projects [3, 4] to build a transition adapted to their territories. These projects focus on the opportunities and impacts of autonomous vehicles and explore different levers to promote their acceptability. The acceptability of a technology can be defined by the intention of use by future users [5], in other words, this is a predictor of its adoption [6]. The solutions to measure and support the acceptability of autonomous vehicles are being studied in the SUaaVE (SUpporting acceptance of automated VEhicle) project, which includes the work presented here to expand on an earlier communication [7]. The 10 partners in this project are looking at new uses and functionalities that can be offered by a "level 4+ AV", i.e. 100% autonomous but still with manual controls. With such a vehicle, the user could rest, watch a film, or telework instead of driving. However, these on-board activities could generate negative conditions (e.g. anxiety, motion sickness, stress) which could be minimized by considering e.g., understanding of the driving situation, dynamics, comfort, etc. These 5 study axes make up the ALFRED concept presented in Fig. 1. Its objective is to optimise vehicle behaviour and level of information according to user needs. The study axis presented here, the Smart Cognitive Assistant (SCA), focuses on the user-centred design of a "cognitive" Human Machine Interface (HMI), i.e. capable of helping the user to construct a mental representation rich enough to understand the driving situation.

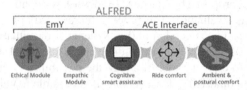

Fig. 1. ALFRED, a travel assistant from 5 axes of study. (Ethical Module, Empathetic Module, Cognitive Assistant, Conduit Comfort, Ambiant and Postural Comfort). ALFRED = Automation Level Four - Reliable Empathic Driver; EmY = EmpathY unit; ACE = Adaptive, Cognitive, Emotional [7].

Mental representation (and situational awareness) emerged as key for understanding both the principle of acceptability assessment and the trust process, but especially for achieving the supposed goal of a so-called cognitive interface. The theoretical concepts discussed are illustrated by the case of taxi use, which has notable similarities to the use of an AV.

1.2   Mental Representation to Situational Awareness in an Autonomous Vehicle

The mental representation of a device (e.g. a taxi) involves the activation in memory of specific concepts (e.g., car, driver, taximeter, yellow) or concepts related to use (e.g., airport, luggage, travel, reserved parking). Implicitly, the bricks that make up this representation are derived from previous experiences. Among these bricks, there are also event schemas [8] (e.g., the way the driver greets the customer and takes care of his luggage). Such a schema is a structure that encodes an action (goal) in memory and the intermediate actions (sub-goals, steps) necessary to achieve it [9].

To build or update a representation, an observer can spontaneously adopt the point of view of an observed actor. This is often referred to as an empathic mechanism, whereby the observer mentally simulates the actor's point of view and actions [8]. It is also an important process in social interactions: it allows e.g. two interlocutors to activate a set of shared representations on which dialogue can be based [10]. This empathic capacity is thought to be based on neural structures called mirror neurons [11, 12] that use observed behaviour to activate known action patterns in memory. The representation of the mental states of others helps the observer to understand what the actor perceives, how he formulates his goals, and how he carries out his actions [13].

These representation theories provide insight into the cognitive mechanisms at work in assessing, for example, a driver's abilities. They also show the limitations faced by the AV's user: if they cannot observe a virtual driver, how can they project themself in the driver's place and understand what they are doing? To go further, these theories are also applicable in the other direction: the driver is able to simulate the mental states of their passenger and adapt their driving. This is an avenue that is being explored in the project to support the user's situational awareness and correct negative emotions (not discussed here).

In the field of transport-related HMI, human factor specialists often substitute the psychological notion of mental representation with the more applied notion of situational awareness. The model proposed by Endsley [14] describes a continuous process of decision making and action evaluation. This process, represented in Fig. 2, is structured by three successive stages: (1) perception of the elements of the situation, (2) understanding of the situation, (3) projection of the future state. This model infers the interest of a cognitive interface to offer the user of an AV the possibility of quickly reintegrating important information on driving. For example, it is possible to help the user to detect an element of the situation (level 1), to understand its nature (danger, delay, discomfort factor, etc.; level 2), and its effects on the behaviour of the vehicle (level 3).

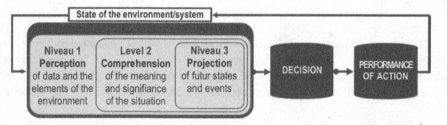

Fig. 2. Simplified model of situational awareness, based on Endsley's model (from [14]).

In addition to the principles of situational understanding, the notion of mental representation also sheds light on the possibility of assessing the acceptability of an AV based on a simulation.

Acceptance of a product is a quality valued by designers as it is closely linked to product success. This quality can be pursued using a variety of methods to improve the user experience of future products [15]. In particular, an iterative design approach can be applied, alternating design and test phases, to gradually adjust the product. During the test phases, the product is evaluated by measuring the user's attitude using questionnaires such as the TAM3 (Technology Acceptance Model, version 3) [16] or the UTAUT2 (Unified Theory of Acceptance and Use of Technology) [17]. These types of tools are designed to obtain a prediction of the acceptance of the future product from a real or simulated experiment carried out by testers (potential users). The testers are immersed in a real or simulated situation in order to construct a mental representation of the object in its context of use as accurately as possible, and then they answer the questionnaire. Each group of questionnaire items is comparable to a probe that extracts a specific fragment of the representation. For example, the first group of TAM3 items extracts the representation of the performance gain offered by the product; another group extracts the perceived ease of use, etc. The TAM3 thus offers a look at the different dimensions of product acceptability such as practical aspects (e.g. perceived usefulness and perceived ease of use), hedonic aspects (e.g. perceived pleasure), or social aspects (e.g. subjective norms), etc.

However, the acceptability of technologies based on forms of artificial intelligence (AI), such as AV, seems to be hampered by the issue of trust [18]. Trust is not addressed head-on in reference models of acceptability such as the TAM [16, 19], UTAUT [17] or the Nielsen model [5]. Nevertheless, the link between trust and acceptability has been studied for a long time and the emergence of AI has enriched the models [20]. Some determinants of trust are close to those of acceptability. Starting with attitude, which is associated with both acceptability [21] and trust [16, 18].

1.3 A View on the Attribution of Trust

On the same principle as acceptability, trust in a system is determined by various factors, including the ability to mentally imagine how it works. But first, what exactly is trust? There are many definitions of trust in a person [22]. A fairly general description would be to associate trust with "expectations, assumptions, or beliefs about the likelihood that another person's future actions will be beneficial, favourable, or at least not detrimental to one's interests" [23]. This prognosis is based on indices of attributes, such as competence [24, 25] or reliability [26].

These attributes are found in the questionnaire proposed by Jian, Bisantz and Drury [27] to measure trust in a system. In their model, they differentiate between non-trust factors (e.g. deceptive, lack of transparency...) and trust factors (e.g. reliable, understandable). The determinants of trust in a system [20, 22] are close to those of trust in a third party, especially for reliability which is fundamental for AVs [26]. Reliability can be assessed over the long term, which introduces a notion of familiarity that is favourable to trust [28]. In this case, it is possible to assign a level of trust to a target (person, group of people, object or type of object) based on observations made over the course of experiences with it. However, some situations are not supported by recurrent experiences. For example, when travelling in a taxi in a foreign country, it is necessary to quickly obtain information on the driver's ability to provide the desired result. For this purpose, it is possible to use action patterns that are based on driving experiences and that allow the user to check whether the observed actions are consistent. If so, confidence can be established. These patterns are building blocks of mental representation or situation awareness, which can be offered to the user through a specific interface.

1.4   Guidelines for an Empathetic and Cognitive Interface

The activities that can be carried out in an AV will divert the user's attention from the road. Cognitive user assistance covers two important aspects of the driving situation: the road situation and autonomous driving [29]. The road situation is composed of a static infrastructure and dynamic elements constituting a flow of information on the environment (e.g. traffic, presence of pedestrians, signs, weather, etc.). Autonomous driving corresponds to the driving actions developed from the information taken by the AV from the environment. The flow of information associated with the actions allows the user to understand the vehicle's behaviour. The processing carried out by the AV is not very visible to the user due to its speed and complexity. However, it is possible to make some of the "objectives" visible (e.g. increasing speed, anticipating a traffic jam) and to share some of the environmental information processed by the AV. This information is useful for passengers to understand the operation of the AV but also to support their representation of the situation. It is possible to communicate information symbolically or verbally through different sensory channels: visual, audio, haptic, etc.

There is a lot of information available about the AV and the road situation. The design of the HMI must respect a certain minimalism to avoid cognitive overload [17, 30]. The sensory channels (auditory, sensory, etc.) and codes (verbal, symbolic) used by the system to communicate must be carefully chosen to inform the user without overly competing with his onboard activities [31]. This is where the empathetic nature of the interface comes into play. This empathy is ideally bidirectional within a communication situation: the user must understand the operation of the AV; the AV must "understand" the state of the user to adjust its level of information. According to the principle of iterative design, the first version of the interface provides a standard level of information. This information level is optimised in a second phase, based on user feedback and future measurements of the passenger's cognitive and emotional states (see Fig. 1: Empathic module).

Within the framework of an iterative design, a first design phase was initiated based on the first principles: informing about the situation and informing about the actions of the AV. An initial interface mock-up was developed, with a view to refining the nature of the information presented and its mode of presentation on the basis of a user test.

2   Interface Description

To follow the above principles, the design of the interface has been made to highlight data on the road situation and on the actions or operation of the AV.

2.1   Information on Traffic Situation

For data on the road situation, functions available on recent vehicles, such as a Tesla, were used i.e. detection of other road users, traffic signs, and weather, and detection of the road configuration (e.g. presence of an intersection). Information on the type of road (e.g. town, country, motorway, car park) is provided to infer appropriate behaviour for the uses and risks of each type of road. A GPS was initially desired, but this function involved developments that were too extensive for the project. However, geolocation information (street name) was added. The implementation of the information presented in Fig. 2 refers to the following functions:

- *The Radar* indicates on a grid the presence of other users around "my car" (blue dot). Other vehicles are shown with a colored dot according to the risk of collision (low = green; medium = orange; high = red).

  Each cell corresponds to a time distance related to safe distances. For example, a vehicle travelling in the same direction is displayed in green (peripheral cells of the radar) if safety distances are respected. If this vehicle is too close, it turns orange and flashes to indicate a risk. If a vehicle follows a different trajectory (perpendicular or opposite) it is displayed in red. The cells in which pedestrians or bicycles are present are highlighted (see the cell in the top right corner of the radar).

  By comparing the radar to a real situation presented, we can see that a glance at the radar captures more information on other road users than a glance at the real environment.
- *The contextual flow* related for example to the presence of an intersection, the state of the road, etc. The displays of the type of road (e.g. urban, motorway) and the weather are permanent, the other information disappears when its becomes obsolete.
- *The signage flow* that impacts driving only (e.g., speed limit, pedestrian crossing). Other signs are ignored (e.g. parking entrance, direction, etc.). Each item disappears when it becomes obsolete.

2.2 Information on the Functioning of the Vehicle

Information about vehicle operation was further considered in view of project constraints and limitations on data from the simulator. First of all, information on the situation was considered as information that the AV is able to process since it is displayed. Secondly, in the European project, information about the vehicle operation was not only about driving, but also about comfort services, such as driving dynamics and empathic functions. Finally, we were not able to recover satisfactory information on actions planned by the simulator: neither on route, nor on speed variations to negotiate a bend, for example. For vehicle actions, only speed information was available, from which the interface was able to calculate accelerations and decelerations. The implementation of this information presented in Fig. 3 refers to the following functions:

- *Traveling (i2 and i3)*, with information about speed, autonomy (battery) and distance remaining. Arrows above and below the speed indicate the acceleration or braking process.
- *The AV*, with a general status icon (i4: mechanical and computer), and an icon related to current driving dynamics (i5: calm, normal, sporty).
- *The passenger*, with an icon for the state of monitoring (i6: operational or not), and an icon for the activity detected (i7: attentive, rest, daydreaming/reflection, oral communication, reading/screen). The emotional state is not displayed so as not to accentuate a possible negative emotion (e.g. fear, sadness, anger).

Fig. 3. Correspondence of the interface fields: i1 = contextual information; i2 = autonomy and remaining distance; i3 = speed, acceleration and deceleration; i4 = technical status of the AV; i5 = dynamics; i6 = passenger status detection capability; i7 = passenger status; s1 = radar; s2 = conditions; s3 = signaling; s4 = location. (Color figure online)

Fig. 4. Visual of the HMI implementation on the ScanerStudio 1.9 simulator. The image (taken from a video) allows to see on the radar the presence of a pedestrian (yellow square) and a distant car on the right lane (green circle). (Color figure online)

3 First Version of the Interface Tested

The first version of the cognitive interface (CI) was connected to a realistic driving simulator (see Fig. 4) and the first test compared acceptability and confidence levels of an AV equipped with the interface vs. without the interface. The second test identified user needs based on an interview.

3.1 Method

After a hands-on phase in manual and autonomous driving, users performed three 100% autonomous driving scenarios of about 15 min each. A total of 40 experienced drivers (minimum 3 years of regular experience) participated, 20 were equipped with the CI, and 20 were not. Of the 40 participants, 4 were excluded from the study after having been cyber-sickness. Participants completed two questionnaires at the end of the driving experiment.

The first questionnaire assessed acceptability based on a French adaptation of the UTAUT [17]. This questionnaire has 9 dimensions (Performance Expectancy; Effort Expectancy; Social Influence; Facilitating Conditions; Hedonic Motivation; Price Value; Habit; Behavioral Intention; Use), each composed of 3 or 4 items. The Price Value dimension was of little relevance at this stage of the study and was removed. The Use dimension predicts the use of different functionalities of a device. This dimension was ignored in this study as the two devices compared were identical, with the exception of the presence of the interface, whose effect on acceptability was being assessed. A final acceptability score was calculated in two steps: a score for each dimension from the average of the associated items, and then the acceptability score from the average of the dimension scores.

The second questionnaire assessed trust [27]. It had 10 items, half of which were negatively valenced. The confidence score was obtained by first inverting the 5 negative scales and then averaging the 10 items.

Finally, the participants were interviewed orally to collect their impressions of autonomous driving. The interviews focused on the following 8 themes (1) Opinion of the experimentation; (2) Opinion of the autonomous vehicles; (3) Opinion of the simulator; (4) Description of the tablet from a visual; (5) Usefulness of the tablet; (6) Defects of the tablet; (7) Additional needs for information or functions; (8) Optional or annoying information on the tablet. The participants were invited to talk freely about the experience, and then they were directed to the targeted themes if necessary. They were then invited to discuss the visual interface.

3.2 Results

• Assessment of Acceptability and Trust

First, analysis of the internal consistency of the scales was carried out using a Cronbach's Alpha test [32]. The test focuses on each of the 7 dimensions of the UTAUT, for which the Alpha was between 0.66 and 0.94 (m = 0.80). The full UTAUT Alpha, calculated from the 7 dimension scores, was 0.85, that is an acceptable consistency. The same analysis carried out on the Trust questionnaire (12 input items) returned an alphla of 0,91; that is near the top threshold suggesting too much consistency.

A second analysis focused on the impact of the tablet on the evaluation of the autonomous vehicle in each dimension. For this, a Friedman ANOVA was carried out (via SPSS) on the scores given by users in conditions WITH tablet versus WITHOUT tablet. The results of the analysis are presented in Table 1. No significant effect of the presence or absence of the HMI appears on the evaluation of the Acceptability (UTAUT) of the autonomous vehicle. Similarly, no effect of the HMI is observed on the assessment of Trust (TR) in the autonomous vehicle, nor on any dimension of acceptability (BI, EE, FC, HM, HT, PE, PV and SI).

A third analysis presents the overall averages per dimension. The objective is to visually identify the dimensions that have the greatest impact on the final score. The graph presented in Fig. 5 shows the score for Trust (TR), Acceptability (UTAUT), and for the 7 dimensions used in the UTAUT. Interestingly, it is possible to distinguish two groups whose dimensions diverge by more than 1 standard deviation from the UTAUT score: on the one hand, EE and FC pull the UTAUT up, and on the other hand, HT, PE and SI pull the UTAUT down.

Table 1. Friedman's ANOVA per dimension: Trust (TR), Acceptability (UTAUT), Behavioural Intention (BI), Effort Expectancy, (EE) Facilitating Condition, (FC) Hedonic Motivation (HM), Habits (HT), Performance Expectancy (PE), Social Influence (SI).

Dimension	ANOVA	Sum of squares	df	Average square	F	Sig.
TR	Inter-G	1,556	1	1,556	1,056	0,311
	Total	51,66	35			
UTAUT	Inter-G	0,607	1	0,607	0,531	0,471
	Total	39,516	35			
BI	Inter-G	8,407	1	8,407	2,696	0,11
	Total	114,432	35			
EE	Inter-G	1,182	1	1,182	1,054	0,312
	Total	39,311	35			
FC	Inter-G	1,259	1	1,259	0,854	0,362
	Total	51,417	35			
HM	Inter-G	0,131	1	0,131	0,043	0,837
	Total	104,083	35			
HT	Inter-G	1,382	1	1,382	0,612	0,44
	Total	78,172	35			
PE	Inter-G	4,696	1	4,696	2,749	0,107
	Total	62,775	35			
SI	Inter-G	1,124	1	1,124	0,549	0,464
	Total	70,775	35			

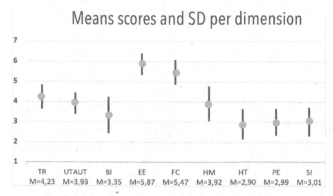

Fig. 5. Means scores (and standard deviation) per dimension: Trust (TR), Acceptability (UTAUT), Behavioural Intention (BI), Effort Expectancy, (EE), Faciliting Condition (FC), Hedonic Motivation (HM), Habits (HT), Performance Expectancy (PE), Social Influence (SI).

Table 2. Example of coding based on the verbatim interviews in the theme Additional information or functions needed. Similar verbatim statements were grouped into counted "ideas" (column n.). The ideas were then categorised into 3 defined sub-themes, and a sub-theme "Other suggestions".

Sub-thematic	Ideas	n.
Navigation information needs	Time and duration of journey	6
	GPS and journey progress	6
	Road anomalies (incidents, risks, traffic…)	7
	Touristic information	1
Need for information and functions related to autonomous driving	Wake up or stop if inattentive/sleepy	7
	Audible + visual alarm in case of emergency recovery	2
	Info if VA mode active, for User and road users	3
	Management of the speed and movements of the VA, to anticipate	6
	Decision process, what the VA understands, how it anticipates	15
	Information on the ability to handle the situation well	10
Information needs to support road situation awareness	Video monitoring (TNY YOLO, LIDAR…)	3
	Types of vehicles: autonomous, manual, trucks, motorcycles, etc	2

(continued)

Table 2. (*continued*)

Sub-thematic	Ideas	n.
	Trajectory of other Vehicles	1
	Road signage	2
	Help the user to locate the road users	11
Other suggestions	Help for understanding/general tutorial	3
	Categorization of information, more visibility	3
	Ejector seat	1
	Music	2
	Check-up, technical information	4

• Data from the Interviews

In sum, 570 ideas were identified and divided amongst the eight themes. Overall, the participants were very satisfied with the experience. They were enthusiastic about the idea of delegating leadership but expressed limited confidence. The main findings are as follows. Firstly, most of the needs expressed by the participants without an interface were on the CI. It should be noted that participants who saw the CI in operation had a good overall understanding of the functions presented, whereas the descriptions were more hesitant and unclear for the others, especially for the RADAR function and the accelerometer. Similarly, an excess of information was reported and a lack of meaning of the icons relating to the status of the passenger and the vehicle. Finally, data on additional information or function requirements was particularly needed to further develop the concept. Table 2 shows the coding of the verbatim reports produced on the theme of maintenance.

4 Discussion

• Discussion on the Assessment of Acceptability and Trust

The analyses did not find any effect of CI on the assessment of acceptability or trust. These results are surprising because the CI frequently met needs identified by users. The explanation put forward here is that users paid more attention to the simulation than to the CI, thus reducing the impact of the CI on the their representation of the AV. To increase the impact of the CI on user mental representation, 3 possibilities are proposed: (1) improving the experimental task to induce the stated need for information in reality; (2) adding sound and visual prompts to draw attention to the CI, (3) adjusting the presentation and level of information to situational needs.

Regarding the overall analysis of acceptability, it is interesting to note that the facilitating conditions (knowledge, information, technical compatibility) and the ease of use are perceived very positively. The real impacts are observed on the side of performance and social influence. In other words, the simulation did not convince the users about the performance of the AVs. The low performance score could be related to the social influence score given the lack of acceptability of the population towards AVs [2].

• Interview Data

The interviews highlighted areas for improvement for the next round of the CI. The design of the new CI will have to meet the challenge of following these improvement paths while integrating new functions related to the other modules developed in the project. The technical architecture (IT) and the main functions (radar, accelerometer) can be preserved and improved. Some examples of improvements are listed below:

- Concerning the radar, the differences in the "with" and "without" interface conditions indicate a learning process. In other words, the radar is not very intuitive. It had a "discrete" display, i.e. it displayed elements of the situation in boxes, to situate them in relation to the vehicle. This display required a recoding of the spatial information from the simulator, which proved to be technically quite complex. To follow the suggestions of some users, it would be interesting to explore a more "continuous" display, for example by presenting the elements of the situation on a dynamic map. This solution seems more complex, but in reality the situation is easily transposable thanks to the OpenDrive protocol [33].
- The level of information will have to be adjusted according to needs expressed by the users. For example, they have indicated that they want to be reassured about the AV's ability to identify signage, rather than being informed about the signs themselves. Currently, 8 items can be displayed simultaneously for 30 s; a solution would be to display only the last sign for a few seconds and then replace them with the default speed limit, or a new sign if necessary.
- Finally, regarding visual density, the current interface highlights too many framed, coloured and juxtaposed elements. More subtle solutions should be explored to give visual priority to the most important elements in a given situation.

Other elements could have a significant impact on the redesign of the CI. Some participants mentioned a lack of appeal of the CI because it is positioned too low. However, raising the CI means hiding the field of vision. One solution would be to place the CI horizontally. Its attractiveness could also be increased with a sound dimension. Based on the empathic module, gentle sound cues could be emitted when the user is not paying attention to the road or the interface. These cues would focus on the location of other road users and emergency manoeuvres, which are frequently mentioned by the participants as being of concern.

Finally, the next version of the CI will be connected to the comfort modules mentioned in the introduction. The changes will include a control and information area linked to these modules. This area will replace elements of the initial CI that were not very functional or well understood, such as information regarding the vehicle and the user.

5 Conclusion

Often, product developments are driven by integration of new technologies into everyday objects or professional tools. In other words, designers look for use cases for technologies designed by their engineers, this is called "techno push" design. This study put into practice the opposite approach: knowledge about humans and their needs in a given situation was the starting point for a so-called "user-centred design". The theoretical foundations around mental representation outlined a first concept of AV control that responded, at least theoretically, to the needs formulated by a sample of users. On the technology side, this approach implies initially using existing software and hardware solutions, and reworking the developments needed to make them work together. The first prototype is not fully functional or very reliable, but it is sufficient to allow users to imagine its use.

In terms of methodology, user interviews proved to be a powerful tool for identifying areas of improvement for the interface, but also, more broadly, for gathering participant opinions on the future technology. At this stage of development, quantitative evaluations did not prove relevant for an object that was not yet fully functional. One explanation could be that the current interface was not functional enough to qualitatively or quantitatively enrich the mental representation of the IL. The next round of development will focus on an interface that is sufficiently finalised to observe an acceptability benefit for the (virtual) autonomous vehicles that are equipped with it.

Acknowledgments. SUaaVE project has received funding from the European Union's Horizon 2020 research and innovation programme under grant agreement No 814999.

References

1. Endsley, M.R.: Autonomous driving systems: a preliminary naturalistic study of the Tesla model S. J. Cogn. Eng. Decis. Mak. **11**(3), 225–238 (2017). https://doi.org/10.1177/155534 3417695197
2. Bel, M., Coeugnet, S., Watteau, P.: Monographie: acceptabilité du véhicule autonome. Manuscrit livré par Vedecom le 25 mars 2019 à la Direction Générale des Infrastructures, des Transports et de la Mer (DGITM) (2019)
3. BRAVE European Project (2021). https://www.brave-project.eu. Accessed 12 Sep 2021
4. Autopilot European Project (2020). https://autopilot-project.eu. Accessed 24 Feb 2020
5. Nielsen, J.: Usability Engineering. Academic Press, Boston (1993)
6. Davis, F.D.: Perceived usefulness, perceived ease of use, and user acceptance of information technology. MIS Q. **13**, 319–339 (1989)
7. Chateau, B., Unrein, H., André, J.-M.: Exploring empathetic and cognitive interfaces for autonomous vehicles. In: Proceedings of the 4th International Conference on Computer-Human Interaction Research and Applications. SCITEPRESS - Science and Technology Publications (2020). https://doi.org/10.5220/0010130701390144
8. Hard, B., Recchia, G., Tversky, B.: The shape of action. J. Exp. Psychol. Gen. **140**, 586–604 (2011). https://doi.org/10.1037/a0024310
9. Zacks, J., Tversky, B.: Event structure in perception and conception. Psychol. Bull. **127**, 3–21 (2001)
10. Knutsen, D., Le Bigot, L.: The influence of reference acceptance and reuse on conversational memory traces. J. Exp. Psychol. Learn. Mem. Cogn. **41**(2), 574–585 (2015). https://doi.org/10.1037/xlm0000036
11. Sinigaglia, C., Rizzolatti, G.: Through the looking glass: self and others. Conscious. Cogn. **20**(1), 6474 (2011). https://doi.org/10.1016/j.concog.2010.11.012

12. Lamm, C., Batson, C.D., Decety, J.: The neural substrate of human empathy: effects of perspective-taking and cognitive appraisal. J. Cogn. Neurosci. **19**(1), 4258 (2007). https://doi.org/10.1162/jocn.2007.19.1.42

13. Davis, M.H.: Measuring individual differences in empathy: evidence for a multidimensional approach. J. Pers. Soc. Psychol. **44**, 113–126 (1983). https://doi.org/10.1037/0022-3514.44.1.113

14. Endsley, M.R., Jones, D.G.: Designing for Situation Awareness: An Approach to User-Centered Design, 2nd edn. Taylor & Francis, London (2012)

15. Lallemand, C., Gronier, G.: Méthodes de Design UX: 30 Méthodes Fondamentales Pour Concevoir des Expériences Optimales. Eyrolles, Paris (2018)

16. Politis, I., Langdon, P., Bradley, M., Skrypchuk, L., Mouzakitis, A., Clarkson, P.J.: Designing autonomy in cars: a survey and two focus groups on driving habits of an inclusive user group, and group attitudes towards autonomous cars. In: Di Bucchianico, G., Kercher, P.F. (eds.) AHFE 2017. AISC, vol. 587, pp. 161–173. Springer, Cham (2018). https://doi.org/10.1007/978-3-319-60597-5_15

17. Venkatesh, V., Thong, J.Y.L., Xu, X.: Consumer acceptance and use of information technology: extending the unified theory of acceptance and use of technology. MIS Q. **36**, 157–178 (2012)

18. Wintersberger, P., Frison, A.-K., Riener, A., von Sawitzky, T.: Fostering user acceptance and trust in fully automated vehicles: evaluating the potential of augmented reality. PRESENCE: Virtual Augmented Reality **27**(1), 46–62 (2019). https://doi.org/10.1162/pres_a_00320

19. Bastien, J.M.C., Scapin, D.L.: Ergonomic criteria for the evaluation of human-computer interfaces. Rapport Technique, INRIA (0156) (1993)

20. Hegner, S.M., Beldad, A.D., Brunswick, G.J.: In automatic we trust: investigating the impact of trust, control, personality characteristics, and extrinsic and intrinsic motivations on the acceptance of autonomous vehicles. Int. J. Hum. Comput. Interact. **35**(19), 1769–1780 (2019). https://doi.org/10.1080/10447318.2019.1572353

21. Davis, F.D., Venkatesh, V.: A critical assessment of potential measurement biases in the technology acceptance model: three experiments. Int. J. Hum. Comput. Stud. **45**(1), 19–45 (1996)

22. Rajaonah, B.: Rôle de la confiance de l'opérateur dans son interaction avec une machine autonome sur la coopération homme-machine. Thèse de doctorat de l'Université Paris 8. 27 février 2006. 234 (2006)

23. Robinson, S.L.: Trust and breach of the psychological contract. Adm. Sci. Q. **41**, 574–599 (1996)

24. Degenne, A.: Types d'interactions, formes de confiance et relations. Revista hispana para el análisis de redes sociales, 16. REDES (2009)

25. Karsenty, L.: Comment maintenir des relations de confiance et construire du sens face à une crise? Le travail humain **78**(2), 141 (2015). https://doi.org/10.3917/th.782.0141

26. Payre, W., Cestac, J., Delhomme, P.: Intention to use a fully automated car: attitudes and a priori acceptability. Transp. Res. F Traffic Psychol. Behav. **27**, 252–263 (2014). https://doi.org/10.1016/j.trf.2014.04.009

27. Jian, J.-Y., Bisantz, A.M., Drury, C.G.: Foundations for an empirically determined scale of trust in automated systems. Int. J. Cogn. Ergon. **4**(1), 53–71 (2000). https://doi.org/10.1207/S15327566IJCE0401_04

28. Rajaonah, B.: Rôle de la confiance de l'opérateur dans son interaction avec une machine autonome sur la coopération humain-machine. Thèse de doctorat de Psychologie Cognitive. Université Paris 8 (2000)

29. Bengler, K., Rettenmaier, M., Fritz, N., Feierle, A.: From HMI to HMIs: towards an HMI framework for automated driving. Information **11**(2), 61 (2020). https://doi.org/10.3390/inf011020061

30. Maeda, J.: The Laws of Simplicity. MIT Press, Cambridge (2006)
31. Wickens, C.: Multiple resources and performance prediction. Theor. Issues Ergon. Sci. **3**, 159–177 (2002)
32. Howell, D., Yzerbyt, V., Bestgen, Y.: Méthodes statistiques en sciences humaines. De Boeck, Bruxelles (2008)
33. Association for Stadardization of Automation and Measuring Systems. ASAMA Open Drive. ASAMA, Standards (2021). https://www.asam.net/standards/detail/opendriv/

Visualizing Critical Objectives in Omnichannel Management Through Mental Models: The Application of an Assortment Integration Context

Gültekin Cakir[1]([⊠]) [iD], Marija Bezbradica[2], and Markus Helfert[1]

[1] Maynooth University, Maynooth, Ireland
{gueltekin.cakir,markus.helfert}@mu.ie
[2] Dublin City University, Dublin, Ireland
marija.bezbradica@dcu.ie

Abstract. Channel Integration is a crucial task for retailers in order to generate a seamless customer experience. This is particularly the case for assortments. Customers expect an identical assortment along all channels or customer confusion can occur, potentially leading to purchase abandonment or postponement and thus to losses in sales. Mental models can help to simplify complex systems and behaviour and can support managers in decision-making processes. This paper builds on a mental model approach to visualize the dynamics and trade-offs of the three critical objectives in omnichannel assortment management: assortment integration, customer confusion reduction, and purchase postponement/abandonment reduction, to assist retailers in decision-making through the depiction of different scenarios and objective achievements. Recommendations for actions are provided for each scenario eventually helping retail managers in improving understanding and decision-making for omnichannel assortment decisions.

Keywords: Omnichannel management · Mental models · Assortment integration · Channel integration · Customer experience

1 Introduction

The retail industry is experiencing tremendous development from different directions and is undergoing a major transformation towards "digital retail", a combination of traditional retail and digital technologies with the aim to integrate all channels in a seamless manner [1–3]. Within this transformation process towards omnichannel retailing which is additionally accelerated by the impact of the COVID-19 pandemic [4, 5], the generation of a seamless customer experience represents the major leading objective for retailers [6, 7]. Channel integration activities can facilitate a seamless transition across channels for the customers and is therefore regarded as key to realize for an omnichannel approach [8]. As studies show, channel integration is positively related to retail performance [9, 10].

A. Holzinger et al. (Eds.): CHIRA 2020, CCIS 1609, pp. 139–156, 2022.
https://doi.org/10.1007/978-3-031-22015-9_8

However, while attempting to implement channel integration, decision-makers in retailing are faced with balancing trade-offs in realizing customer- and shareholder-related objectives [11, 12]. Especially, the integration of the assortment across channels reflects a difficult and complex task in these activities [8, 13]. So far, there is still a lack of supporting tools for retail managers addressing these challenges. The aim of this study is to conceptualize a heuristic method assisting retail managers in reflecting the dynamics and trade-offs between selected assortment integration objectives along with recommendations for actions.

To do so, a mental model approach is applied. The concept of mental models supports the understanding of complex system behavior and can help decision-makers in making appropriate judgements and conclusions, particularly for trade-off scenarios [14]. This article builds on the conceptual propositions from the paper published in the Proceedings of the 4th International Conference on Computer-Human Interaction Research and Applications - Volume 1: WUDESHI-DR [15] that demonstrates a visual mental model approach assisting in understanding the dynamic relationships and trade-offs between the omnichannel objectives "Channel Integration", "Customer Experience Generation" and "Economic Value Creation", understood as high-level critical objectives in achieving transition into omnichannel retailing [15]. We adapt the conceptual basis and apply scenarios of omnichannel assortment integration objectives with corresponding recommendations for actions. The scenarios can help decision-makers to visualize dynamics and retrieve actionable directions in the realization of omnichannel assortment integration.

The article is organized as follows. The next section outlines the relevant theoretical background and provides definitions of the different concepts addressed in this paper. Thereafter, a brief look into related work is discussed, followed by the overview of the methodology and the main part, the proposition of a conceptual mental model capturing different scenarios in the realization of omnichannel assortment integration. Finally, the last section concludes the paper and addresses the limitations and future research of this work.

2 Theoretical Background

2.1 Objectives in Omnichannel Retailing

Omnichannel retailing is understood as the seamless and simultaneous use of all existing channels by customers [16]. The realization of omnichannel is defined as *"the synergetic management of the numerous available channels and customer touchpoints, in such a way that the customer experience across channels and the performance over channels is optimized."* [2, p. 176). Digital technologies represent herby an integral part and support integration as well as customer experience improvement activities. Technologies such as VR/AR, IoT, fog/edge computing, smart mirrors, beacons [e.g., 17, 18, 19]; AI applications [20–22] as well as customer experience-oriented concepts such as personalization [23] are utilized to achieve these goals.

The ability to integrate all existing channels is the crucial task in realizing an omnichannel approach [8, 24, 25]. Channel integration is understood as the degree to which different channels interact successfully with each other [26, 27]. The integration is required to be achieved on different levels such as on an operational level [e.g., 8], on an organizational structure level [e.g., 28] and on a strategic level to begin with [e.g., 29, 30, 31, 32]. Channel integration represents therefore a crucial objective in omnichannel management.

Along with the need for channel integration, customer experience developed to be the most significant aspect in the current retail industry today [2, 3, 33–35] and can be understood as the leading management objective [36]. It is characterized by the fact that it is a strategic objective of non-financial nature unlike typical financial objectives such as profit margin [37]. From a definition point of view, it is described as "*a multidimensional construct focusing on a customer's cognitive, emotional, behavioural, sensorial, and social responses to a firm's offerings during the customer's entire purchase journey ...*" [36, p. 71] and therefore represents a difficult construct to capture and generate.

Trade-off problems occur when goals have a conflicting relationship to each other. This happens when a decision-maker is confronted with trading off the realization of one objective against another [38, Fig. 1].

Fig. 1. Trade-off-relation between two objectives [38].

Figure 1 shows specific decisions (shown by three examples, x1, x2, and x3 on the graph) each depicting a trade-off situation where the degree of the achievement of one objective is sacrificed against the achievement of the other objective. For example, decision x3 reflects a high degree of the realization of objective 2 but a low achievement for objective 1.

It is clear that the realization of an omnichannel strategy entails dealing with conflicting objectives. Predominantly, the aspiration to generate a distinctive customer experience through seamless channel integration can conflict with shareholder-value-related business objectives [11] since a transformation towards omnichannel retailing can require significant realignment and reallocation of business resources, as well as high investments in digital technologies [e.g., 12]. Shareholder-value-related objectives are usually of financial nature and address the task in the creation of sustainable economic value (e.g., return on investment, profit, EVA).

The assumption is that superior customer experience can be achieved once channel integration is realized [e.g., 26], proposing a positive relationship between these two objectives. Ideally, as a result, economic value is created in the long term, eventually establishing the logical link of all three objectives.

2.2 Omnichannel Assortment Integration

Assortment can be described as the collection of goods or services a retailer offers to consumers [39, 40]. Consequently, in an omnichannel context, assortment represents all goods or services provided to consumers in all available channels the retailer utilizes. As a subtask in channel integration, the requirement for integration of assortment along channels is an ongoing and challenging issue discussed in current omnichannel literature [e.g., 8, 13], and an important but complex strategic decision for retailers [12, 41, 42]. The integration is usually measured by the "*[degree of] overlap of assortments between a retailer's different channels*" [43, p. 438].

Next to the degree of overlap, assortment integration between on- and offline channels can appear in different configurations. These assortment coordination types can be divided into three approaches [44]. "No integration" implies an overlap of 0%, which means both the on- and offline assortment differ completely from each other. "Partial integration" or "asymmetrical integration" is characterized by a partial overlap of assortments. Empirical studies show that asymmetric integration is the most common type in retail practice [43, 45]. Finally, "full integration" means that assortment is identical along all channels and reflects the understanding of the seamlessness feature within omnichannel shopping – meaning I as a customer can buy all items in each channel.

2.3 Mental Models

Mental models are concepts of mental representations of external systems used by individuals to describe, explain, and predict certain behavior of those systems [46]. They support and facilitate a decision-maker's judgements and decisions and are of subjective nature [47, 48] since they are created and adjusted through the interactions with real-life business systems they manage (e.g., marketing campaign management) [49].

This implies that there are assumptions and expectations based on experience and knowledge of systems behavior [14, 50]. According to Meadows et al. (1974), "*each person carries in his head a mental model, an abstraction of all his perceptions and experiences in the world, which he uses to guide his decisions…*" [51, pp. 4–5]. Similarly, Zhang-Kennedy et al. (2013) state that a mental model is a simplified internal version of a concept from reality [52].

To provide an example, Warren Buffet and Charlie Munger developed the well-known mental model of the "Circle of Competence" for decision-making in investment contexts (Fig. 2). Based on a Euler Diagram, the visualization of the mental model consists of an inner and outer circle. The inner-circle reflects one's competence as "What you know" whereas the outer-circle represents "What you think you know" [53]. The utility is to show visually the boundaries of competence in decision-making with the principle "only invest in those things you know about". Therefore, to respect your own limitations and to make investment decisions based on your actual knowledge instead of relying on knowledge "what you think you know" [15].

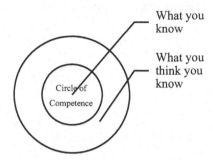

What you know

What you think you know

Fig. 2. "Circle of Competence" mental model [53].

2.4   Mental Model Visualization of Omnichannel Management Objectives

In the article "Visualising Trade-offs of Objectives in Omnichannel Management – A Mental Model Approach", [15], the concept of Venn Diagrams [54] is used to visualize a mental model arranging different scenarios depicting different states of the relationship between omnichannel management objectives, along with shared and overlapping sections. Three circles represent the critical management objectives "Channel Integration" (CI), "Customer Experience Generation" (CX), and "Economic Value Creation" (EV) (Table 1).

Table 1.   Descriptions of omnichannel objectives [15].

Objective	Description
Channel integration (CI)	This objective is realised when channels are integrated in such a way that alignment and interaction among these are ensured and operational. Realisation is driven through investments in e.g. digital technologies, restructuring efforts, or acquisition of relevant know-how
Customer experience generation (CX)	This objective is realised when a seamless transition along the customer journey across all available channels is ensured for the customer. Reflects customer-oriented objectives
Economic value creation (EV)	This objective is realised when the retailer is able to generate financial value (e.g. profitability). Reflects shareholder-value objectives

The relationship between the objectives is visible through the intersections of the circles. The larger the overlap the more complementary the two objectives are to each other, postulating a positive relationship (Fig. 3). For example, a high overlap of channel integration and customer experience would reflect a strong positive relationship.

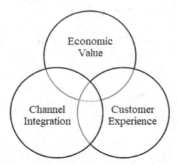

Fig. 3. Mental model visualized as a venn diagram [15].

The mental model can reflect five basic scenarios a decision-maker can be confronted with while pursuing a transition towards an omnichannel approach (Fig. 10, appendix). The following describes each of them briefly.

High CX Generation/Low EV Creation. High CX Generation/Low EV Creation. This scenario postulates a positive relationship between CI and CX. However, the achievement of EV is unsatisfactory and therefore reflects scenarios where a retailer is able to generate a distinct customer experience through effective channel integration but is unsuccessful in staying profitable at the same time. Typically, this scenario can represent retailers with a strong customer focus. The recommendation is to exploit and translate the value created through CX generation into financial outcomes and consider cost-effectiveness in CI activities at the same time to eventually improve EV.

High EV Creation/Low CX Generation. In this scenario, there is a positive relationship between CI and EV. However, there is a lack of substantial CX generation. This indicates that channel integration activities are cost-effective and do not affect profitability strongly negative but also lack distinctive CX generation as a trade-off. Retailers prioritizing profitability goals over CX generation can be associated with this scenario. It is recommended to improve and balance channel integration activities towards successful CX generation. At the same time, additional investments for these activities can be considered as well since this would ensure a sustainable approach towards CX generation.

Low CX Generation/Low EV Creation. This scenario can be regarded as the least optimal constellation since CI is not achieved, leading to no substantial CX generation nor to EV creation as a consequence. The recommendation is to initiate CI activities in order to generate distinctive CX and eventually address the industry narrative and the customers' needs. This scenario represents a pre-omnichannel setting and is not of sustainable nature.

High CX Generation/High EV Creation but no CI Achievement. In this scenario, the retailer is successful in the generation of high CX and stays profitable at the same time (high EV). However, this is not achieved through CI activities and indicates that the retailer provides high CX without relying on integrated channels. This might be the case with retailers having a strong imbalance between channels (e.g., 90% of revenue is generated offline, indicating a strong customer experience generation within a physical context, e.g. through atmospherics). It is recommended to identify and consider the potential positive impact of integrated channels on the CX generation and to improve the EV creation further.

Towards Omnichannel Approach. This constellation represents a balanced scenario between all three objectives and postulates a successful harmonization of all trade-offs. The rationale is that CI achievement leads to high CX generation evident through a high EV output as a consequence. CI activities are regarded as effective. This constellation serves as an ideal scenario and a mental aspiration towards a sustainable omnichannel approach. It is recommended to keep the balanced relationship and optimize further.

3 Related Work

There is scarce work addressing the tension between different objectives while undergoing omnichannel transformation, especially from a mental model view. However, some studies contribute to the discourse from different perspectives. The most relevant ones are discussed briefly below.

[40] propose a framework aiming at aligning strategies and actions from a market, firm, store, and customer perspective. They are linked to the overall objective "retailer profitability". The objectives and their relationships are not discussed explicitly, but the study shows that "customer experience" is a crucial strategic concept influencing the overall objective "retailer profitability". Additionally, a focus specifically on omnichannel is not intended but captured through a general industry lens. Following a qualitative grounded theory approach, [10] demonstrate that cross-channel integration is affecting sales growth positively. The work leaves out a customer experience perspective though. Similarly, [55] shows a relationship between channel integration, enabled by IT, to firm performance and considers human resources at the same time. Empirical findings underline a positive relationship and postulate efficient offering delivery and innovativeness in future offering creation. However, the context is positioned as a pre-omnichannel setting and "customer experience" is being left out in this work as well.

[56] utilize a Venn Diagram approach to decompose the business model concept into the three components value proposition (value offering), resources & competencies (value creation), and economic logic (value capturing). The visualization demonstrates the dynamics between the components with different scenarios with the overlap of all three circles reflecting a "workable business model". The authors consider the same theoretical basis, the Attention-based-view of the firm [61], as [15] and this study. Despite having a very similar approach, the work concentrates on the concept of business models

and therefore does not focus on particular objectives in retailing or omnichannel context. Similarly, [57] develop a mental model approach on the premise of the conflicting relationship between usability and security in software design. The interesting approach aligns design features with user requirements and develops a meta-model relating security, usability, and the user mental model.

Overall, related work shows a gap in linking a mental model approach to the relationships of omnichannel retailing objectives in general and assortment integration objectives in particular.

4 Methodology

Assortment decisions represent a critical and complex task in channel integration activities [8, 12, 13] and are therefore selected as an appropriate context for the mental model development. The overarching goals "channel integration", customer experience" and "economic value" [15] are mapped to the assortment objectives "assortment integration" (AI), "customer confusion reduction" (CCR), and "purchase postponement /abandonment reduction" (PPAR) (Fig. 4). Table 2 provides details and descriptions regarding the mapping. Assortment integration reflects the subset activity for channel integration [13], whereas customer confusion reduction represents a subset for customer experience [43]. An economic perspective is ensured through the concept of purchase postponement/abandonment as a behavioral consequence of customer confusion resulting in lost sales from a financial point of view [37].

The alignment of the assortment across channels represents a major challenge since customers can experience confusion when confronted with inconsistencies [12, 13, 58, 59]. For instance, a customer may identify an item of interest on the web-shop and decide to take a closer look and maybe purchase it at the physical store of the same retailer. The fact that the item may be not found in the physical store can lead to an undesired outcome/unmet expectation and thus to purchase abandonment or postponement in the short-term but also to potential image damage through bad word-of-mouth in the long-term [43, 60]. Consequently, the confusion effect should be reduced in case of identical assortments across channels [43], favoring the "full integration" type of overlap [e.g., 59].

Following [15], the intersections reflect the relationship between the objectives. The larger the overlap the more complementary the two objectives are to each other, postulating a positive relationship. For example, a high overlap of AI and CCR can represent a strong positive relationship. In this study, for simplification purposes, trade-off relationships are considered under certainty, as well as to eliminate uncertain consequences [38]. In this sense, and in line with the subjective nature of a mental model [47, 48], a non-formalized approach is followed [38].

The mental model scenarios attempt to capture the above-mentioned rationale for the relationship between the assortment objectives.

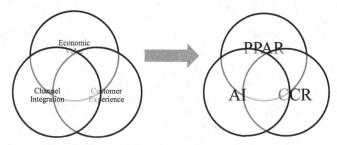

Fig. 4. Adapting high-level omnichannel management objectives into the omnichannel assortment context.

Table 2. Mapping and description of the assortment integration objectives.

Omnichannel objectives	Assortment context	Description	Literature
Channel integration	Assortment integration	The integration of different assortments across all channels. This can be reflected by full integration (assortments are identical throughout all channels), partial integration (there is partial overlap of the assortment between channels), and no integration (both the on- and offline assortments differ 100% from each other)	[8, 12, 13, 43]
Customer experience	Customer confusion reduction	Reflects a subset of customer experience. Cognitive overload can happen in case a large amount of information is needed to be processed within the shopping journey. Comparing assortments can lead to confusion the higher the dissimilarity across channels is evident. It can lead to purchase postponement and abandonment. Reducing the effect represents therefore a critical objective in assortment integration decisions	[43, 60, 62, 63]

(continued)

Table 2. (*continued*)

Omnichannel objectives	Assortment context	Description	Literature
Economic value	Purchase postponement /Abandonment reduction	Economic consequence of the customer confusion effect. The customer refrains from the purchase or postpones due to a dissatisfactory impact during the shopping journey. The aim should be therefore to mitigate the customer confusion effect in order to reduce purchase postponements/abandonments	[43, 64]

5 Mental Model Visualization of Omnichannel Assortment Integration Objectives

The developed mental model is able to reflect five basic scenarios representing different states of assortment integration objectives.

High CCR/Low PPAR.   This scenario shows a positive relationship between realizing AI and achieving CCR (Fig. 5). However, PPAR is not achieved satisfactory and is still evident. This scenario can indicate the fact that despite achieving assortment integration and reducing the customer confusion effect, purchase postponements and abandonments are still occurring, potentially highlighting the fact that other factors might influence the postponement and abandonment behavior (e.g., inefficient searching/filtering process on the web-shop, bad layout and presentation of items in the physical store). The retailers should aim to identify and mitigate those factors and differentiate the effects accordingly compared to the assortment integration activities.

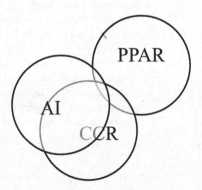

Fig. 5. High CCR/Low PPAR.

High PPAR/ Low CCR. Here, there is a positive relationship between AI and PPAR, meaning assortment integration has effectively reduced postponement/abandonment behavior (Fig. 6). However, CCR is still unsatisfactory and shows potentials for improvement. This scenario indicates that the assortment integration efforts do not mitigate the customer confusion effect but other factors leading to the reduction of postponements/abandonments. In this case, retailers should identify those factors which influence this independent from the customer confusion effect. A possible factor can be the case that not every confusion effect leads to postponement/abandonment).

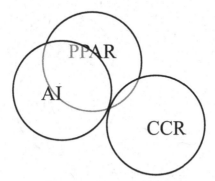

Fig. 6. High PPAR/Low CCR.

Low CCR/Low PPAR. This scenario reflects a pre-omnichannel constellation since AI is not achieved, resulting in the occurrence of the customer confusion effect and consequently purchase postponements and abandonments (Fig. 7). Here, the aim is to initiate AI in order to achieve CCR and therefore realize PPAR.

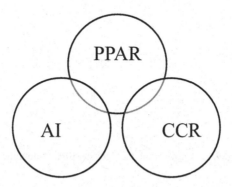

Fig. 7. Low CCR/Low PPAR.

High CCR/High PPAR. This scenario demonstrates a successful PPAR through CCR (Fig. 8). However, the CCR is not achieved through AI activities, indicating other factors mitigating the customer confusion effect. Since AI is not realized, meaning assortments across channels are different (no integration type), the customer confusion effect is not occurring. This might be the case when a retailer provides information for the customer on both channels, for example indicating the fact that "item not available on [channel]" or "item only available on [other channel]", preempting the occurrence of unmet expectations.

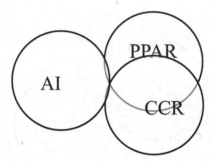

Fig. 8. High CCR/High PPAR.

Towards Omnichannel Assortment Integration. The high overlap between AI, CCR and PPAR shows a balanced and harmonized constellation between all three objectives (Fig. 9). AI leads to effective CCR and consequently to the realization of PPAR. This represents the ideal scenario and serves as an ideal mental representation of the relationships. The retailer should aim to keep the high degree of overlap and optimize further.

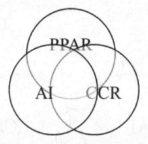

Fig. 9. Towards omnichannel assortment integration.

6   Conclusion

The challenge in realizing an omnichannel strategy is of major relevance for current retailers and demand an understanding of dynamics and trade-off relationships between critical objectives.

This article is motivated by the need for more decision-support in this regard and builds on the mental model visualization approach by [15]. The development of a heuristic method, visualizing the dynamics in omnichannel assortment integration demonstrates its utility in depicting five basic scenarios in the achievement of the assortment objectives "assortment integration", "customer confusion reduction", and "purchase postponement/abandonment reduction". With this, retail managers are able to reflect, understand and predict those scenarios with the aim to act towards the realization of omnichannel retailing.

This paper involves the following limitations. It represents a conceptual idea subject to be further developed and supported by empirical validation, such as through case studies for example. Another limitation is evident through the fact that the proposed scenarios are not capturing all relevant constellations or situations. In addition, a time and evolution point of view can help to link the different scenarios to each other and determine certain paths for omnichannel assortment integration. It is planned to provide empirical validation and further develop the dynamics in future work. Finally, in view of future developments, the concept of personas development through mental model mapping has been successfully utilized to create decision support and user interfaces so far [e.g., 65]. However, with the accelerated application of AI solutions and their limitations ("black boxes"), new approaches need to be considered and developed to account for these requirements. Notable contributions such as Personas for AI [66] demonstrate practical solutions in the domain of mental models and AI and are expected to receive further attention in the future.

Acknowledgements. This project has received funding from the European Union's Horizon 2020 research and innovation programme under the Marie Skłodowska-Curie grant agreement No. 765395, and was also supported, in part, by Science Foundation Ireland grant 13/RC/2094 and co-funded under the European Regional Development Fund through the Southern & Eastern Regional Operational Programme to Lero –the Irish Software Research Centre (www.lero.ie).

Appendix

High CX Generation/ Low EV Creation   High EV Creation / Low CX Generation

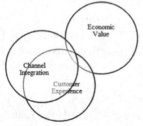   

High CX Generation/ High EV Creation   Towards Omnichannel Approach
but no CI achievement

   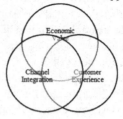

Low CX Generation/ Low EV Creation

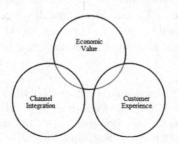

Fig. 10. Five basic scenarios arranging the objectives CI, CX and EV, [15].

References

1. Hagberg, J., Sundström, M., Nicklas, E.Z.: The digitalization of retailing: an exploratory framework. Int. J. Retail Distrib. Manag. **44**(7), 694–712 (2016)
2. Verhoef, P.C., Kannan, P.K., Inman, J.J.: From multi-channel retailing to omni-channel retailing: introduction to the special issue on multi-channel retailing. J. Retail. **91**(2), 174–181 (2015)
3. Brynjolfsson, E., Hu, Y.J., Rahman, M.S.: Competing in the Age of Omnichannel Retailing, pp. 1–7. MIT, Cambridge (2013)

4. Sethuraman, R., Roggeveen, A.L.: How the COVID pandemic may change the world of retailing. J. Retail. **96**(2), 169 (2020)
5. Pantano, E., Pizzi, G., Scarpi, D., Dennis, C.: Competing during a pandemic? Retailers' ups and downs during the COVID-19 outbreak. J. Bus. Res. **116**, 209–213 (2020)
6. Verhoef, P.C., Lemon, K.N., Parasuraman, A., Roggeveen, A., Tsiros, M., Schlesinger, L.A.: Customer experience creation: Determinants, dynamics and management strategies. J. Retail. **85**(1), 31–41 (2009)
7. Hosseini, S., Merz, M., Röglinger, M., Wenninger, A.: Mindfully going omni-channel: an economic decision model for evaluating omni-channel strategies. Decis. Support Syst. **109**, 74–88 (2018)
8. Bijmolt, T.H., et al.: Challenges at the marketing–operations interface in omni-channel retail environments. J. Bus. Res. **122**, 864–874 (2021)
9. Pauwels, K., Neslin, S.A.: Building with bricks and mortar: the revenue impact of opening physical stores in a multichannel environment. J. Retail. **91**(2), 182–197 (2015)
10. Cao, L., Li, L.: The impact of cross-channel integration on retailers' sales growth. J. Retail. **91**(2), 198–216 (2015)
11. Gademann, N., Brandt, G.: Omni-channel strategy. In: Van Woensel, B.: Omni Channel Logistics – state of the art (2016)
12. Zhang, J., Farris, P.W., Irvin, J.W., Kushwaha, T., Steenburgh, T.J., Weitz, B.A.: Crafting integrated multichannel retailing strategies. J. Interact. Mark. **24**(2), 168–180 (2010)
13. Rooderkerk, R.P., Kök, A.G.: Omnichannel assortment planning. In: Gallino, S., Moreno, A. (eds.) Operations in an Omnichannel World. SSSCM, vol. 8, pp. 51–86. Springer, Cham (2019). https://doi.org/10.1007/978-3-030-20119-7_4
14. Kaplan, R.S., Norton, D.P.: Translating strategy introduction the balanced scorecard. Harvard Business School (1996)
15. Cakir, G.: Visualising trade-offs of objectives in omnichannel management: a mental model approach. In Proceedings of the 4th International Conference on Computer-Human Interaction Research and Applications - WUDESHI-DR, pp. 291–298 (2020). ISBN 978-989-758-480-0; ISSN 2184-3244. https://doi.org/10.5220/0010214002910298
16. Shi, F.: Omni-channel retailing: knowledge, challenges, and opportunities for future research. In: Rossi, P. (ed.) Marketing at the Confluence between Entertainment and Analytics. DMSPAMS, pp. 91–102. Springer, Cham (2017). https://doi.org/10.1007/978-3-319-47331-4_18
17. Mosquera, A., Olarte-Pascual, C., Ayensa, E.J., Murillo, Y.S.: The role of technology in an omnichannel physical store. Spanish Journal of Marketing-ESIC (2018)
18. Iftikhar, R., Cakir, G., Wruck, T., Helfert, M.: How can older adults shop online in the future? Developing design principles for virtual-commerce stores. ECIS 2021 Research Papers. 122 (2021)
19. Zimmermann, R., Auinger, A., Riedl, R.: Smartphones as an opportunity to increase sales in brick-and-mortar stores: identifying sales influencers based on a literature review. In: Nah, F.-H., Siau, K. (eds.) HCII 2019. LNCS, vol. 11588, pp. 82–98. Springer, Cham (2019). https://doi.org/10.1007/978-3-030-22335-9_6
20. Cirqueira, D., Helfert, M., Bezbradica, M.: Towards preprocessing guidelines for neural network embedding of customer behavior in digital retail. In: Proceedings of the 2019 3rd International Symposium on Computer Science and Intelligent Control, pp. 1–6 (2019)
21. Cirqueira, D., et al.: Explainable sentiment analysis application for social media crisis management in retail. In Proceedings of the 4th International Conference on Computer-Human Interaction Research and Applications - WUDESHI-DR, pp. 319–328(2020). ISBN 978-989-758-480-0; ISSN 2184-3244. https://doi.org/10.5220/0010215303190328

22. Mora, D., Jain, S., Nalbach, O., Werth, D.: An in-store recommender system leveraging the microsoft hololens. In: Stephanidis, C., Antona, M. (eds.) HCII 2020. CCIS, vol. 1225, pp. 99–107. Springer, Cham (2020). https://doi.org/10.1007/978-3-030-50729-9_14

23. Wetzlinger, W., Auinger, A., Kindermann, H., Schönberger, W.: Acceptance of personalization in omnichannel retailing. In: Nah, F.-H., Tan, C.-H. (eds.) HCIBGO 2017. LNCS, vol. 10294, pp. 114–129. Springer, Cham (2017). https://doi.org/10.1007/978-3-319-58484-3_10

24. Zentes, J., Morschett, D., Schramm-Klein, H.: Strategic Retail Management. Gabler Verlag, Wiesbaden (2007)

25. Rigby, D.: The future of shopping. Harv. Bus. Rev. **89**(12), 65–76 (2011)

26. Herhausen, D., Binder, J., Schoegel, M., Herrmann, A.: Integrating bricks with clicks: retailer-level and channel-level outcomes of online–offline channel integration. J. Retail. **91**(2), 309–325 (2015)

27. Bendoly, E., Blocher, J.D., Bretthauer, K.M., Krishnan, S., Venkataramanan, M.A.: Online/in-store integration and customer retention. J. Serv. Res. **7**(4), 313–327 (2005)

28. Saghiri, S., Wilding, R., Mena, C., Bourlakis, M.: Toward a three-dimensional framework for omni-channel. J. Bus. Res. **77**, 53–67 (2017)

29. Hansen, R., Sia, S.K.: Hummel's digital transformation toward omnichannel retailing: key lessons learned. MIS Q. Executive, 14(2) (2015)

30. Cao, L.: Business model transformation in moving to a cross-channel retail strategy: a case study. Int. J. Electron. Commer. **18**(4), 69–96 (2014)

31. Cakir, G., Iftikhar, R., Bielozorov, A., Pourzolfaghar, Z., Helfert, M.: Omnichannel retailing: digital transformation of a medium-sized retailer. J. Inf. Technol. Teach. Cases. (2021). https://doi.org/10.1177/2043886920959803

32. Climent, R.C. Cakir, G.: Business model themes and product market strategies as value drivers in omni-channel retail: a set of propositions. JBAFP, **2**(3) (2021)

33. Piotrowicz, W., Cuthbertson, R.: Introduction to the special issue information technology in retail: toward omnichannel retailing. Int. J. Electron. Commer. **18**(4), 5–16 (2014)

34. Kranzbühler, A.M., Kleijnen, M.H., Morgan, R.E., Teerling, M.: The multilevel nature of customer experience research: an integrative review and research agenda. Int. J. Manag. Rev. **20**(2), 433–456 (2018)

35. Hermes, A., Riedl, R.: Dimensions of retail customer experience and its outcomes: a literature review and directions for future research. In: Nah, F.-H., Siau, K. (eds.) HCII 2021. LNCS, vol. 12783, pp. 71–89. Springer, Cham (2021). https://doi.org/10.1007/978-3-030-77750-0_5

36. Lemon, K.N., Verhoef, P.C.: Understanding customer experience throughout the customer journey. J. Mark. **80**, 69–96 (2016)

37. Cakir, G., Bezbradica, M., Helfert, M.: The shift from financial to non-financial measures during transition into digital retail – a systematic literature review. In: Abramowicz, W., Corchuelo, R. (eds.) BIS 2019. LNBIP, vol. 353, pp. 189–200. Springer, Cham (2019). https://doi.org/10.1007/978-3-030-20485-3_15

38. Keeney, R.L., Raiffa, H.: Decisions with Multiple Objectives: Preferences and Value Trade-offs. Cambridge University Press, Cambridge (1993)

39. Berman, B., Evans, J.R., Chatterje, P.: Retail Management: A Strategic Approach. Global Edition, Pearson (2018)

40. Kumar, V., Anand, A., Song, H.: Future of retailer profitability: an organizing framework. J. Retail. **93**(1), 96–119 (2017)

41. Cao, L.: Implementation of omnichannel strategy in the US retail: evolutionary approach. In: Piotrowicz, W., Cuthbertson, R. (eds.) Exploring Omnichannel Retailing, pp. 47–69. Springer, Cham (2019). https://doi.org/10.1007/978-3-319-98273-1_3

42. Broniarczyk, S.M., Hoyer, W.D., McAlister, L.: Consumers' perceptions of the assortment offered in a grocery category: the impact of item reduction. J. Mark. Res. **35**(2), 166–176 (1998). https://doi.org/10.2307/3151845

43. Bertrandie, L., Zielke, S.: The effects of multi-channel assortment integration on customer confusion. Int. Rev. Retail Distrib. Consum. Res **27**(5), 437–449 (2017)
44. Emrich, O., Paul, M., Rudolph, T.: Shopping benefits of multichannel assortment integration and the moderating role of retailer type. J. Retail. **91**(2), 326–342 (2015)
45. Van Ameijden, D., et al.: Selling to the multi-channel consumer: strategic and operational challenges for multi-channel retailers (2012)
46. JohnsonLaird, P.N.: Mental Models: Towards A Cognitive Science of Language, Inference, and Consciousness. Harvard University Press, Cambridge (1983)
47. Markman, A.B.: Knowledge Representation. Psychology Press, London (2013)
48. Markman, A.B., Gentner, D.: Thinking. Annu. Rev. Psychol. **52**(1), 223–247 (2001)
49. Capelo, C., Dias, J.F.: A system dynamics-based simulation experiment for testing mental model and performance effects of using the balanced scorecard. Syst. Dyn. Rev.: J. Syst. Dyn. Soc. **25**(1), 1–34 (2009)
50. Lant, T.K., Milliken, F.J., Batra, B.: The role of managerial learning and interpretation in strategic persistence and reorientation: an empirical exploration. Strateg. Manag. J. **13**(8), 585–608 (1992)
51. Meadows, D.L., Behrens, W.W., Meadows, D.H., Naill, R.F., Randers, J., Zahn, E.: Dynamics of Growth in a Finite World, p. 637. Wright-Allen Press, Cambridge (1974)
52. Zhang-Kennedy, L., Chiasson, S., Biddle, R.: Password advice shouldn't be boring: visualizing password guessing attacks. In: eCrime Researchers Summit, San Francisco, CA, pp. 1–11 (2013)
53. Street, F.: The 'Circle of Competence' theory will help you make vastly smarter decisions. Bus. Insider. https://www.businessinsider.com/the-circle-of-competence-theory-2013-12?r=DE&IR=T
54. Venn, J.I.: On the diagrammatic and mechanical representation of propositions and reasonings. London Edinb. Dublin Philos. Mag. J. Sci. **10**(59), 1–18 (1880)
55. Oh, L.B., Teo, H.H., Sambamurthy, V.: The effects of retail channel integration through the use of information technologies on firm performance. J. Oper. Manag. **30**(5), 368–381 (2012)
56. Gross, N., McNamara, P., Ryazanova, O., Connolly, N.: Integrative or autonomous? mental models and experimentation-driven business model innovation. In: Academy of Management Proceedings (Vol. 2016, No. 1, p. 15886). Briarcliff Manor, NY 10510: Academy of Management (2016)
57. Mohamed, M.A., Chakraborty, J., Dehlinger, J.: Trading off usability and security in user interface design through mental models. Behav. Inf. Technol. **36**(5), 493–516 (2016). https://doi.org/10.1080/0144929x.2016.1262897
58. Gallino, S., Moreno, A.: Operations in an omnichannel world: introduction. In: Gallino, S., Moreno, A. (eds.) Operations in an Omnichannel World. SSSCM, vol. 8, pp. 1–11. Springer, Cham (2019). https://doi.org/10.1007/978-3-030-20119-7_1
59. Neslin, S.A., Shankar, V.: Key issues in multichannel customer management: current knowledge and future directions. J. Interact. Mark. **23**(1), 70–81 (2009)
60. Mitchell, V.W., Walsh, G., Yamin, M.: Reviewing and redefining the concept of consumer confusion. Manchester: Manuscript Manchester Sch. Manag. 4 (2004)
61. Ocasio, W.: Towards an attention-based view of the firm. Strateg. Manag. J. **18**(S1), 187–206 (1997)
62. Cooper-Martin, E.: Measures of cognitive effort. Mark. Lett. **5**(1), 43–56 (1994). https://doi.org/10.1007/BF00993957
63. Malhotra, N.K.: Reflections in on the information decision overload paradigm consumer making. J. Consum. Res. **10**(4), 436–440 (1984). https://doi.org/10.1086/208982

64. Mitchell, V.-W., Walsh, G., Yamin, M.: Towards a conceptual model of consumer confusion. Adv. Consum. Res. **32**, 143–150 (2005)
65. Miaskiewicz, T., Kozar, K.A.: Personas and user-centered design: how can personas benefit product design processes? Des. Stud. **32**(5), 417–430 (2011)
66. Holzinger, A., Kargl, M., Kipperer, B., Regitnig, P., Plass, M., Müller, H.: Personas for artificial intelligence (AI) an open source toolbox. IEEE Access **10**, 23732–23747 (2022)

Author Index

Printed in the United States
by Baker & Taylor Publisher Services